Date Due

HISTORY OF MEDIÆVAL PHILOSOPHY

HISTORY OF
MEDIÆVAL
PHILOSOPHY

BY

MAURICE DE WULF

PROFESSOR OF PHILOSOPHY AT LOUVAIN AND HARVARD UNIVERSITIES;
DOCTOR OF PHILOSOPHY AND LETTERS; DOCTOR OF LAWS; MEMBER OF
THE ROYAL ACADEMY OF BELGIUM.

TRANSLATED BY

ERNEST C. MESSENGER, Ph.D.

LECTURER IN LOGIC AND COSMOLOGY AT ST. EDMUND'S COLLEGE, WARE.

VOL. II

FROM ST. THOMAS AQUINAS TO THE END OF THE SIXTEENTH
CENTURY

LONGMANS, GREEN AND CO. LTD.
39 PATERNOSTER ROW, LONDON, E.C.4
NEW YORK, TORONTO
BOMBAY, CALCUTTA AND MADRAS
1926

theology, is no longer questioned by anyone who has come into direct contact with mediæval philosophy.

The second, namely, that scholasticism is not the whole of mediæval philosophy, but the best part of it, that it represents the collective inheritance of the majority of the thinkers of the West, and that it had to encounter fierce opposition throughout the centuries,—this second thesis, while gaining numerous adherents, is still disputed, and we do not intend in this place to undertake to justify it.

To those who reject it because their attention is turned to the differential aspects presented by the mediæval systems of philosophy, we would say that in our opinion, the study of these aspects derives its full value and presents all its fruits only when associated with the study of the common doctrines, and is constantly made clearer when viewed in the light of the latter.

On the other hand, we are glad to note that a parallel study of the civilization of the thirteenth century—the culminating point of the Middle Ages—confirms in a remarkable and unexpected way the correctness of our method of interpretation. In all the spheres of mental life—art, religion, customs and politics—the Middle Ages was governed by collective ideals and great cosmopolitan forces which acted in a similar fashion on the various countries of Western Europe.

The study of the philosophic movements in their surroundings, and in their relations of interdependence with other factors of civilization, is destined to throw a new light on the systems of thought the temporal connections of which have not hitherto been thoroughly understood. We have followed this path, not without some hesitation, for to do so with complete assurance the collaboration of the historians of the Middle Ages would be indispensable. In other words, we are aware of the *lacunæ* which might be pointed out in our work from this point of view.

As in the preceding editions, our attention has been devoted above all to theories and systems.

In our exposition of these, as in the study of their developments, we shall take as our basis the internal logic of a man's thought rather than his intentions. Philosophy is full of examples of thinkers who by their express declarations endeavour to escape the consequences to which the dialectical pressure of their ideas would lead them. Thus all the monists of the

Middle Ages wished to safeguard the co-existence of the One and the Many, and the boldest theologians desired to respect Catholic dogma.

But the intention, revealing as it does temperament and personality, is one thing, and doctrine, the more or less vigorous product of thought, is another. The content of a doctrine is independent of the subjective preoccupations which have inspired it. At all times we find men who err in good faith and who are led by the best of motives to the worst of doctrines. We shall have occasion to make numerous applications of this important principle of exegesis.

The reader will permit us to point out some other modifications introduced in the present edition. The historical introduction devoted to Greek philosophy has been suppressed in order to bring out into more complete relief the philosophy of the Middle Ages. But at the same time it would not have been wise to exclude from a work of this nature all references to the great philosophers of Antiquity, for on the one hand the philosophers of the Middle Ages constantly appealed to them, and indeed were the continuers of the ancient tradition, and on the other hand, the divergent expositions which have been given by modern historians of Greek and patristic philosophy on many important doctrines must be dealt with here and now, failing which all comparison with the corresponding doctrines of the Middle Ages would be sterile. Hence the reader will find scattered up and down the work partial data concerning the philosophies of Plato, Aristotle, the Stoics, neo-Platonists, St. Augustine, and pseudo-Dionysius— to quote only the chief inspirers of mediæval thought.

Similar considerations have induced us to reduce to an indispensable minimum the treatment of the oriental philosophical systems of Byzantium, Africa, and Mohammedan Spain. We are concerned with these vast movements of ideas, so little known up to the present, only in so far as they have penetrated into Western philosophy.

Whole departments of the philosophic history of the Middle Ages depend upon learned research, as for instance all that concerns the life and chronological order of the writings of a philosopher. Important work has been done and is still in progress, of which we have endeavoured to make the best use, without pretending that we have been able to acquaint ourselves fully with the productions of these latter years.

The history of the Latin translations of Greek and Arabian works presents a typical example of the difficulties which face any one who in the present state of knowledge undertakes a general exposition of this subject. Our good friend, Mgr. A. Pelzer, one of the admitted authorities on the philosophic history of the Middle Ages, and whose first-class researches have rendered invaluable services to the subject in question, has been good enough to revise the paragraphs relating to this difficult subject. We beg him to accept this expression of our immense gratitude.

A selected bibliography, which does not pretend to be exhaustive, is appended to each of the various chapters or paragraph sections. It should be taken together with the bibliographical indications in the notes, which for the sake of brevity are not repeated. We have above all aimed at mentioning the works which have appeared since 1915, i.e., since the last edition of Ueberweg-Baumgartner (*Grundriss der Geschichte der Philosophie, Die Mittlere oder die patristische und scholastische Zeit*, Berlin), the documentation of which it is unnecessary to repeat.

A synthetic work on the history of mediæval philosophy ought to be accompanied by a collection of texts, following step by step the divisions adopted : we hope to publish this in the near future.

M. DE WULF.

LOUVAIN,
　　1st June, 1924.

TRANSLATOR'S NOTE

The second French edition of this work appeared in 1905, and an English translation, by Dr. Coffey, of Maynooth, was published in 1909. Since that date our knowledge of mediæval philosophy has been considerably extended, and accordingly Professor De Wulf has recast the whole book. This new English version is based upon the fifth French edition, which appeared in 1924 and 1925. I have not hesitated to adopt the felicitous renderings of Dr. Coffey wherever possible. An Index will be found at the end of each volume.

WARE,　　　　　　　　　　　　　　E. C. MESSENGER.
　　1st October, 1925.

CONTENTS

SECOND PERIOD: MEDIÆVAL PHILOSOPHY IN THE
THIRTEENTH CENTURY.

CHAPTER II: THE GROUP OF SCHOLASTIC
PHILOSOPHIES

Art. V.—Thomas Aquinas.

Art. VI.—The Conflict Between Thomism and the Older
Scholasticism

§ 1.—*The Opponents of Thomism.*

§ 2.—*Supporters of Thomism.*

Art. VII.—Godfrey of Fontaines and Henry of Ghent.

THIRD PERIOD: MEDIÆVAL PHILOSOPHY IN THE
FOURTEENTH AND THE FIRST HALF OF THE
FIFTEENTH CENTURY.

CHAPTER I: GENERAL NOTIONS.

CHAPTER II: THE GROUP OF SCHOLASTIC PHILO-
SOPHICAL SYSTEMS.

Art. I.—General Notions.

Art. II.—The Terminist or "Nominalist" School.

§ 1.—*General Notions.*

§ 2.—*Durandus of St. Pourçain and Peter Aureolus.*

CONTENTS

CHAPTER III : SCHOLASTIC PHILOSOPHY.

CONTENTS

ADDITIONS AND CORRECTIONS

VOL. I

Page 45, line 21   -   - For " Erfort " read " Hereford."

„ 81, line 2 -   -   - Add : In connection with Alfarabi, we must add to the two Latin Versions of the *De scientiis*, his *De ortu scientiarum* (beginning, " Scias nihil esse præter substantiam et accidens ") translated probably by Dominic Gundisalvi (edited by Baeumker, *BGPM*, XIX, 3, 1916).

„ 144, line 8 - - - For " Doscelin," read " Roscelin."

„ 146, line 12   -   - „ " 1910," read " 1010."

„ 159, footnote 4 -   - „ " *ex*," read " *et*."

„ 205   - - -   - Add the following to the last paragraph of section viii : In connection with Peter of Poitiers we may mention Martin de Fugeriis and a group of writers of *Summæ* who flourished at the commencement of the thirteenth century (**214**). Finally, we ought to mention here, as one of the best arranged expositions of doctrine, the *Catholicæ fidei libri quinque* by Alan of Lille, and a work by Nicholas of Amiens ascribed to Alan of Lille. The theological work of these two men was influenced to some extent by their polemics against the Albigenses (**117**).

„ 247, line 24   -   - Delete " and Duns Scotus boasted of having taken him as his guide."

„ 264, line 28   -   - Insert 82.

„ 314, line 9 - - - For " Hereford " read " Herford."

„ 352, line 11   -   - „ " translations of the commentaries " read " translations and commentaries."

„ 394, note 1   -   - For " Michel," read " Michael."

„ 413 - - - - „ " Pacheeu," read " Pacheu."

„ 416, 2nd col., line 33 „ " NMende," read " Mende."

Passim - - - - - „ " Haureau," read " Hauréau."

SECOND PERIOD

MEDIÆVAL PHILOSOPHY IN THE THIRTEENTH CENTURY

CHAPTER II

The Group of Scholastic Philosophies

Art. V—Thomas Aquinas

269. Life and Works.—THOMAS AQUINAS belonged to the family of the Counts of Aquin. He was born about the beginning of 1225[1] at Rocca Secca,[2] and received the first part of his education at Monte Cassino. He completed it at the University of Naples, under the Arts professors Petrus Martinus and Petrus de Hibernia.[3] He became a Dominican at Naples in April, 1244, and set out for Paris the following year in order to attend the lectures of Albert the Great, and from this time his career was closely bound up with that of his master. In 1248 he followed him to Cologne, where a *studium generale* had just been founded by the Dominicans, and remained there till 1252. The Head of the Order then recalled him to Paris to prepare for his mastership in Theology. This was the period of his public lectures, first as Bachelor (1256) and then as Master, in one of the two Dominican chairs (1256-1259). To this period also belongs his vindication of the rights of his Order against William of St. Amour. The recognition of his title

---

[1] In this biographical note we follow in general Mandonnet, *Chronologie sommaire de la vie et des écrits de St. Thomas*, R. sc. phil. theol. 1920, pp. 142-153.

[2] Pellegrini and Scandone, *Pro Rocca secca, patria di S. Tommaso*, Naples, 1903.

[3] Author of commentaries on Porphyry and Aristotle's *Perihermeneias* and *De Longit. et brevitate vitae* mentioned by Pelzer, *Un cours inédit d'Albert le Grand* (R. Neo-scol. 1922, p. 24). In them we notice the twofold method of commenting by *expositio* and *disputatio*. Baeumker had previously published in the form of a *reportatio* made by a listener the *determinatio* by the Irish master about 1260 in presence of King Manfred of the interesting question whether the function creates the organ or whether the organ exists for the sake of the function ? " Utrum membra essent facta propter operaciones vel operaciones essent factae proper membra." See *P. de Hibernia, d. Jugend lehrer d. Th. v. Aquino u. seine Disputation ver König Manfred* (Sitz. bayer Akad. wiss. Phil. Kl. 1920). Cf. Grabmann, *Th. v. A. und P. von Hibernia*, Phil. Jahrb. 1920, pp. 347-362.

3

and that of St. Bonaventure (240) terminated the conflict in favour of the regulars.

After these three years of teaching, Thomas set out for Italy as a professor at the *studium curiæ* set up in 1243-1244 at the Papal Court, and in this capacity he resided at Anagni and Orvieto (1259-1265). From 1265-1267 he taught at St. Sabina's in Rome, and then returned to the Court at Viterbo (end of 1267). About this time he met William of Moerbeke at the Court of Urban IV, and from 1261 was linked in close friendship with the faithful Reginald. Thomas returned a second time to Paris as Professor at the beginning of 1269. This unusual return[1] of a Dominican master to the Paris convent can only be accounted for by his brilliant reputation and the gravity of the doctrinal disputes then in progress. Thomas found himself face to face on the one hand with the Averrhoism of Siger of Brabant, and on the other hand the new attacks by Gerard of Abbeville and Nicholas of Lisieux on the rights of mendicant orders. The second departure of the master for Italy (1272) gave rise to great regret in academic circles. Thomas taught once more at Naples until 1273. He died on the 7th March, 1274, at the Abbey of Fossanova between Naples and Rome while on his way to Lyons, whither Gregory X had summoned him to assist the work of the Council by his learning. He was forty-eight years of age when he died.

The Rector, Procurators and Masters *actu regentes* in the Faculty of Arts at Paris sent their sincere condolences to the Dominicans, and tell us that Thomas when leaving them had promised to send them various translations made by his friend William of Moerbeke which they did not possess.[2]

The recent labours of Mandonnet, Grabmann, Pelster and others on the chronology and authenticity of the works of Aquinas have not resulted in agreement on all points. In deciding the question of authenticity Mandonnet takes as his criterion the catalogue of Bartholomew of Capua, which he

---

[1] " The only other instance, as far as we know, is that of William of Hotham,"—Mandonnet, *Siger*, Vol. VI. 88.

[2] *Commentum Simplicii s. librum de celo et mundo* ; *Expositio Timei Platonis, De Aquarum conductibus*. The reference is not to original works written by Thomas. This point is established by Birkenmajer, who brings forward a new text of the letter, containing the expression " Commentum Simplicii super librum de celo." He attributes the traditions to William of Moerbeke, unhesitatingly in the case of the first two, but, with a reservation for the third. *Der Brief d. Parisir Artistenfakultat über d. Tod des hl. Th.*, in *BGPM*, XX, 5, pp. 1-35.

calls the official catalogue ; Grabmann would compare various
ancient catalogues and examine the manuscripts.[1]   The chronological succession of the master's works is of capital importance
for the understanding of his doctrines, but it is not yet settled
in all its details.

Singling out the works which chiefly concern us in this
history, we can distinguish with Mandonnet[2] :

(i) The works connected with the schools : Commentaries
on the four books of the Sentences (1254-1256),[3] *Quæstiones
disputatæ*,[4] ranging from 1256 to 1272 in the following order :
*De veritate, De potentia, De malo, De spiritualibus creaturis,
De anima, De virtutibus.*   In the *Quæstiones quodlibetales* (the
first six were written at Paris between 1269 and 1272, and the
remaining ones in Italy from 1263 to 1268), we find discussions
of the points which divided scholastics in metaphysics and
psychology, and a study of several Averrhoistic doctrines.
All the controversies of the period find a place.

Besides various sermons,[5] we must mention the philosophical
commentaries on Boethius (1257-1258), and on the *De divinis
nominibus* of pseudo-Dionysius, and the collection of commentaries on Aristotle.   The latter comprise a series composed
in Italy (*Physics, Metaphysics* except the last two books,
De anima, De sensu et sensato, De memoria, Ethics, Politics[6]
and the *Posterior Analytics*), and another series written at
Paris (*Meteors, Perihermeneias, De cælo, De generatione*)

---

[1] Mandonnet, *Les écrits authentiques de S. Thomas d'Aquin.* The exclusion
of the apocryphal works from the official catalogue is deliberate : " Si autem
sibi alia adscribantur, non ipse scripsit et notavit, sed alii recollegerunt post
eum legentem vel praedicantem."   They are "reported" particularly by
Reginald of Piperno and Peter of Andria.—Grabmann, *Die echte Schriften,*
etc., *BGPM*, XXII, 1-2, defends the authenticity of twelve works rejected
by Mandonnet.

[2] *Chronologie sommaire,* etc.

[3] The Catalogue of 1319 mentions another commentary on the First Book of
Sentences.   After writing the commentaries on the Sentences which we
possess, in which Augustinian influences are evident, Aquinas seems to have
treated the subject matter again in a more personal way, and then to have
withdrawn the work from circulation because the same ground was covered
by the Summa. — Mandonnet, *Les écrits authentiques,* etc.

[4] Mandonnet, *Chronologie des Q. d.* (*R. Thom.* 1918, p. 275); Grabmann,
Einführung in d. S. Theologica des hl. Th., 1919. Birkenmajer, *Kleinere
Thomas Fragen.* I. *Ueber d. Reihenfolge u. d. Entstehungszeit d. Quaest.
disputatae des hl. Thom.* (*Phil. Jahrb.* 1921, pp. 31-49), confirms Grabmann's
theses.

[5] Salvatore has published *Due Sermoni inediti di S. Tommaso* (Rome, 1912),
which are rather discourses at the opening of courses, or *principia*.

[6] Books I and II., and chapters 1 to 6 of Book III of the Politics are authentic, the rest is by Peter of Auvergne, Grabmann, *Welchen Teil der Aristot.
Politik hat der h. Thomas selbst kommentiert ?* (*Philos. Jahrb.* 1915, pp. 375-
378).

to which must be added a commentary on the *Liber de causis*.

(ii) Miscellaneous works[1] : *De principiis naturæ* (1255) ; *De ente et essentia* (1256) ; *Summa contra Gentiles* (1258-1260, or 1264 according to Grabmann) ; *De regimine principum*, 1265-66 (Book I, and Chapters 1 to 4 of Book II[2] ; the rest is by Bartholomew of Lucca) ; *De occultis operationibus naturæ* (1269-1272) ; *De regimine Judæorum* (letter to the Duchess of Brabant) ; *De unitate intellectus* ; and *De æternitate mundi* (1270) ; *De substantiis separatis* (1272) ; *De mixtione elementorum* (1273).

The *Summa Theologica*, written " ad eruditionem incipientium,"[3] was commenced between 1267 and 1273. Thomas continued to work at it until his death. He stopped at question 90 of the Third Part. The Supplement to this part was drawn up by Reginald of Piperno. The *Compendium theologiæ*[4] seems to be one of his last works, dating from 1271-1273.[5]

270. Personality.—Thomas Aquinas has been justly called the Prince of Scholastic Philosophers. He owed his philosophical vocation and introduction to Peripateticism to Albert the Great, but in every respect he excelled his master.

(i) *Thomas the commentator.* In place of the running paraphrase of Aristotle which had been employed in popularizing his works, St. Thomas adopted the more critical method of the

---

[1] We do not mention all the authentic *opuscula* here.

[2] Endres (*BGPM*, Festgabe Baeumker, p. 261) denies the authenticity of even this portion of the work, but for reasons which do not appear to us to be convincing.

[3] Prologue.

[4] Mandonnet, *Bibl. thomiste*, p. 15.

[5] Among the apocryphal works often attributed to St. Thomas, we may mention the following : *Totius logicae summa* ; *De potentiis animae* ; *De natura syllogismi* ; *De inventione medii* ; *De demonstratione* ; *De natura accidentis* ; *De natura generis* ; *De pluralitate formarum* (many treatises on forms have been wrongly attributed to him) ; *De intellectu et intelligibili* ; *De principio individuationis* ; *De universalibus* ; *Eruditio principum* ; *De professione monachorum* ; *De usuris*. Later on more than one *compendium* based by some disciple on the authentic teaching of the master, was put forward under the latter's name. It must also be noted that Aquinas borrowed the materials for various *opuscula* from previous works (an example is the *De mixtione elementorum*). Pelster has recently put forward the questionable hypothesis that the harmony of divergent Thomist theories, *Pertransibunt plurimi*, belongs to the old age of Thomas himself. See *Die concordantia Dictorum Thomae, ein echtes Werk aus d. letzten Lebensjahren d. hl. Thomas v. A.*, (*Gregorianum*, 1922, pp. 72-105). The use of the first person would indeed seem to indicate that Thomas is writing of himself. Grabmann on the other hand holds that this is a literary artifice (*Hilfsmittel d. Thomasstudien*, etc., p. 65), found also in the pseudo-Boethian thirteenth century work, *De disciplina scholarium*.

literal commentary, keeping close to the text. "Quodam singulari et novo modo tradendi utebatur," are the words used of him by Ptolomy of Lucca.[1] It was in order to produce commentaries of this kind that he took such pains to obtain faithful versions, and begged William of Moerbeke to devote himself to the revision of existing translations or to the making of new ones.[2] William helped him in the production of his commentaries, and this partly explains why Aquinas had a knowledge of Aristotle more profound and far superior to that of his master Albert. On many points of exegesis he indicated the real teaching of the Stagirite, and refused to regard him as responsible for many an error which others had attributed to him. It is worthy of note that the commentaries of Aquinas contain many ideas which are personal to him, and which may easily be recognized. Thus the prologues to the books are his own work.[3]

(ii) *Thomas the historian.* His historical sense was remarkable for his time. He not only made use of Aristotle : he was also the first the utilize Proclus in William of Moerbeke's translation. He recognized the neo-Platonist origin of the *Liber de Causis* by comparing it with the works of Proclus. He was one of the most faithful exponents of the ideas of the Greeks, the Fathers of the Church, the Arabs and the Jews, especially Avencebrol and Maimonides. Nevertheless, the desire to make use of their authority to support what he thought to be true, and the pre-occupation which he had, in common with other philosophers of his time, of harmonizing contradictory opinions, led him into mistakes. It is interesting to note his attitude towards St. Augustine, from whose teaching he felt compelled to depart on a great number of points. Thomas does not contradict him ; he does not consider him suspect because of his connection with neo-Platonism ; instead he transforms the meaning of his statements, sometimes by slight corrections, sometimes by violent interpretations which do violence to the text.[4] We may add that he was always

---

[1] *Hist. eccles.* XXII, c. 24.

[2] See Vol. I. (p. 243.)

[3] Grabmann, *Die Kommentare des hl. Th. v. A. über die Werke d. Aristoteles* (Louvain *Annales*, Vol. III, 1914, pp. 231-281), deals from the historical and technical points of view with the methods, sources, and personal ideas of Aquinas.

[4] Von Hertling, *Augustinuscitate bei Thomas v. Aquin* (Sitzungsber. d. philos.-philol. und histor. Klasse Acad. Munchen, 1905, p. 558). For instance, Aquinas says : " In multis autem quae ad philosophiam pertinent, Augustinus

between the finite and the infinite, the contingent and the necessary. Pure act implies the plenitude of all perfection ; a being which *becomes*, or is composed of act and potency, implies an acquired perfection, and necessary limitation. All the various compositions found in contingent being, and in particular those of matter and form, substance and accident, essence and existence, must be regarded as functions of change and becoming.

273. Matter and Form.—Thomas broke away from the traditions of the older scholasticism, and restated the theory of matter and form in its real peripatetic sense.

(i) *Prime matter* is an incomplete element of reality and distinct from form. The older scholasticism had a tendency to infer from this that matter is capable of existing apart from form. Thomas declares this to be a metaphysical absurdity. The concept of matter existing of itself is equivalent to the contradictory concept of the determined—undetermined. God himself could not realize that which is intrinsically impossible.[1]

(ii) Here is another important innovation : corporeal being alone is composed of matter and form, for it alone is involved in the profound becoming which transforms substances into different ones. The older scholasticism regarded the composition of matter and form in every contingent being as the precise reason of its contingence. Thomas protested against this doctrine, by which his master was still influenced ; he denounced the *binarium famosissimum* which the classical theory had become.[2] Why explain the being of a spiritual substance, the nature of which is incorruptible, by a composition which is postulated only by corruptibility ? To introduce the notion of prime matter in a spiritual being is to make the former equivalent to that of potentiality : a twofold use of the same term constituting an abuse of the principle of intelligibility.[3] By restricting the composition of matter and form to corporeal beings, in which it is the foundation of diffusion in space and the imperfections resulting there-

---

[1] " Relinquitur ergo quod (materia) non possit esse in actu nisi in quantum participat actum : actus autem participatus a materia nihil est aliud quam forma ; unde idem est dictu, materiam esse in actu et materiam habere formam. Dicere ergo quod materia sit in actu sine forma est dicere contradictoria esse simul, unde a Deo fieri non potest."—*Quodl.* III, I. a. 1.

[2] Vol. I. p. 360.

[3] *Summa contra gentiles*, II, c. 53 and 54.

from, Thomas gives it a dynamic and not a static interpretation.

The *De substantiis separatis* traces the doctrine it opposes back to its real source : while Bonaventure and his disciples appeal to St. Augustine as the father of their theory, Thomas shows that it really comes from Avencebrol,[1] whose *Fons vitæ*, far from being a fount of pure doctrine, contains impurities which contaminate the stream of Aristotelian thought.

(iii) Just as he simplifies the theory of matter, so also Thomas purifies the doctrine of *form* : to the plurality of substantial forms he opposes the celebrated theory of *unity*. It would seem that he himself was influenced at first by the older scholasticism.[2] The Commentaries on the Sentences, in which we find more than one doctrinal peculiarity, contain several texts which hesitatingly suggest that *corporeitas* is the *prima forma substantialis* of a body.[3] But subsequently, throughout all his works, Thomas affirms the unity of the substantial form with an array of powerful arguments which leave no room for doubt as to his opinion, and which were justified by the circumstances of the time. In a being the substance of which undergoes change, one single formal principle satisfies the potentialities of matter and confers the plenitude of substantial perfection. In other metaphysical arguments, the unity of form is linked up with the transcendental unity of being (" nihil est simpliciter unum, nisi per formam unam per quam habet res esse"[4]), and with the very notion of substantial being. In Physics it explains the generation and corruption of substances ; in Psychology the unity of human nature, the solidarity of vital functions, the identity of the individual man before and after the resurrection, etc.

How then are we to explain the manifold perfections, which were referred by the older scholastics to diverse forms ? By the multiplicity of operative powers springing from the substance and directly bound up with the one principle of perfection.

---

[1] Wittmann, *Die Stellung d. hl. Thomas zu Avencebrol*, p. 40.
[2] Peckham could say about the theory : " tenuit hactenus totus mundus.— Ehrle, *J. Peckham*, etc., p. 178.
[3] *In I. Sent.*, d. VIII, p. 5, a. 2, and *In II. Sent.*, D. III, q. 1. a. 1. See De Wulf, *Le traité de l'unité des formes de G. de Lessines*, Ch. III : " L'innovation principelle du thomisme." This collects together the various arguments put forward by St. Thomas.
[4] *S. Theol.* I. q. 76, a. 3.

The theory of the unity of form exercised a far-reaching influence on Thomism, and acted as a bond of union between a number of doctrines. Thomas learnt it neither from his master, who adopted a different solution, nor from the Averrhoists,[1] but owed it to his personal penetration of the peripatetic genius of scholasticism. Here again St. Thomas attributed the origin of the pluralistic doctrine to the Arabs and Avicenna and not to St. Augustine.

(iv) The *individual* and the *common essence*. Each substantial and individual being is identical with itself: Thomas never tires of affirming that " nihil est præter individuum " ; and it is clear that each being is itself by all that constitutes it, that is to say, by its whole essence. A corporeal being is therefore itself by its matter and its form ; a spiritual being owes its individuality to the form, with which it is wholly identical.

It is true that to a certain extent different individual things possess similar characteristics, and that this similarity serves as a foundation for the abstract and general notions by which our knowledge is constituted : we say both of a lion and of a man that they are living beings. Again it is true that corporeal beings, although graded in perfection according to the hierarchy of forms, present a kind of continual multiplication of the same formal perfection : thus we say that men are multiplied within the same species. But in every case, each existing thing is marked with the indelible stamp of individuality. Life in a lion or a man, humanity in Peter or Paul, are individual realities.

We shall see later on that the process of abstraction by which our knowledge is moulded hinders us from grasping the individuality of things. We know that this individuality *must be*, and therefore that it *exists* ; we do not know *what it is* : St. Thomas describes the relation between the common and the individualized essence as that of potency to act.

(v) *Individuation* is a particular problem connected with individuality : it consists in an endeavour to find out what it is that makes it possible for one and the same formal perfection to be realized many times over. St. Thomas holds that, of itself, a perfection is neither one nor multiple; it is realized to the full when it comes into existence. Hence one can see no reason why a form as such should be affected by the limitation

[1] Ch. III, § 1.

which consists in being multiplied in numerous individuations.
If it is multiplied, it is because it is linked up with extension,
or bound up with a quantified state, and ultimately because it is
united to prime matter, which is the origin of this state.   The
presence of *materia signata*, or matter affected with an intrinsic
aptitude to impose a particular extension upon the form
receiving it, renders possible and necessary the multiplicity
of individuals in one and the same species.

The Thomist doctrine has another aspect : if corporeal
forms are subject to individuation by reason of their union
with prime matter, an incorporeal being on the other hand, since
it excludes matter, cannot be multiplied.   This is the case
with the angels, spiritual substances in which each individual
constitutes its own species [1]   To them we apply the saying :
" Forma irrecepta est illimitata " (from the point of view of
number).   More logical than Aristotle,[2] St. Thomas regards
them as separated forms (" forma subsistens ").   For while
matter cannot exist without form, the reciprocal of this is not
true.   In any case, the simplicity of an immaterial substance
is quite compatible with its contingence.

As for the heavenly bodies, which are composed of matter
and form and are nevertheless unique in their species, the
general ideas of scholastic physics must be taken into consideration in order to understand the thought of the Angelic
Doctor.[3]

274.   The substance and its operative powers.—The duality
of potency and act is found not only in the profound region
of matter and form, in which it serves to explain the appearance
and disappearance of a substance, it is likewise found in all that

---

[1] " Individuae ergo sunt substantiae separatae, et singulares ; non autem
individuantur ex materia, sed ex hoc ipso quod non sunt natae in alio esse
et per consequens nec participari a multis."—*De unit. intell.*, p. 485, in De
Maria's edition.

[2] Cf. Zeller, *Die Phil. d. Griechen*, II, 2, p. 339, n. 3.

[3] Since the formal principles in which St. Thomas seeks the explanation of
the specific nature of things are separate and distinct from each other, both
in the realm of bodies and in that of spirits, it follows that real beings constitute a great hierarchy from the lowest form up to God.   Some recent
interpreters of Thomism (for instance, Maggiolo, *Le thomisme*, in *Revue
Thomiste*, 1921, pp. 5-25), lay stress upon this theory of form, and consider
that it furnishes a complete explanation of reality.   This would make the
Thomist metaphysics more or less identical to the neo-Platonist conception
of the degrees of being, a static idea, leaving aside the dynamic aspect, i.e.,
the becoming of things, starting not from below with the observation of facts,
but from above, with the notion of being.   In our opinion, the theory of form
is subordinate to that of act and potency, which is the corner-stone of the
metaphysics of contingent being.

concerns the development of this substance in the course of its existence. A concrete thing *becomes*, and is continually being determined by incessant changes of states and conditions affecting its substance.

Among the accidents, which St. Thomas regards as really distinct from the substance, there are, besides quantity and action (*actus secundus*), a special quality which he calls the proximate principle of action. The question of the distinction between the substance and its operative powers arises chiefly in connection with man : are these powers or faculties identical with the substance of the soul as Augustine held ? St. Thomas does not display the hesitations of his predecessors and contemporaries : God alone acts by his substance ; action cannot belong to the substance of a contingent being, and therefore the proximate principle of action is distinct from this substance. If it were otherwise, we should have to choose one of the following inadmissible consequences : (*a*) a being would expend the totality of its energies in each operation, for the substance of the thing, being identical with its action, would be present therein in its entirety ; or (*b*) all the individuals of one and the same species would all be endowed with the same intensity of action ; or (*c*) the substance of a being would increase and decrease with its activity.

The operative powers are really distinct from the substance (potency), and are determining elements (act). But this distinction does not divide up a thing into a mosaic, for one existence embraces the many elements of reality of which a concrete thing is constituted.

275. Essence and existence are distinct realities.—This important doctrine is not new for we come across it at the beginning of the thirteenth century, but no one before St. Thomas had such a clear comprehension of all that it implies. In an existing being, the constituent reality (*essentia, quod est*) is one thing, the actuality itself by which this reality exists (*esse, quo est*), is another. Whether the existing substance is composed of matter and form (corporeal substance), or is a separated form (immaterial substance), the perfection which makes it an existing thing is distinct from that reality to which it gives existence. Existence is the supreme actuality (*actus secundus*) of the concrete quiddity (*potency*). And as the degree of actuality depends upon potency, it follows that the essence of a concrete thing (*this* man, for instance), substantial and accidental, can only receive existence within the limits of its capacity.[1] Existence is different in different individuals (Peter, Paul), and in different species (man, lion), just as the volume of water in a vessel depends upon the latter's capacity. Existence increases and diminishes in any one being by reason of the variations in its accidental essence. In every case the total essence of the concrete thing forms a limit.

To suppress limitation and contingence, we have only to exclude the real distinction between essence and existence. God alone, the infinite and pure Actuality, exists by His very essence : He is all existence.

The synthetic ideas sketched out above were clearly enunciated in the *De ente et essentia*, and the master constantly made them more precise. If we regard his philosophic system as a whole, we cannot but be struck by the important part played by this fundamental doctrine. Not only does it bring out the contingency of things,—it also explains why the quiddity of a concrete thing, in spite of its real complexity, is unified into one single existing thing instead of consisting of a group of existences, and how this one existence harmonizes with the flux in which the essence is involved.

276. Natural theology.—(i) *Existence of God*. The five ways to which St. Thomas has recourse in order to prove the existence of the Pure Actuality are well known. The first argument, from cosmic change (*ex motu*) is an integration of the Aristotelian proof of the immovable mover : That which changes, does so under the influence of something other than itself. Now it is impossible to allow an infinite series of moving and moved bodies, for this would involve the denial of the existence of any real change, i.e. the denial of a fact. Therefore there must be an immovable mover. A single change would suffice to necessitate the existence of the Immovable Being. The argument is based upon the nature of change, and not upon the plurality of changes.—The second way leads to God by the connection between efficient causes (*ex causa efficiente*) : in any series in which the higher is the cause of the lower ; to deny

---

[1] Speaking of the angels, Thomas writes : " Quia forma creata sic subsistens habet esse et non est suum esse, necesse est quod ipsum esse sit receptum et contractum ad terminatum naturam. Unde non potest esse infinitum simpliciter." (*Summa Theol.*, Ia, q. 7, a. 2, and q. 3, art. 4. See Cajetan's commentary on this passage : " Unde esse earum non est absolutum sed receptum, et ideo limitatum et finitum ad capacitatem naturae recipientis." (*De ente et essentia* cap. 6, Cf. *Contra Gent.* II, c. 52.)

a first cause, or to prolong the chain to infinity, which would amount to the same, would destroy all real causality and therefore contradict the facts.—The third proof, in which St. Thomas follows Maimonides, is based upon the distinction between the " possible " and the " necessary " (*ex possibili*) : the existence of contingent being compels the mind to infer the existence of necessary and permanent being, and if there exists a series of necessary beings, we must come to a first necessary being, itself the cause of all other necessary and contingent beings.—The fourth way argues from the gradations (*ex gradibus*) in the transcendental perfections (being, goodness, truth, unity) of limited beings to the existence of a Being possessing these perfections in the highest degree, from which all others are derived.   Lastly we have the classic proof drawn from the finality and government of the world (*ex gubernatione rerum*)[1]   The Aristotelian inspiration of these arguments is evident.   All start from sensible experience, the analysis of the imperfect world, and argue from the principles of sufficient reason and causality.   Thomas unhesitatingly rejects as without value the *a priori* arguments based upon the concept of the Infinite.   The fourth proof, the sense of which is very much discussed, has indeed a neo-Platonist appearance, but when viewed in connection with the others, it applies to the order of real existence and not to that of mere concepts.

The existence of God is accordingly not evident.   Between Him and us there is the corporeal and contingent world.

(ii) *Attributes*.   We only know God through the world and as author of the world ; but we understand that the Pure Actuality, excluding as it does all possibility of limitation, is infinite.   The Being-in-itself possesses all the degrees of perfection, just as " no degree of whiteness would be lacking to a being which was whiteness in itself."[2]

The perfections which we are justified in attributing to God flow from the fact that His essence is existence (*esse a se, per essentiam*).   They are represented by concepts which are *negative*, inasmuch as they exclude all imperfection, *analogical* since there can be no common measure of the Infinite and the finite, and *transcendent*.   We distinguish between them by a " virtual incomplete distinction " (*distinctio rationis cum*

---

[1] The first two and last two arguments are given at the beginning of both *Summae* ; the third is found only in the *Summa Theologica*.
[2] *Contra Gent.*, I, 28.

fundamento in re) as so many aspects of one and the same infinite reality.

True to his intellectualism, St. Thomas speaks of intelligence as the noblest of all the divine perfections. In God immanent intelligence is infinite, for His activities are identical with His substance. By His own essence God knows Himself (*object primarium*) and all that is outside Him (*objectum secundarium*); and these feeble and distinct resemblances constitute the very nature of contingent things (Divine ideas).

St. Thomas definitely breaks away from the older scholastics and follows Aristotle in defending the famous thesis that the eternity of the world does not imply any contradiction.[1] The indetermination of duration, and therefore the absence of a beginning, does not affect the essential dependence which results from the creative act. Creation *ab æterno* is not absurd in philosophy, although as a theologian, St. Thomas teaches the commencement of things in time. The neo-Platonist theses of the necessity of the creative act and the interposition of intermediaries are rejected as incompatible with the very notion of production *ex nihilo*.[2]

277. Metaphysical pluralism and the notion of being.— Thomist metaphysics is above all a study of the determinations of corporeal being, but it arrives at results which apply also to immaterial being, so that ultimately all reality constitutes its domain.

Being, which belongs to everything real, is profoundly different in the various beings. There is no single formality which is absolutely alike and applies in the same way to the Necessary Being and to contingent things—not even the opposition to nothing. Otherwise being would be a genus to which one could add differences ; this would be impossible, for there could be no difference which is not itself being, and thus we should be led to monism. Everything is *diverse*, even to the profoundest depths of reality. The notion of being, upon which the mind confers an indefinite plasticity (intellectus humanus potest omnia fieri), is not *univocal* ; the reality attained to is *analogous* in its various terms, according to a proportion which constitutes the basis of the analogy. It is thus that the notion of being can be applied to God. Although the Divine

---

[1] *Summa Theol.* I, q. 46, a. 2. " Mundum non semper fuisse sola fide tenetur et demonstrative probari non potest."

[2] *De Potentia*, q. III, a. 4. Cf. Rohner, *BGPM*, XI, 5, pp. 93-133.

being has no common measure with finite being, " God is to
His attributes as the creature is to his." The proportion is
real, although all the terms of the proportion are not equally
knowable. The analogy of proportion (" non simpliciter
eadem, sed proportionaliter eadem ")[1] safeguards pluralism,
the diversity of beings, the transcendence of God and His
knowability.

278. Principles of nature.—(i) *Substantial transformation.*
In consequence of its eternal finality, a body is endowed not
only with a tendency to change its accidental state, but also
with a more profound inclination to make room for other
bodies. St. Thomas regards this substantial becoming as
the simple actuation of a potency, and he excludes the complications with which the older scholasticism had surrounded
the theory. Matter and form are proportioned to each other,
and accordingly a change in the dispositions of the matter
involves in the latter an exigency for the realization of new
forms which were previously only potentialities (theory of the
privatio). Since nothing can pass of itself from potency to
actuality, this change in the plasticity of prime matter and
its reception of a new perfection can only place under the
influence (*virtus activa*) of external agents. The phenomenon
of transformation requires nothing more in order to be intelligible. St. Thomas vigorously combats the doctrine adopted
both by the older scholastics and by Albert the Great, that the
very germs of the successive actuations are deposited in matter
(*rationes seminales*), and are merely drawn out by the efficient
causes. To endow matter itself with active germs is to give a
determination to the undetermined, and to form a concept of
contradictory notions. St. Thomas stresses the passivity of
matter ; its capacity for receiving a series of successive
perfections is a sufficient foundation for the evolution of
substances.[2] The problem of substantial transformation is
thus simplified and saturated with the peripatetic spirit.

(ii) *The theory of light.* St. Thomas rejected the interpretation of the theory of light given by the older scholastics and
the Latin neo-Platonists.

(a) Against St. Augustine[3] and the Augustinians, he teaches

---

[1] *S. Theol.* Ia, q. 3, a. 5.
[2] *Contra Gent.*, III, 22.
[3] In conformity with his method of interpreting Augustine, he writes :
" Nihilominus Augustinus non intendit hoc afferre (i.e., quod lux non sit

that light belongs properly only to bodies, and that accordingly it is only metaphorically applied to purely spiritual beings.[4] Moreover, in bodies it is not a substantial form, but an accidental determination.[5]

(b) Against the neo-Platonists of his time, and in particular the treatise *De intelligentiis*, he denies that a being which acts upon another is light, or that its efficient causality is luminous in character. Here again we have at most a metaphor (" nisi lux metaphorice accipiator pro omni actu "). To speak of a luminous effusion is to make use of a misleading figure.[6]

279. Celestial and terrestrial bodies.—The universe is a closed and finite system. The higher spheres are put in motion not by astral souls playing the part of intelligent and divine forms (Aristotle), but by intelligent movers which are extrinsically united to them.[7] Speaking of the movements of the planets and of the theory of epicycles and eccentrics advanced in order to explain and complete the geocentric hypothesis, St. Thomas makes this significant remark : " Licet enim talibus suppositionibus factis apparentia salvarentur, non tamen oportet dicere has suppositiones esse veras, quia forte secundum aliquem alium modum nondum ab hominibus comprehensum apparentia circa stellas salvantur."[8] This shows clearly that he does not make his metaphysics depend upon a particular astronomical theory.

The stars are unchangeable, but composed of matter and form. The first heaven exercises an influence on all the changes which take place upon the earth, including those in the human body, but has no effect upon the intellect, will, or the spiritual soul.[9] Its general efficiency collaborates with the causality

accidens) quasi fidei conveniens, sed sicut utens his quae philosophiam addiscens audierat." (*II. Sent.*, d. 13, q. 1, a. 3.)

[4] *ibid.*, a. 2. " Quod in spiritualibus non nisi metaphorice inveniatur."

[5] *ibid.*, a. 3. " Nulla substantia est per se sensibilis, quia quod quid est est objectum intellectus. Unde oportet quod lux quae per se videtur, non sit forma substantialis. . . . Lux est forma accidentalis."

[6] " Quamvis liber de intelligentiis non sit auctoritatis alicujus, nec etiam verum sit quod omnis influxus sit ratione lucis nisi lux metaphorice accipiatur pro omni actu." (*Quodl.* VI. q. 11, a. 19). The whole passage is worth noting).

Cf. Baeumker, *Witelo*, pp. 415-421.

[7] " Ad hoc autem quod moveat, non oportet quod uniatur et ut forma, sed per contactum virtutis, sicut motor unitur mobili." (*Summa Theol.* I. q. 70, a. 3).

[8] In lib. II. *De Cælo et Mundo*, lect. XVII. Cf. *Summa Theol.* I. q. 32, a. 1. ad 2.

[9] *Summa Theol.*, I.IIae, q. 9, a. 5.

of particular agents,[1] for the unity of the cosmic order requires
that inferior beings should be governed by the higher.[2] Thomas
Aquinas pronounces against a plurality of worlds, for it is fitting
that there should be one only.[3]

Abstract quantity (mathematical) is indefinitely divisible,
but there is a limit to the divisibility of a natural substance,
and a mininum of size without which it could not retain its
specific nature.[4]

280. The activities of the soul.—*Sensation.*—Questions 75
to 90 of the First Part of the *Summa Theologica* might very
well be detached from the master's work and serve as a manual
of Psychology. He studies in turn the activities of the soul
and its nature. He holds that there is a real distinction
between the soul and its faculties, and between each of the
latter, and adds to arguments metaphysical in character the
further considerations that the adequate diversity of vital
operations implies that of the immediate subject (*faculty*) from
which they are derived. He differs from Aristotle, whose
opinion is not quite clear[5] and from the Augustinians, who
regarded the soul and its faculties as one and the same
reality.

The Thomist theory of knowledge departs from the older
scholasticism on several points.

The sense faculties are passive powers, and are determined
(*species sensibilis*) by exterior objects, the action of which
upon the organ is a real efficient causality. This safeguards
the objectivity of sensation. Inasmuch as the action is
received in the subject, it belongs to the psychic order, and
hence must not be confused with the physical phenomena
which take place in the medium between the object and the
sense organ.

281. Thought.—(i) *Origin and nature.* The human
intellect begins to abstract as soon as it comes in contact
with reality, whether by external or internal sensation.
Abstraction is the law of the human mind, and all the imperfections of our knowledge follow from it. The multiplicity

---

[1] *Ibid,* I, q. 115, a. 3.
[2] *Quodl.* VI, 19.
[3] *De Cælo et Mundo,* I. 19. See a remarkable chapter in Rousselot, *L'intellectualisme de S. Thomas,* p. 156.
[4] "Corpus naturale, quod consideratur sub tota forma, non potest in
infinitum dividi, quia quando ad minimum deducitur, statim propter debilita-
tem virtutis convertitur in aliud." (*De sensu et sensato,* I, 15.)
[5] Piat, *Aristote,* pp. 156, 157.

of concepts relating to one and the same object, and the necessity of judgment and discourse (*ratio*) are all connected with this abstract character of knowledge.

From the historical point of view, there are two important ideological doctrines which St. Thomas maintained against the older scholastics : the causal influence of sensation in the production of thought ; and the absence of any need for a special illumination.

In the first place, Thomas criticizes the ideology of Plato, and declares that the function the latter assigns to the sensible object ("excitant animam intellectivam ad intelligendum ") is insufficient.[1] His criticism applies equally to the explanation given by the Augustinians. St. Thomas holds in common with Duns Scotus, that the corporeal reality acts on the understanding through the intermediary of the sensible image (*phantasma*) ; it exercises an instrumental causality, in conjunction with the efficient causality of an immaterial faculty, the active intellect. With the aid of this higher energy, the sensible image—and in the last analysis the external object—arouses the passive understanding (*species intelligibilis impressa*), the reaction of which results in the immanent activity perfecting thought (*species intelligibilis expressa*).[2] It is hardly necessary to point out that St. Thomas rejects the false theory of the " spiritualized phantasm."[3]

In the next place, Thomas is convinced that in spite of its weakness, the human intelligence is adequate for the acquisition of our knowledge,—" parvum lumen intelligibile, quod nobis est connaturale, sufficit ad nostrum intelligere."[4] It is unnecessary to introduce a special divine help in order to explain the genesis of the higher truths. He regards the Augustinian texts concerning the divine illumination as referring to the ultimate foundations of knowledge, and the resemblance between our intelligence and the Divine Mind.[5]

Many doctors of his time wished to harmonize the Augustinian ideas with the terminology of Aristotle, and had called God the " active intellect of our souls." Thomas, in a text

---

[1] *Summa Theol.* I, q. 84, a. 6.
[2] This terminology is found in the contemporaries of St. Thomas. The latter generally uses *species* in the sense of *species impressa* ; the *species expressa* is usually called the *verbum*.
[3] Vol. I, p. 295.
[4] *Contra Gentiles*, II, 77.
[5] Von Hertling, *Augustinuscitate bei Th.*, pp. 563-601.

in the commentary on Book II of the Sentences which has given rise to discussion[1] mentions an attempt to apply this formula in a theological connection. After pointing out that the majority of philosophers after Aristotle agree in distinguishing substantially between the active and possible intellects, and regard the supreme felicity of man as consisting in his union with the active intellect, he goes on to say : " Quidam catholici doctores, corrigentes hanc opinionem et partim sequentes, satis probabiliter posuerunt ipsum Deum esse intellectum agentem ;   quia per applicationem ad ipsum anima nostra beata est." The last words, together with the context, show that he is referring to the supernatural order. These theologians (" doctores ") call God the active intellect inasmuch as his possession by the understanding constitutes beatitude. In the natural order, God is not the active intellect of our souls. Thomas is careful to prove this in the same article, in order that there should be no misunderstanding of his thought. He concludes: " Et ideo, remotis omnibus prædictis erroribus, dico . . . intellectum possibilem . . . in diversis diversum esse, et multiplicari secundum divisionem materiæ in diversis individuis . . . et superaddo etiam intellectum agentem esse in diversis diversum."[2] When from the ideological point of view Thomas calls the human intelligence a torch kindled by the eternal truth, he is merely adopting the current formulæ, and the theory of light has only the value of a comparison.

We find the same language elsewhere,[3] while in other places Thomas disapproves of the identification of God and the active intellect.[4] The *Summa Theologica* contains another explanation in which St. Thomas, conciliatory as always, endeavours to give an acceptable sense to the formula.[5] But in reality his doctrine is profoundly different from that of Bacon, Marston and others whom he endeavours to excuse (Ch. IV, § 2).

[1] *Dist.* 17, q. 2, art. 1, *in corpore*.

[2] Delorme, article *Bacon* in *Dict. Theol. Cath.*, II, 12. would appear not to have read this passage.   Otherwise how can he invoke Aquinas in favour of Bacon's ideology ?

[3] *De unitate intellectus.* St. Bonaventure also mentions this explanation and considers it orthodox.

[4] *Quaest. disput. de anima*, a. V.

[5] I. q. 79, a. 4. The question of doctrine is clearly enuntiated : " Utrum intellectus agens sit aliquid animae," and the answer is equally definite : " Respondeo dicendum quod intellectus agens de quo Philosophus loquitur, est aliquid animae." Answering an objection based upon the texts of Aris-

On the other hand, when faced by the Averrhoist psychology his indulgence gives place to indignation. Here there is no possibility of coming to terms ; we have to deal not with friends but with enemies : the theory of human monopsychism leads to fatal consequences. We shall outline his polemic on this subject later on.

(ii) *Value.* St Thomas takes as many pains in the fixing of the limits of knowledge as he does in the justification of its value within these limits.

Since reason is bound up with sensation, it is the world of bodies that is its proper object ; the supracorporeal—God, and the nature of the human soul—are known only by indirect methods. The intuitions of the supra-sensible so dear to St. Bonaventure are excluded by the logic of Thomism. The existence of the ego is alone attained in a conscious operation. Even in the corporeal domain, our grasp of reality is weakened by the fact that we get abstract views of everything, the content of which we then proceed to generalize. The human mind knows things by classes. It is condemned to be ignorant of the diversification of essences : what we understand by life and movement, for instance, applies in an identical way to all living and moving things. For the same reason, the intellectual knowledge of that which is individual in a substance must of necessity be beyond us. We understand that there must be in each individual thing—this particular man for instance—something which stamps his whole reality (humanity, actions, etc.) with a particular mark, but we do not know in what it consists. The intellect grasps the individual only in an indirect manner, by means of a reflection on the data of the senses, and the exact nature of this *reflexio* is one of the obscure and difficult points in Thomism.

Still, however inadequately our thoughts may correspond to reality, this correspondence is a faithful one. In order to explain this, Thomas points out that every element of reality may be considered in three states : the natural state, in which it is singular and multiple ; the universal idea of

totle, Thomas says that God, as first cause, could still be called the active intellect of our souls. He is careful to add that we are nevertheless endowed with a created active intellect, the work of the uncreated active intellect. For otherwise man would be the one exception to the law that contingent things contain in themselves the principle of their activities. This is clearly expressed : " Nulla autem actio convenit alicui rei, nisi per aliquod principium ei inhaerens. . . . Ergo oportet virtutem quae est principium hujus actionis (*scil.* facere actu intelligibilia) esse aliquid in anima."

it in the mind, in which it is one, general, and thought of as related to an indefinite number of beings ; and lastly, that which constitutes its abstract quiddity, apart from the singularity or universality which makes its existence real or ideal.[1]   Now this reality, or quiddity, is taken by abstraction from the singular thing : the form of universality results exclusively from the ideal state, since it results from a previous process of abstractive segregation.   Hence we get this synthetic formula : the universal as such (*formaliter*) is a product of the mind, but has a foundation (*fundamentaliter*) in the extramental reality.[2] Like all the great scholastics of the thirteenth century, Thomas maintains the realism of Abelard. Posterity has given this moderate realism the name of Thomistic realism, in order to render homage to the precision and dialectical force of the master.

282. **Appetition. Will.**—The sensible appetite is a movement of our being towards a concrete object presented to us in sensation as desirable.[3] On the other hand, the will is of a superior nature, and has as its object being under the abstract formality of the good, presented by the intelligence. Thomas distinguishes between the necessary and free volition of the good. An irresistible tendency impels us towards the good as such, and leads us to seek to unite ourselves to that which perfects our nature. This profound tendency is necessary, and is always in act. It manifests itself in an initial tendency towards any and every object which appeals to us in the first place as something good. But inasmuch as all the good things among which we are placed are in fact limited, a man has only to reflect to realize their deficiencies. Then we are faced by two contradictory judgments : if it is good to will a particular thing for certain reasons, it is also good not to will it for other reasons. It is the will that brings the deliberation

---

[1] *Quod.*, q. 1, a. 1.

[2] *In Sent.* I. D. 19, q. 5, a. 1. He speaks in the following terms of the fundamental error of exaggerated realism now definitely shown to be untenable. " Credidit (Plato) quod forma cogniti ex necessitate sit in cognoscente eo modo quo est in cognito, et ideo existimavit quod oporteret res intellectas hoc modo in se ipsis subsistere, scilicet immaterialiter et immobiliter."— *S. Theol.* Ia, q. 84, a. 1.

[3] In a study on the *De passionibus animae*, Meier groups the sources of St. Thomas as follows : Aristotle, 226 quotations ; St. Augustine, 56 ; pseudo-Dionysius, 12 ; St. John Damascene, 9.   In accordance with his usual custom, St. Thomas endeavours to harmonize these with each other and with Aristotle. —Meier, *Die Lehre des Th. v. A. de passionibus animae in Quellenanalytischer Darstellung*, BGPM, XI, 2, 1912.

to an end by deciding to choose one of the two alternatives, not because it is the *greatest* good, but because it is *a* good. Or again, a particular thing seems to us to be the greatest good by the very fact that the will chooses it. Thus liberty is founded (*radicaliter*) in a reflecting judgment, but culminates in the will. It consists in the power of judging our judgment, and of choosing one of two values presented to us by two contradictory judgments. The Thomist theory of freedom is thus a form of intellectualism.

283. Intellectualism.—This term is used to designate the doctrine which places all the intensity and value of mental life in the act of understanding.[1] No scholastic philosopher is more intellectualist, more " noe-centric " than that of Thomas Aquinas. He departs from the old doctrine of St. Augustine, and introduces new theories which give rise to ardent discussions during the last quarter of the thirteenth century :

(i) The intellect is superior to the will in its manner of attaining its object. It is the faculty which *grasps* ; the will is that which *tends*. To possess something is more perfect than to tend towards it.

(ii) The intellect gives rise to the necessary consent of the will when it presents something wholly good, " voluntas de necessitate movetur " ; freedom itself has its root in the practical judgment.

(iii) Thomist moral philosophy is intellectualist : the end of man is above all to *know*, that is, to exercise the most noble of all activities ; the acquisition of beatitude (*formaliter*) is of the intellectual order, not of the volitional.[2]

(iv) The intellectualism of Thomas Aquinas is again manifest in the extent of the normal power of the intelligence, and the criticism of the theory of a special illumination (p. 21)

(v) It has analogical repercussions in the study of the angelic and the Divine life. In particular it explains why St. Thomas is so careful to make the order of essences and the natural and moral law dependent on the Divine knowledge. Just as in metaphysics Aquinas studies being as such, commencing with corporeal being, so in psychology he studies the function of knowledge and will, not only in man, but in all spiritual beings.

---

[1] See Preface in Rousselot, *op. cit.*
[2] Again, the *habitus* of faith resides in the intellect (*op. cit.*, p. 374, note).

284. Human nature.—The spiritual soul is the one substantial form of the body. This doctrine is alone capable of accounting for the unity of human nature and explains why the intensive exercise of one activity may interfere with that of others. Similarly it ensures the identity of personality after the resurrection, inasmuch as the soul is identical throughout. St. Thomas answers the arguments of his opponents by the theory of the hierarchy of forms and that of transitory forms. A higher determining principle—the spiritual soul for instance—can fulfil the functions of an inferior principle—the corporeal form. On the other hand, human generation consists of a series of successive transformations. The transitory forms which mark the various stages, lead the human embryo to a state of perfection such that it calls for information by the spiritual soul, which is then produced by a Divine intervention.[1]

In order to prove the spirituality and the consequent immortality of the soul, Aquinas bases himself chiefly on the immaterial nature of intellectual activity.[2]

No Scholastic has laid more stress than St. Thomas on the bonds which closely unite soul and body : the soul needs the body in order to exercise its normal activity ; they together form one being. Although destined to survive the body, the soul is naturally inclined to desire it when separated from it. The union of the two is different and more intimate than in the philosophy of St. Bonaventure.

285. Moral philosophy.—St. Thomas built up a complete system of ethics which is justly looked upon as one of the best parts of his philosophy. The general outline is to be found in qq. 1-60 of the IaIIæ of the *Summa Theologica*, which give a concise treatment of the three great questions dealt with in ethics (185).

The real end of man, his highest good, is the possession of God, Who is the supreme object of the highest human activity, that of knowledge. A man who seeks his real good is *en route* towards the Deity, even if he does not yet realize that his real

---

[1] De Wulf, *Le traité de unitate de G. de Lessines*, pp. 53-58.
[2] At the same time he makes use of the following argument, which does not harmonize very well with his thesis on the natural union of soul and body, and seems to be a concession to traditional ideas : the more the soul is freed from the body, the more capable does it become of high speculation. Hence death, or complete detachment from the body, cannot involve the annihilation of the soul. (*Contra Gentiles*, II, 79.)

good is God.[1] Moral goodness, or ethical value, applies not
only to the fundamental tendency leading all men to seek for
what is suitable for them—a tendency which may be diverted
but cannot be altogether destroyed—but also to the voluntary
and free acts which a man is able to subordinate to his real
perfection if he so chooses, provided they converge towards
his real end.[2] The morality of an act consists in a relationship
based upon the very nature of man, which is immutable like
the order of essences. Furthermore, morality applies to the
same elements (intention, object willed, circumstances) as
those which complete the ontological reality of the volitional
act.

Moral obligation, which St. Thomas strictly confines to the
means indispensable for the obtaining of our end, is in the
last analysis an echo of the *lex æterna* or providential plan in
the Divine mind, which makes God the end of every creature.
This plan is reflected in each being according to its own proper
nature (*lex naturalis*), so that everything is subject to a Divine
attraction, " imprimit principia actuum totæ naturæ."[3]
The natural law of man is a participation of the eternal law
applied to a rational creature and made known to us by reason.[4]
It ordains that man shall tend towards God, but at the same
time respects his nature as a free being. It is the same
always and in all, in its *dictamen* and immediate corollaries,
although its detailed application may vary according to circumstances.

The *synderesis*, which determines the content of obligation,
is a " habitus continens præcepta legis naturalis,"[5] and from
the subjective point of view, a *virtus* of the possible intellect,
a light " per quod cognoscimus quid agendum et quid vitan-
dum." Conscience applies precepts to particular cases, and is
the means by which the law gives rise to a concrete act of the
will. It binds us in virtue of the knowledge we possess of the
law : hence an erroneous conscience binds in the same way as
a correct one, and anything which lessens the clearness of
knowledge likewise diminishes the obligation. St. Thomas

---

[1] *Summa Theol.*, Ia, q. 2, art. 1.
[2] " Dominus actuum ducens ad finem,"—*ibid.*, q. 1, art. 1.
[3] *Summa Theol.* IaIIae, q. 19, a. 2.
[4] " Lex naturalis nihil aliud est quam participatio legis æternæ in rationali
creatura," (*ibid.*, q. 91, a. 2). " Prima regula (commensurans voluntatem)
scilicet lex æterna quæ est quasi ratio Dei ; regula propinqua et homogenea
scilicet ipsa humana ratio " (q. 71, art. 6.)
[5] q. 94, a. 1.

gives a lengthy treatment of the moral virtues or permanent tendencies in the will towards the accomplishment of the good. Prudence, the " recta ratio agibilium," penetrating all other virtues, and justice, which is the permanent disposition to render to each one his *jus*[1] are the subject of noteworthy developments.

Moral philosophy is supplemented by religion and dogma, for the life of the elect consists in an intellectualist and complete possession of God through the beatific vision.

286. Political and social philosophy.—Since the group life exists only to help individuals to realize their moral end (188), it has itself an ethical character. St. Thomas studies by preference two groupings following from the nature of man, namely, the family and the State.

The State to which he refers (*provincia, regnum*) is neither the little Greek city of Aristotle, nor the solidly organized nation, which did not as yet exist in the thirteenth century, but a political entity which would seem to correspond more or less to the feudal principalities of his day—duchies, countships, municipal republics, or even the great European kingdoms then in process of formation.

(i) Power or sovereignty, without which there can be no social life, comes from God, and belongs to the people, that is to say, to the collection of citizens. This is logical, for the group is not an entity in itself, and the only social reality is the individual citizen. St. Thomas adopts John of Salisbury's comparison of the state with the human organism. But neither he nor the other scholastics ascribe to this simile the real significance accorded to it by modern organicists.

The State is the people, but the latter delegates its authority by a kind of contract, essentially revocable, either to one (monarch) or to many persons " who govern in the name of the community."[2] Election, civic education, and popular control follow from this principle.

(ii) Power is an *officium*, or function to be used for the *bonum commune*.[3] This common good, which supplies the insufficiency of the individual for the attainment of his well-

---

[1] " Perpetua et constans voluntas jus suum unicuique tribuendi," IaIIae, q. 58, a. 1.   This *jus* (a juridical term which St. Thomas identifies also with the justum or δίκαιον of Aristotle) is " aliquod opus adæquatum alteri secundum aliquem modum (*ibid.*, q. 57, a. 1).

[2] *Summa Theol.*, IIaIIae, q. 90, a. 3.

[3] *De Regim. principum*, I, c. 1-13.

being, is possible only by means of organization, and hence the latter without the acquisition of the good by the individual would be compromised. The common good is superior to the individual good " as the whole is superior to its part," but is nevertheless subservient to it.[1] The *De Regimine Principum* draws up a detailed programme of the duties of the prince,[2] and the *Summa Theologica* describes the social justice which it is the prince's duty to promote.[3] This social justice, resulting from the common exercise of all activities for the good of all, is a magnificent affirmation of solidarity. It is based upon the principle that every action of an individual has its repercussion on the group, and ought to be put to the service of the group. But by reason of the individualism which characterizes his philosophy throughout, St. Thomas attributes to the human person the benefit of all his acts, for they are his means of attaining to his end, and accordingly there must be some compensation restoring the equivalent (*jus*) of the labours of the individual on behalf of the community.[4]

This Thomist philosophy of the State applies to every form of government, and the mode of delegation of the authority must be decided by circumstances. St. Thomas himself gives his preference to a monarchy tempered by a wide participation in government by an aristocracy or even by the people.[5]

St. Thomas deals with some special questions concerning social life, such as the right to wage war, and the theory of property. Only the government of a State can declare war (*auctoritas principis*), and then only for a just cause (*justa causa*) and with the upright intention of obtaining reparation for the injury suffered (*intentio bellantium recta*). Thus the end or object of war is the re-establishment of peace.[6] These doctrines provided the basis for a Christian conception of the right of war.

Individual property is a natural right, for the *jus gentium*, from which it follows, is itself only the extension of the *jus naturæ*.[7] In this way St. Thomas harmonizes the point of view of the Roman lawyers and the Fathers of the Church, who states

---

[1] *Summa Theol.* IIaIIae, q. 57, a. 5.
[2] I, c. 15.
[3] IIaIIae, q. 57, a. 6.
[4] IIaIIae, q. 58, a. 5, 6, 9. Cf. *Mediœval Philosophy Illustrated from the System of Thomas Aquinas*, Ch. XV.
[5] IIaIIae, q. 90, a. 1.
[6] IIaIIae. q. 40, a. 1.
[7] *ibid.*, q. 66 and q. 57, a. 3.

that property is a human institution, with the doctrine that it is natural and essential for the normal functioning of the group life.

There is not much trace of feudal and communal life in St. Thomas's economic theories. He condemns usury, and the lending of money otherwise than for a commercial operation, and he subjects all transactions to the laws of justice.[1]

Lastly, St. Thomas proclaims the superiority of the Church over civil society, in virtue of the principle that the religious welfare of the people is superior to their temporal good.[2]

287. Philosophy and Theology.—St. Thomas was also the prince of the speculative theologians of the thirteenth century. He widened the scope of doctrine, and on many questions put forth new or synthetic solutions, and above all he built up the data of Catholic theology into a system which has won the admiration of posterity. We find in his work the two constructive methods of scholastic theology : that of authority and the apologetic method.[3] He has never been surpassed in his philosophic apologia for Christianity, his utilization of metaphysics in the service of dogma, and his combination of arguments based on reason with those of faith.

For a long time scholastics had held the distinction between theology and philosophy, and the autonomy of each (120). But St. Thomas was the first to systematize the relations between the two branches of knowledge in a chapter of scientific methodology. The specific character of a science results from the way in which it knows its object and not from the object itself : " diversa ratio cognoscibilis diversitatem scientiarum inducit."[4] The distinction between philosophy and theology is accordingly based upon the distinction between the points of view (*secundum quod ; ratio formalis objecti*, formal object) from which they study their subject matter (material object). The prohibitive attitude adopted towards philosophical con-

---

[1] q. 77, a. 4.

[2] Is it temerarious to suggest that the manifold interventions of the Papacy in the internal affairs of kingdoms were in some sort an application of these political theories in the thirteenth century ? The people were practically defenceless against the suzerains and kings, and the Pope became their protector and mandatory for the exercise of their rights on their behalf. See De Wulf, *Les théories politiques du moyen âge* (*Revue Neo-Scolastique*, 1924, p. 249).

[3] See the Prologue to the Commentary on the Sentences, art. V. Cf. Gardeil, *La Réforme de la théologie catholique*, *La documentation de Saint Thomas* (*Revue thomiste*, May-June 1903), pp. 199 *et seq.*

[4] *Summa Theol.*, Ia, q. 1, a. 1, and also the rest of q. 1.   Cf. the Prologue to the *Contra Gentiles*.

clusions threatening or contradicting a dogma is merely a particular case of the general law of logical solidarity.[1]

St. Thomas is equally original in his application of these principles. No scholastic goes further in the partial compenetration of the respective domains of the two sciences. In the first place, many revealed truths belonging to the theological order are at the same time given a philosophic demonstration (for instance, the existence and attributes of God). Again, when reason bows before a mystery, it does not disclaim all competence, for it shows that the supra-rational is not the anti-rational. Aquinas the philosopher did not think it necessary to prove all the conclusions of the theologian : his ideas on eternal creation are a striking example of this.

288. Doctrinal characteristics of the Thomist philosophy.— (i) *Its systematic character.* What strikes one above all in Thomism is the close connection and solidarity of its doctrines. Everything is interrelated and unified. The constructive genius of this master of thought has compelled the admiration of posterity.

(ii) *New theories.*[2] St. Thomas introduced into his synthesis some new theories which were in complete opposition to the ideas of his contemporaries and predecessors : to the plurality of forms he opposed the unity of the substantial principle ; to the hylomorphic composition of spiritual substances the doctrine of subsistent forms[3] and the peripatetic idea of matter ; to the Augustinian theory of the identity of the soul with its faculties, that of the real distinction between a limited substance and its operative powers ; to the confusion of existence and essence, that of their real distinction[4] ; to the theory

---

[1] " Aliæ scientiæ certitudinem habent ex lumine rationis humanæ quæ potest errare ; hæc autem (sacra doctrina) certitudinem habet ex lumine divinæ scientiæ quæ decipi non potest " (*ibid.* art. 5).

[2] It has often been pointed out how strongly his disciple and biographer, William of Tocco, emphasized these innovating tendencies : " Erat enim novos in sua lectione movens articulos, novum modum et clarum determinandi inveniens et novas reducens in determinationibus rationes, ut nemo qui ipsum audisset nova docere et novis rationibus dubia definire, dubitaret, quod eum Deus novi luminis radiis illustraret, qui statim tam certi cœpisset (esse) judicii, ut non dubitaret, novas opiniones docere et scribere." (Acta SS. VII martii, n. 15).

[3] This doctrine is already found in John de la Rochelle, and accordingly St. Thomas is not the first to maintain it. So Minges, *Philos. Jahrb.* 1914, p. 224. But in any case the theory is new in virtue of the place it occupies in Thomism and the consequences which St. Thomas is the first to derive from it.

[4] Grabmann says in the *Theological Review*, 1916 (*Grundsätzl. u. Kritisches zu neuen Schriften über Th.*) that the discussion on the nature of the distinction

Neo-Scolastique for 1920, pp. 217-245. There have also been many editions of separate works, especially of the *Summa Theologica*. De Maria published *Opuscula philosophica et theologica*, including many apocryphal works, in three volumes (Citta di Castello, 1886). The Louvain Institute of Philosophy has published St. Thomas's Commentary on the *De Anima* (1901). Hedde has published the *Questiones disputatæ de anima* (Paris, 1912) ; Cathala the commentaries on the *Metaphysics*. There are also many editions of the *Quodlibeta* (Paris, and Turin). The *De Pulchro et Bono* which Uccelli publishes from a MS. which he claims to have been written by St. Thomas himself is simply an extract from Albert the Great's Commentary on the *De Divinis Nominibus* of pseudo-Dionysius (Naples, 1869), as has been shown by Jungmann in *Zeitschr. f. Kathol. Theol.* 1885, pp. 241-262, 278 *et seq.* Schütz, *Thomas-Lexicon* (2nd edit. Paderborn, 1895) is very useful. There is in preparation a *Lexique Thomiste* by Blanche.

There is a French translation of the *Summa Theologica* by Lachat, in 14 vols. (Paris, Vives, 1854), and an English one by the Dominican Fathers (London, 1911-1922, 18 vols.). There is also an English Dominican translation of the *Contra Gentes* (in course of publication), and a French translation by Vedrinne and Fournet in 6 vols. (Paris, Vives, 1854). Father Rickaby, S.J., has published the greater part of the *Contra Gentiles* in an English translation with notes under the title *God and His Creatures* (London, 1905).

General Studies : The works of Jourdain, Plasmann, Froschammer (1858) are inadequate. Willmann, *Gesch. d. Ideal.* II, 74-79. Excellent study by Rousselot, *L'intellectualisme de S. Thomas* (Paris, 1908, new edition 1924). This much-discussed book is studied in the *Revue Neo-Scolastique* for Feb. 1909. Sertillanges, *S. Thomas d'Aquin*, 2 vols., Paris 1910, excellent ; Grabmann and Endres, *op. cit.* ; E. Gilson, *Le thomisme*, Paris, 1923, English translation of 3rd French edition by E. Bullough (Cambridge 1924) ; Duhem, *Le systeme du monde*, Vol. V, ch. XII, a remarkable study ; see critique of Duhem by Geny, *La cohésion de la synthèse thomiste*, in *Xenia Tomistica*, III (Rome 1925) ; Durantel, *Le retour à Dieu par l'intelligence et la volonté dans philos. S. T.*, Paris 1918, claims that St. Thomas is a Neo-Platonist ; De Wulf, *Mediæval Philosophy illustrated from the system of Thomas Aquinas*, (Harvard, 1922).

Rosarius Janssen *Die Quodlibeta d. hl. Th. v. Aq. Ein Beitrag zu ihrer Wurdigung u. eine Beurteilung ihrer Ausgaben,* Bonn, 1912 ; J. Destrez, *Les disp. quodlib. de S. Th. d'après la tradition manuscrite (Melanges Thomistes,* see later on) ; articles by Pelster (*Gregorianum* 1924) and Glorieux (*Revue sc. philos. théol.* 1925) on the Quodl. XII of St. Thomas ; A. Dyroff, *Ueber d. Kulturbegriff d. Quæst. disput. de veritate d. hl. Thomas (Phil. Jahrb.* 1923, pp. 82-92), calls them the first majestic work of the master ; P. Minges, *Abhangigkeitsverh. zwischen d. Summe Alexanders v. Hale u. d. hl. Th. v. A.* in *Franz. Studien,* 1916, Vol. III, pp. 58-76 ; Grabmann, *Einfuhrung in die Summa Theol. des hl. Th.,* Fribourg, 1919 ; *Die Schrift De Ente et Essentia u. die Seinsmetaphysik des hl. Th. v. A.* (Beitr. z. Phil. u. Pedag. Willmann Festschrift, 1919). Among the doctrinal monographs, which are constantly increasing in number, we may mention the following : Dehove, *Essai sur le réalisme thomiste* (Lille, 1908) ; Schütz, *D. hl. Thomas u. sein Verstandniss d. Griech. (Phil. Jahrb.,* 1905) ; M. Asin y Palacios, *El Averroismo teologico de Sto Tomas de Aquino* (Extracto d. homenaje a Fr. Codera), Zaragoza, 1904, pp. 271-332 ; J. Maréchal, *Le point de départ de la Metaphysique,* Vol. I, De l'Antiquite à la fin du M. A. (Museum Lessianum, 1922), a remarkable comparative study of the problem of knowledge in St. Thomas, Duns Scotus, and William of Ockam ; A. Vacant, *Etudes comparées sur la philos. de S. Th. d'Aquin et sur celle de Duns Scot* (Paris 1897) ; Huit, *Les éléments platonic. de la doctrine de S. Th. (Revue Thomiste,* 1911) ; Guttmann, *De. Verhaltniss d. Th. v. A. zur judischen Litter.* (Gottingen 1891). On the relations between St. Thomas Aquinas and Siger of Brabant see Mandonnet, *op. cit.* For the proofs of the existence of God see the following : Baeumker, *Witelo,* pp. 317-339 ; Grunwald, *op. cit.,* pp. 133-161. Nys, *La notion de temps d'après les principes de S. Th.d'Aq.,* (Louvain, 1925). *La notion d'espace* (Brussels 1922). Endres, *Die Bedeutung d. hl. Th. fur das wissenschaftlich Leben seiner Zeit (Histor. Polit. Blätter,* 1911, p. 801). Maurenbrecher, *Thomas v. Aquino's Stellung z. Wirtschaftsleben seiner Zeit* (n. 1, Leipzig 1898), endeavours to find echoes of the communal organization in Thomist doctrines ; J. Vialatoux, *L'idée de civilisation dans philos. S. Th.* (Lyons) ; N. Thoemes, *Commentatio de S. Th. A. operibus ad ecclesiasticum, politicum, socialem statum reipublicæ christianæ pertinentibus* (Berlin 1874), good ; J. Zeiller, *L'Idee de l'Etat dans St. Thomas*

peacefully side by side : from henceforth doctrinal conflicts separated them. The older party also included secular teachers, and even a certain number of Dominicans whose formation dated from the pre-Thomist period.   John Peckham tells us that in the hey-day of Thomas's teaching at Paris (1269-1271), his colleagues criticized his thesis on the unity of the substantial form—" etiam a fratribus propriis arguebatur argute." [1] Similarly at Oxford a Dominican was for many years the soul of the opposition to Thomism.   Lastly, the latter met with opposition on the part of certain mystics who disliked the extreme intellectualism of the master.

The opposition to Thomism manifested itself in written works and in censures.

(i) Incidental refutations of Thomist doctrines are found in the works of writers like MATTHEW OF AQUASPARTA, but between 1277 and 1282 a prominent teacher, WILLIAM DE LA MARE (248) published a formal criticism, under the title *Correctorium fratris Thomae*.   This book, in which the author criticizes a hundred and seventeen points of doctrine found in Thomas's works, is a veritable manifesto of the Franciscan school,[2] and a declaration of war by the older scholasticism against Thomism.

The theory of the unity of form was one of the most frequently opposed.   RICHARD OF MIDDLETON wrote a treatise *De gradu formarum* (unpublished) in defence of the doctrine of plurality. JOHN PECKHAM, who was all his life a vigorous opponent of Thomas, relates in a boasting manner how he debated the question of the unity of forms with Thomas Aquinas in a disputation (about 1269-1271) at which the Bishop of Paris and the masters of theology were present.   According to him, he alone defended Aquinas as far as the truth would allow, and St. Thomas was in the end forced to submit his theses to the censure of the Faculty.[3]   This account should not be

---

[1] Letter of John Peckham, 1st June, 1285. *Chart.*, I. 634.

[2] This is shown by the title of a compilation containing a number of these criticisms : *Articuli in quibus minores contradicunt Thomæ in secunda secundæ*, and by similar declarations by John of Paris. See Mandonnet, *Premiers travaux de polémique thomiste*, in *R. sc. phil. Théol.*, 1913, p. 58; Ehrle (*Der Kampf um die Lehre d. hl. Thomas von Aquin*, 1913, S. 306 and 272) mentions fragments of a second edition of the *Correctorium*.

[3] " Nos soli ei adstitimus, ipsum prout salva veritate potuimus, defendendo; donec ipse omnes positiones suas, quibus possit imminere correctio sicut doctor humilis subjecit moderamini Parisiensium magistrorum." (Letter to the Bishop of Lincoln, 1285. *Chart.* I, 634).

taken too seriously. BARTHOLOMEW OF CAPUA, a witness at
the process of Canonization of St. Thomas, gives a different
version. Peckham apparently tried to exasperate his opponent,
who nevertheless countered his strong language only with
words of sweetness and humility.[1] We have already pointed
out[2] that there is no allusion to this debate in Peckham's
Quæstiones.

We also possess a letter of the Dominican Robert Kilwardby
to his colleague Peter of Conflas, Archbishop of Corinth,
pointing out the many difficulties to which the new doctrines
give rise.

(ii) The official proscriptions of Thomism form the subject-
matter of lively pages in the university annals of Paris and
Oxford.

291. Condemnations of Thomism.—Already in 1270, on
the occasion of the inquiry preceding the Averrhoist condemnation of the 10th December (**329**), there was a question
of condemning by implication two Thomist theories, namely,
the unity of substantial forms in one of its theological applications, and the doctrine of the simplicity of angels.[3] That
same year Thomas had maintained, in his third Quodlibetic
disputation, almost all the new theories which separated him
from the older scholasticism.

This first attempt to condemn him failed, but seven years
later a similar plan succeeded. On the 18th of January, 1277,
Pope John XXI, to whom complaints had been made about the
Averrhoist errors taught at Paris, charged the Bishop of Paris,
Stephen Tempier, to institute an inquiry. The prelate went
beyond his mandate. After convoking an assembly of masters
of theology and of " prudent men," he drew up on March 7th,
1277, a syllabus of two hundred and nineteen propositions
which he condemned as errors, excommunicating whosoever
held them. This act had extensive consequences. Although
directed chiefly against Averrhoism, as we shall see it also
affected doctrines taught by Roger Bacon, Giles of Rome,
Thomas Aquinas and others. So far as Thomism is concerned
the censure applies to the theories of the unity of the
world, the individuation of material and spiritual substances, and the dependent theory of the localization of

---

[1] *Ibid.*, 635.
[2] Vol. One, p. 378.
[3] We owe this information to Giles of Lessines.

spiritual substances and their relation with the physical world.[1]

It will be noticed that the Thomist doctrines censured are associated with Averrhoist peripateticism, and that in this way Averrhoism and its declared adversary are included in a common condemnation. This censure was principally due to the secular masters who upheld the older scholasticism, but it is likely that many of them were animated by hostility towards the mendicant Orders and saw here an opportunity of striking a blow at one of their redoubtable opponents. In any case it was an abuse thus to censure theories which could not be regarded as heterodox.

Bishop Tempier's condemnation had no binding force outside the University and diocese of Paris. But it was not an isolated incident : it formed part of a plan of campaign the ramifications of which extended to Oxford. This English University was under the jurisdiction of the Archbishop of Canterbury, and was a great centre of opposition to Thomism. The defenders of the older scholasticism were successively led by two Archbishops, the Dominican Robert Kilwardby, and the Franciscan John Peckham, and hence are referred to in contemporary documents as " Cantuarienses."[2]

On the 18th of March, 1277, a few days after the decree of Bishop Tempier, ROBERT KILWARDBY, who had waged war against Thomism among the English Dominicans, caused the Masters of the University of Oxford to prohibit a number of theses *in naturalibus*, among them being the Thomist theories of generation, the passivity of matter, the unity of the soul in man, and the introduction of new forms in the human body after death.[3] To ensure respect for this prohibition,

---

[1] Prop. 34 : " Quod prima causa non potest plures mundos facere." Prop. 96 : " Quod Deus non posset multiplicare individua sub una specie sine materia." Cf. n. 81. Prop. 77 : " Quod si esset aliqua substantia separata, quæ non moveret aliquod corpus in hoc mundo sensibili, non clauderetur in universo." (*Chart.*, I, pp. 543-560). It is interesting to note that the 7th Proposition condemned teaches the Platonist and Augustinian psychology : " Quod intellectus non est forma corporis, nisi sicut nauta navis, nec est perfectio essentialis hominis." Cf. nos. 13, 14.

[2] Giles of Lessines, *De unitate formae*, p. 14 : " Sic arguunt cantuarienses."

[3] " (2), Item quod forma corrumpitur in pure nichil ; (3), item quod nulla potentia est in materia ; (4), item quod privatio est pure nichil . . . ; (7), item quod intellectiva introducta corrumpitur sensitiva et vegetativa ; (12), item quod vegetativa, sensitiva et intellectiva sint una forma simplex ; (13), item quod corpus vivum et mortuum est equivoce corpus, et corpus mortuum secundum quod corpus mortuum sit corpus secundum quid ; (16), item quod intellectiva unitur materie prime ita quod corrumpitur illud quod precessit usque ad materiam primam." (*Chart.*, I, 558). The Thomist theory of the *privatio*

Kilwardby had recourse not to excommunication, but to threats and promises.[4] " I do not condemn them as heretical, but I forbid them as dangerous," he wrote to the Dominican Peter of Conflans.[5] The latter attempted to defend Thomas, but drew from the Archbishop a long letter in justification of his attitude[6] which serves as a commentary on the decree itself. The Thomist interpretation of the unity of forms is described as " fatua positio vel imaginatio phantastica."[7] It is not even an " opinio,"[8] while pluralism is a scientific truth.[9]

It is probable that there was an understanding between Kilwardby and Tempier concerning this double condemnation, for we know that during this same year 1277, the latter thought of proscribing other theses, particularly that of the unity of form. But just then John XXI died, and as the Bishop of Paris was engaged in intrigues in the Roman curia during the vacancy in the Apostolic See (20th May to the 24th November), an order was issued by some of the Cardinals requesting him to postpone his action. The Oxford decrees were given a wide publicity in Paris, and were discussed there as keenly as Tempier's own prohibitions.

The opposition reached its height at Oxford under Archbishop Peckham, who succeeded Kilwardby. But the constitution of the conflicting parties was not quite the same. After the decision of the General Chapter at Milan in 1278, Thomism became at Oxford as elsewhere the official doctrine of the Dominicans. On the 29th October, 1284, Peckham

is affected by propositions 3 and 4. The 13th is opposed to the doctrine of Thomas that " Corpus Christi mortuum et vivum non fuit *simpliciter* idem numero, quia non fuit *totaliter* idem. . . . Corpus mortuum cujuscumque alterius hominis non est idem simpliciter, sed secundum quid." (*Summa Theol.*, 3a, q. 50, a. 5, *in corpore*, and *ad* 1m). But then, retorted his adversaries, we should have to hold that the bodies of the saints which are venerated by the faithful are not the ones which belonged to them when alive : " nec aliqua sanctorum corporum tota vel secundum partes aliquas in orbe existere vel in Urbe, sed quædam alia quæ non genuerunt matres sanctorum." (Letter of Peckham to the Chancellor of Oxford, 10th November, 1884. See Ehrle, *Zeitschr.* etc., p. 174).—Already in 1271 Nicholas of Lisieux similarly characterized as erroneous the doctrine " oculum mortuum esse æquivoque oculum." (*Quodlib.*, III, a. 4).

[4] A Burgh. MS. adds to Robert's decree the words : " quicumque hec dicta non sustinet nec docet, habet a fratre R. archiepiscopo XL dies de indulgentia, qui autem dictas positiones defendit . . ." (*Chart.*, I, 560, n. 3).

[5] Born in 1220/40, a Bachelor of Paris, Archbishop of Corinth (1268), translated to Cosenza in 1278.

[6] See p. 47.

[7] Ed. Birkenmajer, p. 62. Cf. **258**.

[8] " Nec de hoc opinio esse poterit," p. 64.

[9] " De ipsa non est opinio sed scientia vera " (*ibid.*)

confirmed the act of his predecessor, and the tone of his letters shows how bitter the controversy had become.[1] Later on, in consequence of provocation on the part of the Dominican prior (Richard Klapwell or Clapoel), he again on the 30th April, 1286 prohibited the controverted Thomist theses.[2] The eight propositions condemned affected the Thomist thesis of the unity of the substantial form in its principle and in many of its consequences : " . . . istos igitur articulos hæreses esse damnatas in se vel in suis similibus . . . denunciamus."

Peckham inveighs passionately against the " profanas vocum novitates " of philosophers whom he calls " elatiores quam capaciores, audaciores quam potentiores, garruliores quam litteraciores." He advocates a return to " the sound and solid doctrine of the sons of St. Francis, Alexander of Hales and St. Bonaventure."[3] He would apply to a cancerous sore the balm of his pastoral intervention.[4] He warns all against the " dangerous " theory of the unity of forms, and suggests that it may well be of Averrhoist origin.[5] In addition to the plurality of forms, " quam et tenuit hactenus totus mundus,"[6] he recommends the *rationes seminales*, the *rationes æternæ*, and the theory of the identity of the substance and powers of the soul : " . . . que quicquid docet Augustinus de regulis æternis, et luce incommutabili, de potentiis animæ, de rationibus seminalibus inditis materiæ et consimilibus innumeris."[7] He is not condemning philosophy itself, but only its abuse : " novitates (reprobamus) quæ contra philosophicam veritatem

---

[1] On Dec. 7th, 1284, he writes as follows to the Chancellor of Oxford concerning the Dominicans : " Quidam fratres ejusdem ordinis prædicatorum ausi sunt se publice jactitare, doctrinam veritatis plus in suo ordine quam in alio contemporaneo viguisse ; . . . jactant iam esse falsam, quod non esset difficile declarare, nisi esset comparatio odiosa, comparando scilicet scripta scriptis, personas personis et labores laboribus satis notis." The interesting texts of Peckham's letters are collected by Spettmann, *op. cit.* No. 249, p. xvii.

[2] D'Argentré, *Collectio judiciorum*, Vol. I, pp. 234-238. Prop. VIII : " Quod in homine est tantum una forma, scilicet anima rationalis et nulla alia forma substantialis : ex qua opinione sequi videntur omnes hæreses supradictæ." *Chart.*, I, 634.

[3] *Chart.*, I, 634.

[4] " Volentes huic cancerosæ prurigini quam poterimus adhibere pastoralis officii medicinam. (Ehrle, *Zeitschr.*, 176). According to Peckham, even some of the Franciscans allowed themselves to be led away by the Thomist theories. (*ibid.*, 191).

[5] " Nec eam credimus a religiosis personis, sed secularibus quibusdam duxisse originem cujus duo præcipui defensores vel forsitan inventores miserabiliter dicuntur conclusisse dies suos in partibus transalpinis." (Ehrle, *op. cit.*, p. 175). Olivi goes further still and suggests that Averrhoism was introduced by the Dominicans. (Mandonnet, *Siger*, VI, 101).

[6] Letter of the 7th Dec., 1284.

[7] *Chart.*, I, 634.

sunt in sanctorum injuriam citra viginti annos in altitudines theologicas introductæ." The latter is dated the 1st of June, 1286. The " novelties " were therefore introduced from 1265, which takes us back to the second period of St. Thomas's teaching at the University of Paris.

§ 2. Supporters of Thomism

292. The Dominican evolution towards Thomism.— Unbending opposition to St. Thomas from some called forth earnest and unflinching adherence from others. In the Dominican order the hostility was shortlived, and soon gave way to an unbounded admiration for the master. In one particular group of older Dominicans we notice a progressive evolution towards Thomism. An example is found in RAY-MUND MARTIN. He was trained in Rabbinic Hebrew and Arabic in several Spanish schools, where the Provincial Chapter of Toledo (1250) had decided to institute chairs for the teaching of oriental languages. He wrote an apologetical and controversial work, *Pugio fidei adversus Mauros et Judæos*[1] in which he made great use of Arab works. Many passages in this treatise are taken almost word for word from the *Summa contra Gentiles* of St. Thomas.[2] In a previous work, *Explanatio simboli Apostolorum ad institutionem fidelium edita* (about 1256), Raymund rejected the possibility of creation *ab æterno*, which he admitted in the *Pugio fidei* (1278). This would seem to show that under the influence of Thomas Aquinas, Martin leaned towards a theory which before his time had certainly not been defended in the Order.[3]

---

[1] Printed in 1687.
[2] According to M. Asin y Palacios, it was St. Thomas who made use of the work of Raymund Martin and profited by his knowledge of Arabic, just as he profited by the Greek knowledge of William of Moerbeke. (*El Averroismo teologico de Sto Tomas de Aquino* in Homenaje a D. Fr. Codera, Zaragoza, 1904, pp. 322-324, and *La Suma Contra Gentes y el Pugio fidei*, Vergara, 1905). The thesis of Asin has been opposed by Getino, *El averroismo teologico de Santo Tomas de Aquino*, (Vergara 1905), and *Por los mundos del tomismo* (*Cienza Tomista*, 1911, p. 46). Mandonnet (*op. cit.*, VII, p. 47) points out that the *Pugio fidei* is later than 1276, and that the question of its dependence upon Thomas is settled. M. Asin holds another thesis, basing himself on the Arabic text of the *Tehafot* and the *Quitab falsafa*, namely, that Averrhoes established a system of harmonious relations between Mohammedan doctrine and philosophy which inspired that of St. Thomas. He has been answered by Manser, (*Jahrb. Phil. spek. Theol.* 1908) and Mandonnet (*Siger*, VI, 148).
[3] *ibid.*, VII, p. XXVIII.

A similar evolution of ideas is found in the unknown author of a *Correctorium corruptorii fratris Thomæ*, edited many times and wrongly ascribed to Giles of Rome. He tells us that after having held the plurality of forms, he was converted to the Thomist theory. The same influence is manifest in the anonymous author of the *De erroribus philosophorum*, whose sympathies for Aristotle betray a Dominican origin, but who follows the older scholasticism in the question of forms.[1] When Albert the Great set out for Paris at the age of eighty to defend his disciple, opposition must have to a great extent ceased at the convent of St. James. Proud of the reputation which Thomas had acquired, the Chapter of Milan (1278) discountenanced the reaction of which the Oxford house was the centre ; another, held at Paris in 1279, forbade those who did not hold Thomism to speak against it ; the Chapter of Paris in 1286 went one step further and suspended from their charge those who regarded the new doctrine as suspect. The question of the obligation to teach Thomism did not arise till 1309 and 1313, at the Chapters of Saragossa and Metz.[2]

293. The Dominican Defence.—The attacks of WILLIAM DE LA MARE called forth from the Dominicans a number of defenders, and under the same form of *Correctoria* they refuted the *Correctorium* or, as it was called, the *Corruptorium* of the Franciscan master. A first *Correctorium*, wrongly attributed to Giles of Rome,[3] reproduces the complete text of the opponent, and refutes it step by step. A second type of correctorium ascribed by Mandonnet to HUGH OF BILLOM (Archbishop of Ostia, died 1297), and by Ehrle to DURANDUS OF AURILLAC (Durandellus) sets out the attack of the pamphlet in a freer form, and refutes it in a calmer tone. JOHN QUIDORT (Dormiens) or JOHN OF PARIS (died 1306) commenced a third

---

[1] Mandonnet for this reason puts its composition between 1260 and 1274 (*ibid*, p. 30).

[2] *Monumenta ord. Prædic.*, ed. Reichert. Acta capitulorum gen. Romæ, I, 199, 204, 255, II, 38, 64. In spite of these injunctions, there were always Dominicans who on important points differed from Thomism, returning to the older theories or else defending new solutions. See later on, under Theodoric of Freiberg, Durandus of S. Pourcain, Eckhart.

[3] Mandonnet, *Premiers travaux de polémique thomiste* (*R. sc. phil. theol.*, 1913, p. 55) suggests as the author Richard Clapell (Clapwell) or William of Macclesfield. Ehrle, (*Der Kampf um die Lehre d. h. Thomas von A. in den ersten funfzig Jahren nach seinem Tod. Zeitschr. f. Kath. Theol.*, 1913, p. 316) puts in the first place R. Clapwell and Robert of Tortocollo (or Colletorto), and secondly Hugh of Billom and William of Macclesfield. Recently Pelster suggests the name of Robert of Colletorto, (*Thomas von Sutton*, etc., p. 371). The work also exists in an abridged form, see Ehrle, *op. cit.*, p. 284.

Correctorium corruptorii. It was written shortly after the attack of William de la Mare in a very original manner, but never finished.[1] Lastly, we know of an *Apologeticum pro S. Thoma* by Robert of Bologna (died 1308), which is the most perfect and most developed of all the *Correctoria*.[2]

The Franciscans replied, for there exists a *Responsorium ad Correctorium*, dating from the beginning of the fourteenth century, the author of which attacks the Dominican position and defends the attitude of William de la Mare. Thus we find a hand-to-hand struggle between the ancient doctrines and the new ideas.

In addition to these defensive works, the Dominicans attacked the eclectic teachers who directly or indirectly departed from Thomas Aquinas on various matters. The Catalogue of Stams tells us that BERNARD OF AUVERGNE, Bishop of Clermont, at the end of the thirteenth and beginning of the fourteenth centuries, wrote polemical works against the *Dicta* of Henry of Ghent, Godfrey of Fontaines, and James of Viterbo,[3] and a Vatican MS. contains *Impugnationes Bernardi* against Giles of Rome. Two English teachers, WILLIAM OF MACCLESFIELD and ROBERT OF HEREFORD, are also worthy of mention. The former wrote *Contra Henricum de Gande quibus impugnat Thomam*, and *Contra Corruptorum Thomæ*, and the latter *Contra Dicta Henrici de Gande* and *Contra Primum Egidii*. We shall see later on that Thomas of Sutton attacked Henry of Ghent, Robert Cowton, and Duns Scotus. Similar works were written by HERVÆUS OF NEDELLEC and other Dominicans at the beginning of the fourteenth century.

294. Thomism and the Dominicans.—Bernard of Trilia.— While one group of Dominicans replied to the critics of the master, others expounded and developed his doctrine. This group of philosopher-theologians who wrote in the last years of the thirteenth century is remarkable in many ways : their style is concise and clear, they go straight to the point of vital questions, and in adopting the new doctrines which had given rise to so much discussion, they discover new aspects, appli-

---

[1] Grabmann, *Le Correctorium Corruptorii du dominicain Johannes Quidort de Paris*, in *Revue Neo-Scolastique*, 1912.

[2] Ehrle, (*op. cit.*, p. 297) mentions a fifth *Correctorium* at Merton College, Oxford.

[3] Denifle, *Quellen*, etc.

cations, and corollaries. Their works have the stamp of originality.

We find this originality already in PTOLOMY OF LUCCA, who attended the lectures of Thomas Aquinas in 1272 ("ipsius auditor fui ") and who completed his *De regimine principum* ; WILLIAM OF HOTUN or HOZUN, Bishop of Dublin, who died in 1298 ; HUGH, Archbishop of Ostia (died in 1297, wrote *Contra Corruptionem Thomæ*) ; and BERNARD OF AUVERGNE, Bishop of Clermont.

The same is true of BERNARD OF TRILIA (la Treille) who wrote his *Quolibeta* in 1279-1287, and hence must be numbered among the first Thomists. He was born at Nimes about 1240, became Master in Theology at Paris, and taught at St. James. He was then called to other work, and died at Avignon in 1292. In addition to the *Quolibeta* which he did not finish, the Catalogue of Stams ascribes to him *Quæstiones de spiritual-ibus creaturis, De potentia Dei, De anima Conjucta, De anima Separata.*[1] We recognize Thomism in his exposition of the theories of knowledge, matter, the unity of form, and of beatitude. It is worthy of note that Bernard gives a lengthy and ordered treatment of the question of the real distinction between essence and existence, which the master never com-pletely expounded in any single passage.

295. Giles of Lessines and John Quidort.—A special mention is due to GILES DE LESSINES. An intimate friend of Albert the Great, whose lectures he attended, probably at Cologne, he taught as bachelor in the convent of St. James. It was he who wrote to Albert in 1270 ("patri ac domno Alberto, episcopo quondam ratisponensi ") to warn him of the threatened condemnation of Thomism (**260**). He asked for and obtained from his old master an explanatory treatise *De quindecim problematibus,* in which Albert is not very explicit about Thomist doctrines. A treatise *De usuris,* often ascribed to St. Thomas, a lost *Tractatus de præceptis,* a *Tractatus de crepusculis,*[2] another *De concordia temporum* (a chronology of

---

[1] G. S. André, (*Les Quolibeta de Bernard de Trilia,* in *Gregorianum* 1921, pp. 226-265). studies and gives extracts from some quodlibetic questions. " Quolibet," " Quodlibet," " Quotlibet " are three mediæval forms. See Ehrle, *Thomas Sutton* (Festschrift v. Hertling, 1913, p. 426). Notes on the manuscripts of Bernard of Trilia and of William of Hozun will be found in the *Revue Sc. phil. Théo.,* 1914, pp. 467-476.

[2] Mandonnet, *G. de L. et son traité de crepusculis,* in *Revue Neo-Scolastique* 1920, p. 190 ; Grabmann, *Aegidius v. Lessines,* in *Divus Thomas* (Fribourg, 1924).

events down to 1304, whence Quétif and Echard conclude that
Giles died about this time), and a treatise *De unitate formæ*,
constitute the literary output of Giles of Lessines. The last-
mentioned work, dated July, 1278, is a polemical work directed
against Robert Kilwardby (*Cantuariensis, Archiepiscopus*).[1]
In point of fact, Giles's exposition of the pluralistic theory,
his particular interpretation of it (functional subordination of
forms), and the arguments which he adduces in support, are
found word for word in a letter which Kilwardby wrote in
defence of his own teaching to Peter of Conflans[2] which Giles
must have had before him when writing his work, and which
had probably been sent to him from Greece by his colleague.

The treatise of Giles contains, in addition to the exposition
of Kilwardby's theory, two other parts, consisting respectively
of (*a*) general notions of matter and form, (*b*) statement and
proof of the theory of the unity of form, followed by a refutation
of the opposite view. The constructive part of the work
re-states the arguments of Thomas Aquinas, but as the treatise
is mainly controversial, it dwells at greater length on the difficulties of pluralism. The style is concise, and the reasoning
clear. In the closing portion especially the author gives us
the benefit of his own personal views (" de quo principaliter
describimus secundum intellectum nostrum "). The *De unitate
formæ* of Giles of Lessines occupies a leading place, if not the
very foremost, in the rich literature of the end of the thirteenth
century on the controversy concerning forms.[3]

There were also other works concerning Thomist doctrines
particularly attacked : *De immediata visione Dei, De differentia esse et essentie, De eternitate mundi, De intellectu et voluntate.*

JOHN QUIDORT (Dormiens)[4] was born about 1269, taught for
a long time in the Faculty of Arts and became a Licentiate
in Theology in 1304, two years before his death. He also was
one of the earliest Thomists, and gave important developments

---

[1] Edition in *Philosophes Belges*, pp. 13 and 14.
[2] Birkenmajer has published the last part of the letter (not given in Ehrle)
from a Vienna MS. (Bulletin Acad. sciences Cracovie, 1917, p. 74), and
BGPM, XX, 5.
[3] Giles of Rome, and, according to the Catalogue of Stams, William
of Hotun, Hugh of Ostia, and Thomas Sutton wrote works on the unity of forms
at the end of the thirteenth century. Among later ones are the treatises
by Johannes Faventinus (fourteenth or fifteenth century) and Janinus de
Pistorio.
[4] Grabmann, *Studien zu J. Quidort von Paris* (Sitz. bayer. Akad. Wisench.
Phil. Phil. Kl., 1922, Abh. 3).

not inoperative, for as soon as they receive the efficient stimulus from without they react [1] Again, Thomas of Sutton stresses the passivity of the will in the sense that God, the " motor universalis," has placed in us a tendency towards the good, and that liberty affects only the choice of means—which seems a particular way of setting out the Thomist solution.[2] Finally, he maintains with St. Thomas that contingent futures have a " veritas determinata " for the Divine knowledge inasmuch as God knows them in the eternal vision of his own essence, and that this truth does not rest on the decree of the will calling them into existence, as held by Scotus. Thomas Sutton strongly opposes the latter on this point and on many others. This leads us to another aspect of his personality as a philosopher, that of the controversialist.

He contrasts his opinions and those of his master with solutions set forth by other philosophers of renown, which makes his work of considerable interest for the understanding of the philosophical discussions of this latter part of the century. The majority of those referred to are laconically mentioned as *alii*, *quidam*, but we recognize Henry of Ghent in the " quidam magister in diebus nostris,"[3] of whom the English professor criticizes many theories, particularly those concerning the *species impressa*, the principle of individuation, the distinction between essence and existence,[4] the Divine attributes, and the Divine ideas (303). Thomas of Sutton again

---

[1] Pelster writes : " The position of Aquinas certainly amounts to this, that external sensation is an *entirely* passive phenomenon. See Quodl. 8, a. 3." (p. 378). Such is not our opinion. Before discussing the subject in the passage referred to, St. Thomas lays down the general principle : " Respondeo dicendum quod anima humana similitudines rerum quibus cognoscit, accipit a rebus, *illo modo accipiendi quo patiens accipit ab agente*." Now this *modus* always implies the vital reaction of the cognitive act.

[2] Cf. a note of Père Martin, *Pro tutela doctrinæ S. Th. Aquinatis de influxu causæ secundas*, in *Divus Thomas* 1923, fasc. 3, on Pelster's misunderstanding of the texts of Sutton.

[3] *Quodl.*, III, q. 4. Cf. Ehrle, *op. cit.*, p. 15, n. 2.

[4] p. 14. Pelster mentions the following among the first Dominicans who upheld the real distinction between essence and existence : Robert of Colletorto, Bernard of Trilia, John of Lichtenberg ; and among the opponents, besides Thomas of Sutton, Hervæus of Nedellec, John the Teuton, Bernard Gannat, and James of Metz. (*op. cit.*, p. 373). The text relating to John the Teuton is published by Grabmann, (*Die Lehre d. J. Teutonicus ueber den Unterschied von Wesenneit u. Dasein in Jahrb. Phil. u. spek. Theol.*, 1902, p. 43 *et seq.* The life and *Quæstiones disputatæ* (Cod. Vat. lat. 859) of John Picard of Lichtenberg, lector at Cologne and afterwards licentiate at Paris (1310), have been treated at length by A. Landgraf, in *Zeitschr. fur. Kath. theol.*, 1922, pp. 510-555. Cf. Grabmann, *Doctrina S. Th. de Aq. de distinctione reali inter essentiam et esse documentis ineditis sæc. XIII illustrata*, in *Xenia Thomistica* III. pp. 131-190.

attacks Duns Scotus, not only in his last *Quodlibeta*, but also in a treatise entitled *Thomas Anglicus contra primum Sentent. J. Scoti*.[1]

Lastly, he attacks also a contemporary of Duns Scotus, the Franciscan Robert Cowton, in the three last books of *Quæstiones* in the Codex Rossianus IX, 121.[2] A more complete study will perhaps bring out allusions to Godfrey of Fontaines, the colleague and contemporary of Henry of Ghent. Ehrle has collected a certain number of references to works by Thomas of Sutton in the writings of the scholastics of the fourteenth century.

NICHOLAS TRIVET, whom we know through a recent study by Ehrle,[3] belonged to a feudal family, and after studying at Paris taught for two lengthy periods at Oxford, the second being from 1314 to 1324, after the conflict which had arisen between his order and the University. He had an open and a varied mind, and was a writer of remarkable fecundity : he commented on the *De consolatione philosophiæ* of Bœthius, and perhaps also on pseudo-Bœthius, explained Seneca and other classical works, wrote the *Annales sex regum Angliæ* and a universal history, commented on the Sentences of the Lombard, and also left *Quolibeta* and *Quæstiones disputatæ*.[4] We have here, then, a man who is interested in everything and reminds us of the mental outlook of Albert the Great. On the unity of substantial form, the causal intervention of the senses in the production of thought, and other questions, he speaks as a faithful Thomist. Nevertheless, there are slight differences which it would be interesting to study.[5] Thus Nicholas endeavours to deal with the current objection against the theory of the real distinction between essence and existence, namely, that existence cannot add anything to the essence, and finally proposes to take *esse* to mean the concrete subject

---

[1] Hitherto commonly attributed to Thomas of Jorz, restored to Thomas of Sutton by Pelster. Published at Venice in 1523.

[2] *ibid.*, p. 214 *et seq.* Pelster says that he made use of the *Opus Oxoniense* of Scotus, but did not adopt Scotism.

[3] *Nikolaus Trivet, sein Leben, seine Quolibet und Quæstiones ordinariæ*, Festgabe Bæumker, 1923.

[4] See the description of the MSS. of Bale and Worcester in which Ehrle found these two works, p. 23 *et seq.* The *Quolibeta* were written before 1323, the 28th question after 1304, the 4th Question of the third after 1305. The Worcester MS. also contains unpublished *Quolibeta* of other Oxford theologians: the Chancellor Henry Harclay, the Carmelite Robert Walsingham, and Kikeley, belonging to the first two decades of the fourteenth century.

[5] A doctrinal study has not yet been made. Ehrle's article deals chiefly with questions of erudition.

works on medicine, he wrote the *Summulæ Logicales* which will be referred to later.

The condemnations of Thomism did not prevent its spread. The Oxford censures never had the force of law at Paris, and even the prohibitions of Stephen Tempier did not prevent the free discussion of Thomist doctrines, nor affect their fortune in the schools. Various contemporaries, Giles of Rome,[1] Nicholas Trivet, Godfrey of Fontaines,[2] John of Naples,[3] and later on William of Ockam[4] passed severe judgments on the censure of Thomism, and this was moreover withdrawn by Bishop Stephen of Borrete on the 13th February, 1325, after the canonization of St Thomas. There is no trace of a similar withdrawal at Oxford, but gradually the fact superseded the law. The tension between the Dominicans and Peckham relaxed after 1288 ; the succeeding archbishops did not confirm the Oxford prohibitions, and it was suggested that their silence was equivalent to a withdrawal.[5] Nicholas Trivet tells us that in 1314 it was no longer forbidden to maintain the theory of the unity of form.[6]

The title of " doctor communis " (*the* scholastic doctor) which appears at the end of the thirteenth century, bears witness to the rapidity with which the doctrines of St. Thomas spread, and the great impression he created in the schools. Thomas of Sutton writes thus of him : " in ore omnium communis doctor dicitur frater Thomas."[7] His disciples and admirers formed a party or group, and already in 1304 a physician and mystic, Arnold of Villeneuve, speaks of the " Thomatiste," a strange expression which was apparently replaced by the designation " Thomist " at the beginning of the fourteenth century.[8]

---

[1] " Plures de illis articulis transierunt, non consilio magistrorum, sed capitositate quorumdam paucorum," (*In II. Sentent.*, Venetiis, p. 271).

[2] See our study on Godfrey of Fontaines, p. 47.

[3] See Echard, *Script.* I. 476.

[4] *Dialogus*, Lugdini, 1495, Pars I, lib. II, c. 22.

[5] So argues Robert of Primadizzi (or of Bologna, died 1308), quoted by Ehrle, *N. Trivet.* p. 32.

[6] *ibid.*

[7] Ehrle, *op. cit.*, p. 12, n. Mandonnet, *Les titres doctoraux de S. Thomas d'Aquin* in *Revue Thomiste*, 1909, p. 604. The oldest title is that of " doctor eximius " (1282). Mandonnet ascribes the title of " angelical doctor " to the first half of the fifteenth century, (*ibid.* p. 606).

[8] Arnold of Villeneuve († 1311) was the author of a treatise (*Misterium cimbalorum*) in which he announced the coming of Antichrist, and which he wrote at Montpellier in 1297. He was attacked by the Dominican Joannes Vigorosi (1303) and replied (1304) in a pamphlet *Gladius jugulans Thomatistas.* Other Dominicans, and in particular John Quidort († 1306) wrote against

We know also that Thomism gradually penetrated into the general atmosphere of ideas, that Vincent of Beauvais made great use of it in his writings, that Dante was inspired by it, and that art testified to its predominance in western culture.[9]

299. Bibliography.—§ 1 Studies by Ehrle and Spettmann, 249. Peckham's Letters are also published in Wilkins, *Concilia magnæ Britanniæ et Hiberniæ*, II, 107 ; *Registrum epistolarum J. Peckham*, edited by Martin, III, 840. Some are given in *Chart.*, I. Cf. Little, *The Grey Friars in Oxford* (1892). Denifle, *Quellen z. Gelehrtengesch. d. Predigerord.*

§ 2 Works mentioned in notes. De Wulf has edited the *De unitate* of Giles of Lessines (Vol. I, p. 41) from two manuscripts at Paris and Brussels, and added a study. Ehrle, *Die Ehrentitel d. Schol. Lehrer d. M. A.* (Sitz. berichte d. Bayer Akad. Wiss. Philos Kl. 1919, 9). Editions of the *Speculum Quadruplex* of Vincent of Beauvais appeared at Venice in 1484, 1494, 1591, and at Douay in 1624. On Vincent of Beauvais, see a study in *R. des quest. histor.*, Vol. 17. On Dante see Vol. I, p. 324. On Humbert of Preuilly, see *Hist. litt. de la France*, Vol. XXI, pp. 86-90 ; on Peter of Auvergne, *ibid.* Vol. XXV, pp. 93-118 ; Denifle and Chatelain, *Chartul Univ. Par.*, II, pp. 65, 71 ; A. Pelzer, in *Revue Neo-Scol.*, 1920, p. 219 ; 1922, p. 357.

Art. VII—Godfrey of Fontaines and Henry of Ghent.

300. An independent group.—The followers and opponents of Thomas Aquinas belonging to the last years of the thirteenth century displayed a certain individuality in their fight for or against the pre-eminence of Thomism. This individuality was especially prominent in Godfrey of Fontaines and Henry of Ghent, who were concerned even more with striking out a path of their own than with taking up a position in the controversy. Both set forth more or less important groups of new

---

him. The word "Thomatista," Arnold tells us, came from his friend Jacob Albi. The first scholastic to speak of "Thomists" was the Franciscan Petrus of Tornaparte, about 1337. The word "Thomatiste" reappeared in 1474 in a Nominalist work written against the decree of Louis XI. See the excellent study by Ehrle, *Arnoldo de Villanova ed i Thomatiste* in *Gregorianum*, 1920, p. 475.

[9] Vol. I, nos. 208, 210.

and original solutions. At the same time they were influenced by their surroundings : on certain questions Godfrey preferred to side with Thomism, while Henry returned to the older scholasticism. These thinkers, the one a Walloon and the other a Fleming, were in close relationship : they were together at Paris, and attacked each other in their public discussions. The philosophy of Giles of Rome would seem to be less original, possibly because it is less known. James of Viterbo was influenced by it.

On the other hand, Richard of Middleton was an important philosopher, whose individual characteristics will be better realized when a complete study has been made of his works. He anticipated Duns Scotus in several respects.

The list of these eclectic or independent thinkers belonging to the period between Thomas and Duns Scotus will doubtless be extended as a result of research.[1]

301. Godfrey of Fontaines was born at Fontaines-les-Hozémont near Liége. He was a master of theology at Paris in 1286, and *actu regens* for thirteen years, including the year 1292. He became a Canon of Liége, of Paris, and Cologne, and was chosen in 1300 as Bishop of Tournai, but renounced his rights as the election was called in question. Godfrey was a member of the Sorbonne, to which he left a large and valuable collection of manuscripts which are now in the Bibliothèque Nationale. He died after 1303.

The *XIV Quodlibeta* of Godfrey are probably his sole scientific work. They exist in numerous manuscripts, and were greatly used in the schools of France, England and Italy. The third quodlibetic disputation took place in 1286, and the twelfth after 1290. We also possess some sermons by him. It is not certain whether he wrote the treatise against the mendicant orders and a series of questions found at the end of a copy of the *Summa contra Gentiles* bequeathed by him to the Sorbonne.[2]

---

[1] For instance, there is JAMES OF DOUAY, a little-known thirteenth century writer, author of a commentary *De Anima* (Hauréau, *Hist. Litter. France*, Vol. XXI, p. 157). According to the extracts given in Hauréau, James was a moderate realist, but Hauréau's analyses are inadequate, and only deal with the question of universals. See De Wulf, *Histoire de la Philosophie Scolastique dans les Pays-Bas*, p. 281. Similarly, Grabmann mentions a treatise *De principiis naturæ* by the Parisian master JOHANNES DE SICCA VILLA, (*Neu aufgefunde Werke d. Siger v. Brabantia*, etc., p. 15 of the separate reprint).

[2] He certainly conducted *disputationes ordinariæ*. MS. 122 in the Vatican contains *Quæstiones disputatæ* which the copyist ascribes to

Like all the masters of theology of his time, Godfrey was a many-sided figure. He was in turn a dogmatic theologian, moralist, jurist, canonist, philosopher, pamphleteer, and a public man. He gave his opinion on matters of discipline which were then the subject of animated discussion in University circles with an independence of language which it would be difficult to surpass. He openly criticized Stephen Tempier on account of his hasty condemnations of Thomism, and more vigorously still Tempier's successor, Simon de Bucy, for not removing the censures. He also criticized the condemnations by John Peckham, and informs us that they were disregarded at Paris. On the other hand, he sided very definitely against the privileges of the mendicant orders.

Thomism forms the basis of Godfrey's philosophy. He is a resolute opponent of the Dominicans in ecclesiastical matters, but gives an enthusiastic eulogy of Thomas as a philosopher. Still, Godfrey's Thomism is tinged with individual characteristics : he has his own solutions for a number of subsidiary questions, he adopts a hostile attitude towards the contemporary masters of repute in the faculty (Giles of Rome, James of Viterbo, Thomas of Sutton, and especially Henry of Ghent),[3] and lastly, he manifests a certain reserve and hesitation on the innovations which Aquinas introduced into Scholasticism.

302. Philosophical teaching.—(i) *Metaphysics and natural theology.* There is no real distinction between essence and existence. On this important point he sides with Henry of Ghent against Thomism. He does not shrink from any consequences of his principle, and multiplies the existential actualities in a concrete being, even in the accidental order : " tot sunt esse quot essentiæ."[4] At the same time he criticizes and rejects the formulæ of Henry of Ghent, and holds that the distinction of essence and existence arises simply from language.

Godfrey. Pelzer has shown that they belong in great part if not wholly to Hervæus of Nedellec. See his excellent study, *Godefroid de Fontaines : Les manuscrits et ses quolibets conservés à la Vaticane et dans quelques autres bibliothèques* (Revue Neo-Scolastique, 1913).

[3] An old table, which will be published in the appendix to the *Quodlibeta* of Godfrey of Fontaines, points out the principal points of doctrine on which he differs from St. Thomas, Giles of Rome, James of Viterbo, and Thomas Sutton. It does not necessarily follow that Godfrey carried on a controversy with them on the points referred to. The table is simply a synoptic work by some studious person, taking the philosophy of Godfrey's philosophy as a term of comparison.

[4] *Quodl.* III, 1, p. 305 in De Wulf and Pelzer's edition. " Præter hoc esse (substantiale) sunt plura esse secundum quid et tot quot sunt ibi formæ accidentales." (*Quodl.* III, 4, p. 311).

The principle of individuation is not prime matter (against St. Thomas) but the substantial form. The hierarchy of contingent essences has its limits : an infinite series such as that suggested by Giles of Rome, implies a contradiction. In the same way as Henry of Ghent and for the same reasons, Godfrey does not allow that there is in God a proper idea of individuals as distinct from that of their species.

(ii) *Physics*. Godfrey defends the hypothesis of the simplicity of astral substances.[1] To account for the evolution of corporeal things he suggests a theory of transubstantiation supplementary to that of generation, which is peculiar to himself : an existing body can be converted into another existing body in such a way that the substance of the first thing when converted remains wh'ole and entire in some way in the second, both existing prior to the change. Nature does not present such phenomena, but God can realize them, for His omnipotence can bring about anything that is not contradictory. Since the thing to be converted must be the other thing in potency, in virtue of a metaphysical principle, the two beings must agree *in materia*.[2] That is why God could change an egg into an ox, but not a material body into an angel or *vice versa*. In our opinion the theory of *generatio* is sufficient as a scholastic explanation of the evolution of nature, and the *transmutatio* of Godfrey is needless and strange.

(iii) *Psychology*. Godfrey's preferences are for the problems of the time, and those discussed between the various schools. In virtue of the principle " quidquid movetur ab alio movetur," he gives a vigorous refutation of the Augustinian ideology professed by James of Viterbo,[3] the special illumination of Henry of Ghent,[4] and the false interpretation of the intentional species upheld by the last mentioned and many others.[5] Godfrey's ideology is clearer and more penetrating than that of any other scholastic.[6] In order to harmonize the classifications of Aristotle with the tripartite division of St. Augustine, he identifies the *memoria* of the latter with the two intellects of the former.[7]

[1] Vol. One, p. 289.
[2] *Quodl.* V, 1, and X, 1.
[3] *Quodl.* IX, 19.
[4] *Quodl.* VI, 15.
[5] *Quodl.* IX, 19.
[6] *Quodl.* V, 10.
[7] *Quodl.* V. 8.

In the study of the will, even more than in that of the intellect, Godfrey directly attacks Henry of Ghent. Almost the whole of the sixth *quodlibet* is devoted to the exposition and criticism of Henry's voluntarism, to which Godfrey opposes the most complete intellectualism, more thorough-going even than that of Aquinas himself. For not only is the will not *simpliciter activa* (Henry of Ghent), but Godfrey will not allow self motion, even in the free volition of means to an end, and he is very severe on the Thomist solution.[1] The will is *simpliciter passiva*, it is always determined by the understanding, even when it freely follows this determination. After this it is unnecessary to add that Godfrey stresses the other aspects of intellectualism.

While retaining his preference for the Thomist theory of the unity of form in man, Godfrey declares that he is unable to refute the arguments for pluralism. He never gets beyond a hesitating attitude on this question.

The personal teaching of Godfrey soon gave rise to philo-sophical discussions. Bernard of Auvergne criticized him point by point.[2] During the first half of the fourteenth century some upheld his views and others opposed them.[3] This is still more the case with his compatriot Henry of Ghent.

303. Henry of Ghent.—Recent research has completely altered the biography of Henry of Ghent, the "doctor solemnis,"[4] and has exploded the old legend which made him a member of the Goethal family of Ghent, who entered the Servite order, and afterwards became a member of the Sorbonne. The year of his birth is unknown. He was a Canon of Tournai in 1267, and Archdeacon of Bruges in 1276, and from this time onwards played a prominent part in the University of Paris. He was in part responsible for many important decisions. In particular, in 1282, he openly took sides against the ecclesiastical privileges of the mendicant orders. He was a Doctor of theology in 1277, and died in

---

[1] " Qui vero ponunt quod movetur (voluntas) ab uno quasi a fine et non ab aliis videntur ponere irrationabilia et contradictoria : ubi invenitur eadem ratio movendi ponendum est quod si unum movet quod et aliud ; et mani-festum est autem quod voluntas deliberativa nunquam vult aliquid nisi secundum modum et formam apprehensionis." (*Quodl.* X, 14, according to the manuscript in the Bibl. nationale at Paris, no. 15842).

[2] Pelzer has found the text of these criticisms in a manuscript at Florence (*op. cit.*, p. 19).

[3] Third Period, Chap. II, art. V.

[4] " Magister solemnis, qui tunc actu disputabat et habuit totum studium," says Theodoric of Freiberg (**340**). Krebs, *Meister Dietrich*, etc., p. 10.

1293. His chief works are the *Summa Theologica*, and above all the *XV Quodlibeta*, which give us an interesting description of the questions discussed at Paris at the end of the thirteenth century.[1] Several of his quodlibetic disputations synchronized with those of his compatriot, Godfrey of Fontaines, and the correspondence of the theses defended by the one and criticized by the other cannot be doubted.

Like Godfrey of Fontaines, Henry of Ghent was a complex personality. As a philosopher he was more original than the former, and in every respect more remarkable. His important position in the history of scholasticism results from a series of personal doctrines which he defended with great brilliance but did not succeed in getting accepted. He devoted his attention especially to certain scholastic questions, to which he returned again and again. They are derived for the most part from metaphysics and psychology. He has been called an Augustinian, but he was rather an eclectic peripatetic. He adopted a compact group of theories in vogue in the older scholasticism, gave them an interpretation of his own, and adapted them to the rest of his system. Certain Thomist doctrines made a great impression on him, for instance that of the unity of forms, and while he did not altogether agree with the opinions of the great Dominican teacher, he took no part in the intrigues directed against him.

304. **Philosophical teaching.**—(i) *Natural Theology and Metaphysics*. Henry of Ghent determines the question of the relations between philosophy and theology in full harmony with the ideas of St. Thomas. In fact, the commencement of the *Summa*, in which he expounds these relations, is a model of its kind.

In *Natural Theology* he rejects the Thomist thesis of the possibility of eternal creation ; he believes that God can directly produce the operations of secondary causes, and, in opposition to Duns Scotus, that the human mind can demonstrate this possibility. His conception of the Divine attributes and of God's knowledge is peculiar. There are *potentiæ passivæ* in God, but their presence can be harmonized with His infinite perfection. The Divine ideas, or pos-

---

[1] A commentary of his on the *Physics* of Aristotle and a Treatise on Logic have come down to us in manuscript. The Escurial Library possesses his *Quæstiones super metaphysicam Aristotelis*. The *Liber de Scriptoribus illustribus*, for a long time ascribed to him, is probably not his work.

sible imitations of God, are limited in number. Since God
is not an *intellectus practicus*, He has no *scientia practica*.
Again : God has no idea of number, but rather of the *continuum* as such : in the same way he does not know individuals
by a distinct idea, but by the common idea of the species
(*species specialissima*). It is difficult to see how this teaching
can explain the individuality of natural beings, which the
Doctor of Ghent holds as a principle in conformity with
scholastic pluralism.[1]

On the other hand, this conception of Henry of Ghent fits
in with his theory on the principle of individuation. In
opposition to the Thomist doctrine, which had just been
condemned by authority, he holds that individuals have no
essential positive properties other than those of the species.[2]
The principle of individuation is not matter ; it consists of
a property of the *suppositum* as such which ensures its distinction from every other being. Form and matter, act and
potency, are pairs of correlative terms. They are not, however,
absolutely convertible, for the angels are subsistent forms,
and on the other hand, matter could exist without a substantial
form if it pleased the Creator to derogate from the natural
law (against Thomas Aquinas). Since quantity is an attribute
of the *compositum* and not of matter, the possibility of the
separate existence of matter involves that of the existence
of a vacuum.

Even in the substantial compound, matter has its own
existence, in virtue of the principle, on which Henry delights
to dwell, that " Esse sunt diversa quorumcumque essentiæ
sunt diversæ." To every real element belongs a distinct existence. This is the negation of the real distinction between
essence and existence, which differ only in the thought attaining
to them : (" sunt diversa intentione ").[3] In man, who possesses
prime matter, a form of corporeity and a spiritual soul, existence is a conjunction of three partial existences. This brings
us to Henry's psychology.

(ii) *Psychology.*—On the nature of man, his most original

---

[1] Duns Scotus, who is ever ready to criticize Henry of Ghent, attacks
him triumphantly on this point. See *In I. lib. Sent.*, dist. 36, q. 4, p. 102
in Venice edition 1598.

[2] " Nihil rei addunt individua super essentiam speciei ad id quod est reale
in ipsa." (*Quodl.* VII, 1 and 2).

[3] There are traces of a medium between the real distinction and that of
pure reason, a kind of *distinctio a parte rei* anticipating formalism. (*Quodl.*
V, 6, 12 ; X, 7 ; XI, 3).

thesis is that of the *forma corporeitatis* which exists side by side with the soul, and which is necessary in Henry's view to ensure for the parents on the one hand and God on the other an efficacious intervention in the production of a human being.[1] This is the sole exception to the Thomist principle of the unity of form allowed by Henry, but it is sufficient to differentiate the metaphysics of the two philosophical systems.

In the theory of knowledge we see yet again the false notion of the *species impressæ*.[2] Henry introduces a substitute of the object in the phenomenon of sensation ; on the other hand, in the genesis of intellectual knowledge he rejects the species as unnecessary, because, as he says, the sensible species " transformed " by the active intellect is sufficient to determine the understanding.

Other theses in psychology recall the pre-Thomist scholasticism. Thus the intellectual memory is given an important place together with the intelligence and the will. The Solemn Doctor holds with the Bishop of Hippo that the faculties of the soul are not really distinct. Lastly and above all, the beginning of the *Summa Theologica* contains a brilliant and original paraphrase of the theory of exemplarism. Henry grafts on to the traditional Augustinian teaching (60 (iii)) a theory of special illumination which reminds one of Dominicus Gundissalinus and William of Auvergne. By the spontaneous work of the intelligence we get to know things and hence can attain to truth. Nature suffices for this fundamental part of human knowledge, and God intervenes here only by reason of his *concursus generalis*.[3] But " aliud tamen est scire de creature id quod verum est in ea, et aliud est scire ejus veritatem."[4] To grasp the truth of things in its ultimate foundation, that is, the transcendental relation between the intelligible essences and the Divine ideas, God must bestow upon our minds an increase of light. The intellect would be incapable of this synthetic view of things if God were not to endow it with a special light over and above the general divine *concursus*,

---

[1] Henry invokes other arguments, notably the necessity of explaining the incorruptibility of the body of Christ during the period between His death and resurrection, and its identity with His body during his lifetime. See De Wulf, *Hist. de la phil. scol*, etc., pp. 111 *et seq.*

[2] Vol. One, p. 293.

[3] " Absolute ergo concedere oportet quod homo per suam animam absque omni speciali divina illustratione potest aliqua cognoscere et hoc ex puris naturalibus. . . . Dico autem ex puris naturalibus, non excludendo generalem influentiam primi intelligentis, etc." *Summa Theol.*, I, 2, n. 11.

[4] *Ibid.*, n. 13.

thus increasing its original keenness and enveloping it with a serene clarity.[1]

Henry of Ghent is a voluntarist. The hierarchical relations between the will and the reason, he writes, are those of a master and servant, but it is nevertheless true that the servant precedes his master and carries the torch to light the latter's steps.[2] The respective domains of the two great psychic faculties being thus determined, the philosopher of Ghent follows out his voluntarism into all its applications. In order to establish the superiority of the will, one of his arguments is based on the very manner in which the will acts : while the intelligence is passive before being active, the will is *simpliciter activa*, and the exercise of its act is not subjected to any determination from outside. In free volitions, of which he gives a keen analysis, as in necessary volitions, the presentation of the good, whether in part or complete, is only the *conditio sine qua non* of the voluntary act, and hence it exercises no efficient causality upon it.

We saw above that Thomas Sutton and Bernard of Auvergne were contemporary critics of Henry's opinions. Duns Scotus attacked him constantly, and the fourteenth century paid great attention to his personal solutions.

305. Bibliography.—De Wulf and Pelzer, *Les quatres premiers quodlibets de G. de Fontaines* (Vol. II of the *Philosophes Belges*, Louvain, 1904), a critical edition from four MSS. of a "reported" text. De Wulf and Hoffmans, *Les Quodl. V-VII* (Vol. III of same series); J. Hoffmans *Le Quodl. VIII* (Vol. IV, Part One). De Wulf, *Etudes sur la vie, les oeuvres et l' influence de G. de Fontaines* (Louvain, 1904, memoir crowned by the Belgian Academy). *L'intellectualisme de G. de Fontaines, BGPM*, Festgabe Supplementbd ; Pelzer, *Godefroid de Fontaines*, etc. (*Revue neo-Scolastique*, 1913), good. The *Quodlibeta* of Henry of Ghent have been published at Paris (1518) and at Venice (1608, 1613); the *Summa Theologica* at Paris (1520) and Ferrara (1646). All these editions are now very scarce. Biographical researches and a critical account of doctrine will be found in De Wulf : *Hist. de la Philos. scolast. dans les*

---

[1] " Nunc autem ita est quod homo ex puris naturalibus attingere non potest ad regulas lucis æternæ . . . non tamen ipsa naturalia ex se agere possunt ut attingant illas, sed illas Deus offert quibus vult et quibus vult substrahit." (*Ibid.*, n. 26). See the detailed account of these theories in De Wulf, *Etudes sur Henri de Gand*, Ch. IV.

[2] *Quodl.* I, 14, *in fine.*

Pays Bas et la Principaute de Liége jusqu'a la Révol. franc.
(Louvain, 1895, memoir crowned by the Belgian Academy);
C. Hagemann, *De Henrici Gandavensis quam vocant ontologismo*
(Munster, 1898).

Art. VIII—Giles of Rome and James of Viterbo.

306. Giles of Rome (Aegidius Romanus, called " Colonna "
by an Augustine of the fourteenth century) was born in or
before 1247 and died in 1316. He was known as the " Doctor
Fundatissimus," and was the first philosophic personality of
note in the newly founded order of the Hermits of St. Augustine
(1260). He followed the lectures of Thomas Aquinas with close
attention, and after the latter's departure exercised the
functions of a bachelor, doubtless under a secular master.
He had the title of bachelor in 1276-1277, when critical
events upset his professorship. Stephen Tempier, after forbidding several Thomist theses, proposed to give the force of
law in his diocese to the Oxford censures. Giles indignantly
took up the defence of Thomas Aquinas, and, not content with
severely criticizing the Bishop's counsellors ("capitosi," p. 54),
wrote a treatise *Contra gradus et pluralitates formarum* in
which he went so far as to even describe the doctrine of
pluralism, which Tempier wished to establish in the schools,
as contrary to the faith.[1] The Bishop apparently demanded
a retraction from the bold bachelor, and as this was refused,
proceeded to apply to him the penalty with which Kilwardby
threatened recalcitrant professors : refusal to confer the
Mastership on the bachelors in question, and their exclusion
from the university. We know that Giles was absent from
Paris from 1281 to 1285 and returned under not very honourable
conditions. A letter of Honorius IV enjoined the Paris authorities to confer the licentiate upon Giles provided he made a
public retractation, the terms of which were to be fixed by
the Bishop, the Chancellor and the masters of theology.[2]
This retractation, which doubtless was concerned with the
question of forms, took place probably in 1285, and Giles

---

[1] " Ponere plures formas contradicit fidei catholicæ." Venice edition,
1502, fol. 211; v.
[2] Mandonnet, *La carrière scolaire de Gilles de Rome*.

received the *licentia docendi*.[1] During his lifetime a General
Chapter held at Florence in 1287 testified to his worldwide
reputation (" doctrina mundum universum illustrat ") and
enjoined those wearing the habit of the Order to subscribe not
only to the doctrines which he had taught in books, but even
to those which he should teach in the future (" sententias
scriptas et scribendas ").[2] He was elected General in 1292,
became Archbishop of Bourges in 1295, then returned to Paris
as General Director of Studies, and was in close relations with
Simon de Bucy and Philip IV.[3]

The six *Quodlibeta* of Giles, representing his teaching as
master, are well known and have been published in many
editions. The *relatio* on the Council of Paris in 1286, supposed
to be by Godfrey of Fontaines, tells us that after this date
(*postea*) Giles could be heard dealing with the question of
privileges in a *Quodlibet* that won for him no ordinary praise :
" qui modo melior de tota villa in omnibus reputatur," [4]
and in which, curiously enough, he declared against the
thesis held by the mendicant orders.

Among the other works of Giles we may mention commentaries on the logical works of Aristotle and on the *Physics,
Rhetoric, De Anima, De Generatione*; *Quæstiones de materia
cœli, De intell. possibilis pluralitate* (against Averrhoes),
Quæstiones metaphysicales de regimine principum, commentaries
on the first three books of the *Sentences, Q. de esse et essentia,
de cognitione angelorum, de partibus philosophia essentialibus.*

Giles professed an eclectic Thomism, not sufficiently known.
His eclecticism was the fruit of a weak mind, and he displayed
no personality like that of a Henry of Ghent or a Godfrey of
Fontaines. He adopted the fundamental solutions of Thomism
(real distinction between essence and existence and between
substance and its faculties, substantial simplicity of immaterial
beings, the function of *materia signata* in individuation,
possibility of eternal creation) but with indecision and in-
coherence. The retractation forced on him evidently affected
him. He changed his opinion in the question of forms and on
various doctrines affected by the Paris condemnation. On

---

[1] *Chart.*, I, 406, 626, 633 and 634. Cf. D'Argentré, *Coll. judic.*, I, 235.
[2] *Chart.*, II, 12. Same prescriptions in the Chapter of Ratisbon in 1290,
II, 40.
[3] II, 39, 61-62.
[4] II, 10.

F

the other hand he returned to the thesis of the *rationes seminales* and introduced inconsistent elements into the ideological theory of the two intellects.[1]

The treatise *De partibus philosophiæ essentialibus* reproduces the classification of philosophical sciences in vogue in the thirteenth century. Giles brings out the psychological basis of this classification, and from this point of view the treatise has original features. According to Baur, it is the last work of its kind of which that can be said.[2]

As for the *De regimine principum*, written shortly before 1285 for the future Philip the Fair, we find therein a list of the duties of the prince as a man, as head of a family, and at sovereign. This treatise which was widely read, abridged, and translated, is based on Aristotle and on the similar work by Thomas Aquinas In addition, about 1310 Giles wrote a large work, *De ecclesiastica sive de summi pontificis potestate* in which he endeavoured to justify the pre-eminence of Papal authority by means of Thomist principles.

307. James of Viterbo.—When Giles was proclaimed the official doctor of the Augustinian Hermits, he became the head of a *Schola* which grew very much in the following century, One of his first disciples was JAMES CAPOCCI OF VITERBO (Jacobus de Viterbo, " doctor speculativus "), who was likewise one of the foremost men in his order, since in 1293 he was entrusted with a chair at Paris. He taught side by side with his master, and like the latter exchanged the doctor's cap for a bishop's mitre,[3] and produced quodlibetic disputations. In the

---

[1] In order to harmonize the Augustinian triad of the powers of the soul (memoria, intellectus, voluntas) with Aristotle's ideology, Giles seems to have identified the active intellect with the possible intellect. According to Werner, who attributes this theory to him (*Der Augustinismus des späteren Mittelalters*, pp. 23, 130), Giles elsewhere maintained the real distinction of the two. Again, the image of the Holy Trinity in us would not affect the essence of the soul, but simply its powers of operation ; and this would differentiate his doctrine from that of St. Thomas (p. 20). While allowing that the existence of God is proved *a posteriori*, Giles holds that the proposition " God exists " is *per se nota*, at least for the learned. Werner's account is difficult to follow. In theology Giles stresses the affective and practical aspect, and afterwards the speculative. This is another peculiar feature in Giles.

[2] Baur, *op. cit.*, pp. 380-384. Here is Giles's classification : Philosophia :
I. Scientia de entibus causantibus nostram scientiam (speculativa) : Physica—Mathematica—Theologia.
II. Scientia de entibus causatis a nobis (practica) : de intentionalibus (logica),—de realibus (moralibus).
Baur mentions as devoid of all originality, a treatise of ARNULPHUS PROVINCIALIS and certain anonymous tracts dealing with the same subject.

[3] He was Archbishop of Benevento in 1302, then of Naples (1302, died 1308). *Chart.*, II, p. 62.

official assessment of the academic library drawn up by the University on February 25, 1304, we see that the *Quodlibeta* of James are placed with the works of Giles of Rome and Godfrey of Fontaines among the classic works of the time. James also composed a compendium of the Sentences of Giles. In 1295 the Order requested him to publish his own works *in sacra pagina*.[1] James seems to have followed in general the teaching of Giles. His works have not been published.

308. Bibliography.—The chief works of Giles of Rome exist in very many Italian editions of the fifteenth and above all the sixteenth century : they are enumerated by Werner (see below), pp. 16 and 17, note. Lajard, *Gilles de Rome (Hist. Littér. Franc.*, Vol. 30, pp. 421-566) deals only with his life and works ; Werner, *Der Augustinismus d. späteren Mittelalters*, (Wien, 1883), Vol. III. of the collection *Die Scholastik d. späteren Mittelalters*, studies above all the doctrines of Giles of Rome and Gregory of Rimini ; Mattioli, *Studio s. Egidio Romano* (Rome, 1896) ; R. Scholz, *Aegidius von Rom* (Stuttgart, 1902), taken from *Die Publicistik zur Zeit Philipps d. Schönen. u. Bonifaz VIII* (Stuttgart, 1903) ; Oxilia-Boffito, *Un trattato inedito di Egidio Colonna* (De Ecclesiastica Potestate), Florence, 1908 ; Mandonnet, *La carrière scolaire de G. de Rome (R. Sc. theol. et philos.*, 1910, p. 480). A group of writers (Nik. Kaufmann, etc.) published in 1904 *Aegidius Romanus de Colonna, Joh. Gersons. Dionys. d. Karthausers u. J. Sadolets pädagogische Schriften*, in a German translation. A catalogue of the works of Giles of Rome is given by John of Paris (Quétif-Echard, *Scriptures. I*, 503). Dyroff, *Aegidius von Colonna ? Aegidius Conigiatus (Philos. Jahrb*, 1925, pp. 18-25); P. Mackaay, *Der Traktut d. Aegidius Romanus über die Einzigkeit der substantiellen Form dargestellt u. gewürdigt (Wurzbourg, 1924)*

Art. IX—Richard of Middleton.

309. Richard of Middleton (de Mediavilla).—After having studied at Oxford, Richard occupied the Franciscan chair at Paris about 1281. In 1283 he was one of the judges of Peter John Olivi. Later on he became tutor to the son of Charles II. at Naples. He died between 1300 and 1308. The list

[1] *Ibid.*

of his works contains three *Quodlibeta*, commentaries on the Sentences, and *Quæstiones Disputatæ* of great value, only one of which has so far been published.

Richard is a disciple of St. Bonaventure on some points, but follows the Thomist doctrine on others. On the one hand he holds the temporal creation of the world, the identity of the soul with its faculties, and the plurality of forms, and agrees with the majority of those holding this view that the *forma completiva* not only confers the supreme perfection but also determines and completes the inferior forms in their being and causation.[1] He denies the real distinction between essence and existence, but the arguments he adduces are not very clear ; he refuses to regard prime matter as the principle of individuation ; he hesitates as to the existence of matter in spiritual substances. On the other hand he follows Thomism in rejecting the doctrine of the seminal reasons and in combating the Anselmian argument for the existence of God ; he interprets the Augustinian theory of the *rationes æternæ* in the same sense as St. Bonav nture and St. Thomas.[2]

But Richard also holds two very personal theories which give him a place apart and make him a precursor of William of Ockam and of Duns Scotus. The first is that the universal does not exist in any way in nature, in which everything is individualized (" universale . . . secundum rei veritatem singulare est ")[3] : it is a purely logical construction with no foundation in reality, and hence science, constituted as it is of universal notions, does not attain to reality. This opens the door to idealism.

In the second place, the cognitional determinant or *species* by means of which scientific knowledge is built up, does attain to extramental individual essences, and at the same time serves as a starting-point for the logical construction of the essence conceived as abstract and universal. In this way the intellect has an intuitive knowledge of the singular, and as the latter is endowed with objectivity Richard thus returns to the dogmatic and objective tendency of the scholastic epistemology.[4] He

---

[1] *De gradu formarum*, cod. 15962 lat. Paris, Nationale. Cf. De Wulf, *Gilles de Lessines*, Ch. VI.

[2] See the extracts from the *Quæstio Disputata* published in the *De hum. cognit. rat.* etc., pp. 220 *et seq.*

[3] *Sent.* II. D. III, princ. III, q. 1. Venice 1509, fol. 16 v.

[4] " Quamvis autem universale non existat, tamen ejus species realiter in intellectu existit. . . . Et etiam quod est universale, quamvis realem existentiam non habet sub ratione qua universale, tamen habet esse repræsen-

is perhaps the first scholastic in whom we find these two theories, which become so prominent in the following century.

The authority of Richard of Middleton was great in the Franciscan Order, of which he was the most prominent master during the period between Bonaventure and Duns Scotus. He was given the title of *doctor solidus, fundatissimus*.

310. Bibliography.—Hocedez, S.J., *Les quæstiones disputatæ de R. de Middleton*, Extractum. (undated). The *Quæstiones disputatæ* of Richard of Middleton are in preparation at Quaracchi. The *Quodlibeta* and the Commentaries on the Sentences were published several times in the sixteenth century. Studies by Michalski and Minges are mentioned in previous notes. Hocedez, *R. de Middleton, sa vie, ses œuvres, sa doctrine*, in *Spicilegium Lovaniense*, 1925. Lampen, *De patria R. de Mediavilla*. in *Archiv. Franc. Hist.*, 1925, pp. 298-300.

Art. X—John Duns Scotus.

311. Life and Works.—JOHN DUNS SCOTUS was born in Scotland in 1274 according to some, 1266 according to others.[5] He was admitted into the Franciscan Order when quite young (1290), and studied at Oxford.[6] There he was influenced by the prestige of the mathematical and experimental sciences, and also by the anti-Thomist spirit.

He himself taught at Oxford, and from thence went several times to Paris. He commenced his studies for the baccalaureate at the latter place about 1293-1296,[7] and had as his master

tatum, quod esse sufficit ad movendum intellectum mediante prædicta specie." (Fol. 17-20. We quote according to Michalski, *Les courants philos. à Oxford et à Paris pendant le XIVe s.*, Cracovie, 1921. Cf. Seeberg, *Die Theol. d. J. Scotus*, pp. 33 *et seq.*). Minges, (*Scotistisches bei R. d. M.* in *Theolog. Quartalschr.*, 1917, p. 60-79, and 1919, p. 269-304) mentions the following theories : absence of a real distinction between essence and existence ; possibility of matter existing without a form ; the presence of matter in spiritual beings ; the identity of the soul with its faculties ; and the *forma corporeitatis*. With the exception of the two theories we have mentioned above, this group of doctrines is not characteristic of Scotism, but rather of the pre-Thomist scholasticism.

[5] A. Callebaut, *L'Ecosse, patrie du Bienheureux J. D. Scot*, in *Arch. franc. hist.*, 1920, p. 78-88.

[6] William of Ware was not his master. Pelster, *Handschriftliches zu Scotus mit neuen Angaben über sein Leben*, in *Francisk. Stud.*, 1923, pp. 1-2. Cf. E. Longpré, *France Francisc.*, Jan.-March, 1922.

[7] A. Callebaut, *Le B. J. D. Scot, étudiant à Paris, vers 1293-1296*, in *Arch. franc. hist.* 1294, pp. 3-12.

Gonzalvo of Balboa ; in 1302 he taught there as bachelor of the sentences, became a doctor, and taught up to 1307. In this year he went to Cologne, and died there on November 8th, 1308.

Scotus wrote his best known works when at Oxford : the great commentary on Peter Lombard, *Quæstiones in libros IV Sententiarum*, called the *Opus Oxoniense* ; the treatise *De primo principio* ; and the *Quæstiones in metaphysicam*. While at Paris he wrote the *Collationes Parisienses* and a *Quolibet*. In addition, he gave lectures in Paris on the four books of the Sentences and these were collected by his disciples, whence the name of *Reportata Parisiensia* given to this second commentary, of which there exist different *reportationes*. It is commonly thought that the *Reportata* are later than the *Opus Oxoniense*. In the manuscripts, the first book of the *Reportata* is dated 1302 and the beginning of 1303, the fourth is dated 1303. From the fact that the Oxford commentaries allude to a Bull of 1304 Pelster concludes that they were written after the Parisian work. But this question of chronology is not yet definitely settled.

There exist some unpublished disputations of Duns Scotus. In particular Pelster mentions a question which as a master he debated with Godin in 1305 : " Utrum materia sit principium individuationis."[1]

The works just mentioned are the only ones from which up to the present quotations have been found in disciples or opponents of Scotus between 1308-1330 (Longpré), and their authenticity is well established. On the other hand, recent criticism has very much curtailed the scientific output hitherto attributed to him. Thus he is no longer regarded as the author of the commentaries on the *Physics* and the *Meteorology*,[2] the *Conclusiones metaphysicæ* (Gonzalvo of Balboa),[3] the *Expositio in XII lib. metaphysicorum* or *Metaphysica textualis* (Anthony André) the *Theoremata* (posterior to William of Ockam),[4]

---

[1] Pelster, *ibid.*, p. 15, and Pelzer, *J. D. Scot et les études scotistes*, in *Revue Neo-Scolastique*, 1923, p. 418.

[2] Duhem, *Sur les Meteorolog. I. IV. faussement attribués à J. D. Scot*, in *Arch. franc. hist.*, Oct., 1910.

[3] E. Longpré, *Le primat de la volonté, Question inédit de Gonzalve de Balboa* (Et. francisc. 1925).—*Bartolomeo di Bologna, un maestro franciscano del sec XIII*, in *Studi Franciscani*, 1923.

[4] Deodat Marie (*Les Theoremata de Scot*, in *Arch. franc. histor.*, 1918, pp. 3-31), questions the authenticity of this work because no manuscript of it is in existence. Wadding is the only one who ascribes it to him, and its teaching presents certain analogies with Ockamism.

the *Quæstiones disputatæ de rerum principio* (before Scotus),[1]
the *Grammatica speculativa* or *De modis significandi* (Thomas
of Erford).[2] The attribution of the *Quæstiones de anima* and
the logical works remains uncertain. Finally, it has not been
established that Scotus held a solemn disputation at Paris
in favour of the Immaculate Conception.[3]

These important results of the critical examination of the
works of Duns Scotus cast a new light on his philosophy.
Contradictions disappear, the links with the past are seen,
the constructive merit is more evident, and the whole setting
is very different from that in which the genius of the Franciscan
teacher has hitherto been placed.

312. General features of the philosophy of Duns Scotus.—
(i) *His critical and constructive mind.* Scotus was an unusually
forceful critic. He attacked the majority of his contemporaries, the Averrhoists, Thomas Aquinas, Giles of Rome,
Roger Bacon, Richard of Middleton, Godfrey of Fontaines, and
above all Henry of Ghent. He rarely named his opponents,
but those familiar with his polemics could not mistake the
person referred to. This critical attitude, though courteous,
was bound to make his teaching lively and popular. It makes
his works a repertory of contemporary philosophy of incom-
parable doctrinal value. At the same time Scotus had a sense
of tradition. Besides the scholastics he combated, there are
others to whom he appealed, notably St. Bonaventure, and
William de la Mare.

He did not criticize for the sake of criticizing, but in order to
construct. In various places he stressed the mental necessity
for unity and synthesis, and in his doctrine he was able to
introduce this co-ordination, without which there can be
no real philosophy.

(ii) His *language* is concise, but not always clear. Its under-

---

[1] Minges, *Die scotistische Litteratur des XX. Jahrh.* in *Franc. Stud.*, 1917,
p. 185, and recently E. Longpré, *La Philosophie de D. Scot. Extrait des
Et. franc.*, 1924, pp. 22-51 and 288. In addition, J. Carreras y Artau, *Ensayo
sobre el voluntarismo de J. D. Scot* (Gerona, 1923, pp. 74-84), regards it as
spurious, by reason of the opposition in certain passages to authentic texts
of Scotus. Longpré's study was occasioned by the work of Landry, who
advanced the gratuitous hypothesis that the work was written by Scotus
in his youth. In our treatment of the philosophic work of Scotus we follow
the excellent work of Longpré.

[2] Grabmann, *De Thoma Erfordensi auctore Grammaticæ quæ Joanni
Scoto adscribitur speculativæ*, in *Arch. franc. histor.*, 1922, pp. 273-277. The
work is studied at length by M. Heidegger, *Die Kategorien u. Bedeutungslehre
d. D. Scotus* (Tubingen, 1916).

[3] Denifle, *Chartul. univ. Paris*, Vol. II, p. 118.

standing requires a thorough initiation into scholastic terminology and teaching. Faults in the method of exposition
make certain works difficult to read, and the absence of good
editions increases the difficulty of their study.

(iii) In his commentaries on the thought of Aristotle, Scotus
does not always agree with St. Thomas. Like the latter, he does
not follow the Stagirite blindly, as will be seen from the following brief exposition of the Scotist synthesis.

313. Metaphysics.—Underlying his metaphysics, we find
once more the fundamental principle of the Scholastic pluralism : the individual is the only existing thing. It is the being
of this individual, in all its plenitude, which is investigated
by metaphysics. Again, it is according to the richness of
their being that individual things make up one vast hierarchy
with God as its summit.

The interpretation which Scotus gives of this richness of
being makes his individualism an original one. He perfects
and generalizes a metaphysical method the idea of which had
been suggested by some of his predecessors : while insisting
on the unity and identity of the individual he divides it up
into metaphysical sections corresponding to the conceptual
elaboration to which the mind subjects it. This method
appears at its best in the study of form, which at once takes us
to the problem of becoming (165), but it also affects the explanation of various static aspects of being.

(i) *The cleavage of the form into formalitates.*—The theory
of prime matter is treated after the manner of the older
scholasticism,[1] and from this point of view Scotus is a follower
of the Franciscan tradition. It is not certain from the authentic
works that the composition of matter and form extends beyond
corporeal substances.[2]   But apart from this important
restriction, Scotus incorporates into the Aristotelian notion of
matter all the additions which we have pointed out in the
predecessors of Thomas Aquinas : in the corporeal being matter
is the element of initial indetermination, the capacity for
various states which matter desires and which the union with

---

[1] The theory of the three states of matter, attributed to Scotus (*primo
prima*, or fundamental potentiality of every limited being ; *secundo prima*,
or the same element of indetermination endowed in corporeal substances with
the attributes of quantity ; *tertio prima*, or the substratum of accidental
modifications of an already constituted body) is not found in the authentic
works, but in the *De rerum principio*, q. 7 and 8. In this work also occurs
the often quoted phrase : " Ego ad positionem Avencebronis redeo."
[2] Longpré, *op. cit.*, p. 265.

successive forms confers upon it (Aristotelianism). As such it is an entity, very exiguous but still real.[1] Hence it is not pure potency. Its actuality is the object of a distinct idea in God,[2] and of a univocal and proper concept in man (Augustinianism). Furthermore, the *potentia absoluta* of God could call it into existence without uniting it to an informing principle.[3]

We see already that the metaphysics of Scotus is different to that of Thomas. The conflict is evident in the theory of form. Scotus introduces a complication into this, not because he accepts the real plurality of forms (another traditional doctrine which he utilizes in certain cases, such as the explanation of living beings), but because he makes an objective division of one and the same form into several formalities, with which the form is identified.

Take for instance the formal perfection of man, or *humanitas*. It is true that, as it exists outside of the mind, it is characterized by individuality : each man has *his* humanity (pluralism). It is equally true that the abstract and universal notion of humanity is a product of the mind, so much so that in his conclusions Scotus is a realist like Thomas Aquinas and the other scholastics.[4] Nevertheless, this *humanitas*, which is necessarily characterized either by singularity in the order of extramental existence, or by universality in that of our concepts, is identified with generic (life, sensibility) and specific elements (rationality) of which one is not the other, and which, independently of the double state conferred upon them by extramental or ideal existence ("ante omnem actus intellectus, circumscripto omni intellectu") have an ontological value in the individual. The *res* or individual comprises *realitates* or *formalitates*, each with its own proper place in this individual.[5]

Scotus, then, does not multiply forms as R. Kilwardby or Richard of Middleton did, but he introduces into one and the same form several metaphysical sections. At the same time he affirms their unity and identity *in re*, by means of the *distinctio formalis a parte rei*.

[1] *Ox*. IV, d. 11, q. 3, n. 12.
[2] *I. Sent*. d. 36, a. 3, q. 1.
[3] "Non video quod sit contradictio" (*Ox*. II, dist. 12, q. 2).
[4] These ideas are clearly expounded in P. Minges, *Der angebliche exzessive Realismus des Duns Scotus*, BGPM, VII, 1, 1908.
[5] "Quodlibet commune et tamen determinabile adhuc potest distingui, quantumcumque sit una res, in plures realitates, formaliter distinctas, quarum hæc formaliter non est illa." (*Ox*., 1. 2, d. 3, q. 6, n. 15).

(ii) *The individual unity can be harmonized with the multiplicity of its metaphysical elements*. Each element (*formalitas*) in human perfection has no doubt its own entity, and is invested with a corresponding unity, but its entity is weak and fragile, for it melts as it were into that of the form ; its unity is less (*minor*) than the terminal unity of the individual being,[1] for the *realitates* or *formalitates*—ontological sections " quarum hæc formaliter non est illa "—are united in the *res* or individual being " just as the specific form of white forms but one with the generic essence of colour." [2]   The individual alone appears and disappears in nature.   The *realitates*, such as animality, corporeity, are neither separated nor separable.

This enables us to understand what Scotus means by the subtle and celebrated *distinctio formalis a parte rei*. In addition to the *distinctio realis* existing between two entirely distinct elements such as matter and form, and the *distinctio rationis* which multiplies the concepts of one and the same thing in order to consider it either from different points of view (*distinctio rationis cum fundamento in re*) or else from the same point of view (*distinctio rationis sine fundamento in re*), the *distinctio formalis a parte rei* refers to the objective *formalitates* which are realized in one and the same individual substance independently of any intellectual act.

(iii) *The principle of individuation*.   A last formal determination, " ultima realitas entis " restricts the specific form and completes it.   It impresses its definitive seal upon it (*contrahere speciem*), and in uniting itself to particular matter is the ultimate reason of individuation, *ad esse hanc rem*.   Scotus calls it *hæcceitas*.   Individuation, then, is not as in Thomism connected with quantity, the attribute of bodies, and accordingly immaterial creatures—separated human souls and pure forms—are multiplied in their species just as corporeal things.   The *distinctio formalis a parte rei* assures to this *hæcceitas* a certain measure of ontological independence, and at the same

---

1 " Aliqua est unitas in re realis absque omni operatione intellectus, minor unitate numerali sive unitate propria singularis." (*Rep*. I. 7, q. 18, n. 7). " Licet enim (natura) nunquam sit realiter sine aliquo istorum, non tamen est de se aliquod istorum, ita etiam in rerum natura secundum illam entitatem habet verum esse extra animam reale : et secundum illam entitatem habet unitatem sibi proportionabilem, quæ est indifferens ad singularitatem, ita quod non repugnat illi unitati de se, quod cum quacunque unitate singularitatis ponatur." (*In II Sent.*, dist. 3, q. 1, 1).

2 *Rep*. I, 2 dist. 12, q. 8, no. 8.

time explains the fundamental unity of the form of which it is the ultimate *realitas*.

(iv) *Other applications of formalism.*—We have followed Scotus in his study of the *forma* and the elements which organize it from within. It is above all to this domain that the doctrine of *formalitates* or *realitates* applies. But it also affects the whole study of extramental reality, for it intervenes wherever there is room for a detailed treatment of the metaphysical richness of any being. Thus it applies to goodness and truth, which are different *formaliter*, and identical *in re*.[1] It applies again to the faculties of the soul, which are so many aspects of reality constituting the soul itself.[2] A similar explanation is given of the connection existing between the Divine attributes. Everywhere we get the classical formula : " identice unum, formaliter distinctum," and everywhere unity accompanies being : "cuilibet gradui reali entitatis correspondet realis unitas."[3] Metaphysical formalism also affects the psychology of Duns Scotus : we shall see that it is precisely this variety and multiplicity of *formalitates* constituting one concrete reality that accounts for the intuitive knowledge of the individual by the understanding.

Was the theory of *formalitates* an innovation on the part of Duns Scotus? Longpré has recently shown that it was anticipated in scholasticism prior to the thirteenth century.[4] We may link it up with the doctrine of the *rationes reales* taught by Olivi and above all by Peter de Trabibus, and we can also see a suggestion of the idea in the Bonaventurian distinction between the soul and its faculties.[5] But it cannot be denied that it was Duns Scotus who gave to this theory of *formalitates* its fullest extension ; he developed it in such a way as to make it one of the central points in his metaphysics.

---

[1] " Alia perfectio realis, alietate inquam, non causata ab intellectu," (*In Metaph.*, lib. 7, q. 2, n. 24). " Ita concedo per identitatem veritatem esse bonitatem in re, non tamen formaliter veritatem esse bonitatem." (*Ox.*, I, d. 8, q. 4, n. 18).

[2] " Non quod sint [the reference is to the *intellectus* and the *voluntas*] essentia ejus formaliter sed sunt formaliter distinctæ, idem tamen identice et unitive," (*Ox.*, 2, d. 16, q. 1, n. 18).

[3] *In Metaph.*, VII, q. 13, n. 19.

[4] Longpré, *op. cit.*, p. 235 *et seq.*

[5] Different opinions have been put forth on the *distinctio formalis a parte rei*, which is neither a real nor a mental distinction, but occupies a place between the two. Is not Scotus taking as his basis the very way in which the mind organizes the content of its concepts when expressing reality, and if so, is he not applying to extramental reality the process of mental analysis ? If this is so (and this is our opinion), it would be difficult not to see in Scotus' theory a return to a form of exaggerated realism, which, how-

(v) Scotus would not allow a real distinction between *essence* and *existence*. " Simpliciter falsum est quod esse sit aliud ab essentia." [6] From this it follows that every element of reality has its own existential being : " omne ens habet aliquod esse proprium." [7]

(vi) The *generic and specific concepts* utilized by the mind in its scientific constructions attain to univocal realities and have the same value in the indefinitely numerous beings to which these concepts apply. Even the notion of being, which we apply to substance and accident, to creatures and to God, is characterized by univocity, and corresponds, in the measure in which it signifies opposition to nothing, to a homogeneous determination in all that is or can be. Scotus endeavours to harmonize this with the transcendental and analogical character of being, for he strongly affirms that being is not a genus (since there is nothing outside being which could differentiate it) and that in the order of existence being is characterized by different modalities (*modi*).

(vii) There are many other subjects treated in the metaphysics of Scotus, and a comprehensive study could alone treat these adequately. In view of the discussions to which they gave rise among the Ockamists, we must mention the important place occupied by action and passion, the dynamical relations which unite beings in one vast network of reciprocal dependence. He always looks upon action and passion as additions either from without or from within (*extrinsecus* or *intrinsecus advenientes*) to the substance which they modify.[8]

314. Natural Theology.—Reason proves the existence of God *ex necessariis*. From the contingence and ontological poverty of the beings which surround us we infer the existence

---

ever, does not prevent him from accepting the conclusions of the moderate realism of thirteenth century scholasticism, inasmuch as the individual substance alone exists outside our minds. Other interpreters, more favourable to the *distinctio formalis*, treat the matter in a different way ; it is because the *formalitates* are in a being before and apart from the work of the mind that the latter grasps them ; they are apprehended by an intuitive concept, and this first contact, confused but real, constitutes an argument in favour of the presence of the *formalitates a parte rei*. To this the opponents of the Scotist distinction reply that that is precisely the point at issue, and that this pre-existence is a postulate which is unnecessary, and that the virtual distinction of the Thomists is sufficient to ensure the real objectivity of our metaphysical concepts.

[6] *Ox.*, I, 4, d. 13, q. 1.
[7] *Ibid.*, d. 43, q. 1.
[8] *Rep.* I, d. 27, q. 1. Cf. Longpré, *op. cit.*, p. 43.

of the Necessary Being ; we analyse the metaphysical require-
ments of change and by the principle of causality attain to the
existence of the Unchangeable. Scotus insists that in the
causal ascent from one efficient cause to another an infinite
series is impossible, " omni modo est aliquod simpliciter
primum effectivum "[1] and the same is true in the order of
finality and eminence.[2]

He rejects the *a priori* arguments, but endeavours to
" colour " the Anselmian argument in order to give it an
acceptable sense.[3]

His study of the nature and attributes of God is a bold and
vigorous piece of constructive theism. God is the Absolute,
the Infinite, " ipsum esse."[4] On to this fundamental and
common doctrine, Scotus grafts some new thesis in accordance
with his metaphysics and psychology.

(i) *The univocal character of the concept of being.* In the
real order, God possesses being primarily or *per se*, creatures
secondarily. The being of God is the *measure*, the being of a
creature is *measured*, and it is only in virtue of an analogical
participation that being belongs both to the Creator and the
creature. But of these two kinds of beings, so different in
character, the mind possesses a common abstract concept,
applying to both in a univocal way, and having as its content
the formal reason or aspect of being, and not its concrete modes.
Otherwise all knowledge of God would be impossible : " omnis
inquisitio de Deo supponit intellectum habere conceptum
eumdem univocum quem accipimus ex creaturis " :[5] being
is univocal in the logical domain, analogical in the realm of
reality.[6]

(ii) A second directing principle of the Scotist Natural
Theology is the introduction of the *distinctio formalis a parte
rei* into the Divine perfections. These perfections are indeed

---

[1] *Ox.*, I, d. 2, n. 14, etc.
[2] *Ibid.*
[3] " Per illud potest colorari illa ratio Anselmi de summo cogitabili, Prosl.
2, et intelligenda est ejus descriptio sic : Deus est, quo cogitato sine contradictione majus cogitati non potest sine contradictione," (*In Sent.* I, d. 2, q. 2).
Again, the existing is more intelligible than the non-existing, because it
comes within the domain of intuitive knowledge (*ibid.* See Psychology).
Cf. Daniels, *Quellenbeiträge*, etc., pp. 106-107.
[4] *Rep.* I, d. 8, q. 1. Cf. Belmond, *Dieu, existence et cognoscibilité* (Paris,
1913, pp. 174-202).
[5] *Ox.* I, d. 2, q. 3, n. 3.
[6] Cf. P. Minges, *Beiträge z. Lehre des D. Scotus über die Univokatio des
Seinbegriffes* (*Philos. Jahrb.*, 1907, pp. 306-323).

unified in the Divine essence from which they flow[1] and are
identified with it in an eminent degree. All is unity in the
Absolute. Nevertheless, the one is not the other.[2] It is the
influence of the mystery of the Trinity and the desire to
penetrate its richness that inspires Scotus in this transposition
into the study of God of a theory originating in the metaphysics of contingent being.

(iii) Once in possession of the notion of the Infinite, Scotus
dwells at length on the Divine attributes. Reason establishes
the divine unity.[3] He includes the following among the
attributes which reason teaches us *naturaliter* concerning God :
life, involving intelligence and will,[4] truth,[5] general Providence,[6] justice, infinite and creative power, all the great
affirmations of the traditional theology. It was against the
theses and arguments of Scotus that William of Ockam directed
his dialectical bombardment. After proving the infinite
power of God, Scotus makes the reservation that reason—or
perhaps the Aristotelian philosophy—cannot prove either
a priori or *a posteriori* that God could produce *quodcumque
possibile* without the help of some immediate cause.[7] We
must content ourselves with probable arguments.[8] Similarly,
the Divine omnipresence is not capable of rigorous demonstration,[9] and influenced by the condemnation in 1277 of the
theory that " angelus est in loco per operationem," Scotus
criticizes St. Thomas's reasoning on this point.

The Divine intelligence, and above all the will, constituting
the Divine life, are the object of very full developments.

(iv) The basis of the Divine life is the act of intelligence.
It dominates the whole order of volitions and free decrees :
" Deus est agens rectissima ratione."[10] God knows Himself,
and all the possible imitations of His essence : whether these

[1] See *Quodl.* 5, for instance.
[2] " Quia vera identitas, imo verissima, quæ sufficit ad omnino simplex
potest stare cum non identitate formali." (*Ox.*, 4 d. 46, q. 3, n. 4 and 5.
[3] Against William of Ware. Cf. Longpré, *op. cit.*, p. 113.
[4] " Tu vivas vita nobilissima, quia intelligens et volens." Cf. Longpré,
pp. 117 *et seq.*
[5] *Ox.*, 3 d. 25, q. 1. n. 5.
[6] *Ox.*, 4 d. 17, q. 1. n. 7. See Longpré, pp. 113-124.
[7] *Quodl.* XVII, n. 11, 12, 21. The *Rep.*, I d. 42, q. 2, n. 7. add : " Licet
suppositis principiis Philosophorum non possit probari Deum posse producere
immediate quidquid est possibile produci, tamen aliter dicendum est secundum fidem."
[8] *Ox.*, 1, d. 42, q. 1. n. 3 and 4.
[9] *Rep.*, 1 d. 37, q. 2, n. 10.
[10] *Rep.*, IV, d. 1, 1. 5, n. 9.

are of the rational order (*imago*) or otherwise (*vestigium*), their reality is " secundum determinatum exemplar."

The Divine ideas are not the very essence of God, for according to Scotus this would imply an objective dependence of the Divine essence upon the creature before any act of intelligence. Formally they are objective presentations of the creature in the Divine mind.[1] It is the essence of God that determines the act of understanding (*objectum motivum*) and constitutes its principal content (*objectum terminans primario*), so that beings which imitate God and constitute the secondary term of the Divine knowledge (*objectum terminans secundario*)[2] have also the foundation of their reality in God. This is a variant of the theory of examplarism.

(v) In conformity with his general theory on the activities of spiritual substances, Scotus stresses God's will rather than His intelligence, and makes liberty an essential attribute of every Divine volition. But here again we must not interpret the Divine indeterminism in the sense of a despotic and capricious will. Without doubt the Divine will is not determined by anything in His external works (" quia voluntas est voluntas "), but God cannot will the impossible or the irrational : " quodlibet tenendum est esse Deo possibile quod nec est ex terminis manifestum impossibile."[3] To act against reason would be to cease to be.

Minges also points out that in many passages in which Scotus stresses the autonomy of the Divine will, he is considering not the order of possibles but that of existing things. The existence of creatures rests on a decree of the Divine liberty. Now that which exists has alone a proper and real goodness. In this sense the goodness of things, their nature, and in particular the limits of the natural and supernatural life, the moral law, and the constitution of civil society depend on the will of God and not upon His intelligence. Otherwise the ideal goodness and nature of things would compel God to realize them, which cannot be allowed. In other words : the existence

---

[1] *Ox.*, IV, d. 50, q. 3, n. 4. " Per quid cognoscuntur illa ? . . . oportet quod per illam essentiam quæ perfectissime omnia repræsentat." Cf. Klein, *Der Gottesbegriff des J. D. Scotus*, p. 65.

[2] *Rep.* I, d. 36, q. 2, n. 5. " Nullum objectum aliud ab essentia divina potest movere divinum intellectum." Again, n. 7 : " Sicut essentia divina primo movet intellectum, ita primo movet ad se. . . . Aliquid aliud a Deo potest esse objectum et intelligibile ab ipso, terminans ejus secundario."

[3] *Oxon.*, IV, d. 10, q. 2, n. 5. Cf. : Non potest aliquid velle quod non possit recte velle.

of contingent things depends on the will of God, but His will
is not determined without reason, for the act of intelligence is
primordial in the Divine life. It would not have been otherwise even if God, making use of His absolute power (*potentia
absoluta*) of realizing anything not intrinsically impossible,
had created a world other than that the existence of which
has been decreed by the *potentia ordinata* : the Divine will
would have been rational and ordered.[1] God can will only
that which is good. The order of existences, and therefore the
actual world as it is, is good. Here we have the fundamental
solution of Thomism.[2]

(vi) Reason can establish that God has created the contingent
beings existing outside Him, but Scotus combats the arguments employed by Henry of Ghent in order to demonstrate
the temporal character of creation, and leans towards the
Thomist solution. Lastly, anxious as he is to safeguard the
essential liberty of every act of will in man, Scotus is undecided
in the question of physical premotion.

We see that Scotus' natural theology is conceived in the
spirit of dogmatism,[3] and ranks among the noblest which
thirteenth century scholasticism produced. It constitutes a
science, in the Aristotelian sense of the word.[4]

315. Philosophy of Nature.—Scotus frankly rejects the
theory of seminal reasons dear to the old Franciscan school ;
he criticizes the chief argument[5] on which St. Bonaventure
relies in order to establish an *inductio formarum* in matter.
His ideas on place and movement had their repercussion in the
history of the sciences.[6]

Vital activities cannot be reduced to the plasticity of the
body in which they manifest themselves. They denote a
superior perfection. That is why, in addition to the form of
materiality, every organism has a vital form. Scotus goes

---

[1] Klein, *op. cit.*, p. 187 ; Longpré, *op. cit.*, p. 80.

[2] Minges concludes that there is an essential agreement between Scotus's
idea of God and his ostensibly proved Exaggerated Indeterminism (Ch. V.,
Wien 1906). According to Minges, Vacant has misunderstood the Divine
Indeterminism.

[3] It is in the *Theoremata* that we find the manifold doubts cast upon the
rational arguments for a series of Divine attributes. There is therefore no
longer question of finding in Scotus the germs of scepticism.

[4] See a fine passage of the Prologue to the *Reportata*, q. 1, n. 43-48.

[5] " Neque est necessaria hæc ratio seminalis ad vitandam creationem aut
annihilationem," (*Rep.* Lib. II, Dist 18). Scotus gives to the *ratio seminalis*
a restricted and special sense.

[6] Duhem, *Le mouvement absolu et le mouvement relatif* (Montligeon, 1909),
pp. 56-69, 281.

further than Henry of Ghent, but he does not admit the
necessity of multiplying the substantial principles in a compound (Alexander of Hales, Albert the Great), or, *a fortiori*,
in simple bodies (St. Bonaventure).

316. Psychology.—Before we indicate the original doctrines
in the psychology of Scotus, it is important to stress the fact
that he is in agreement with the other great scholastics in
holding the distinction between sensation and thought, the
absence of innate ideas, the function of internal experience,
the spirituality of the soul, and the other fundamental solutions
of the scholastic patrimony. He combines these with personal
opinions on the nature of the intellect and the will, the intrinsic
constitution of the human being, and the immortality of the
soul. The *distinctio formalis a parte rei* which Scotus introduces
between the soul and its faculties is merely an application of the
metaphysical system already dealt with.

(i) *Extension of the domain of the intellect.* Careful to secure
for the understanding the immediate perception of individual
reality, Scotus allows, in addition to the abstract and universal
knowledge which is *distinct*, a preliminary intuitive knowledge
representing a concrete and singular thing in a *confused*
manner (*species specialissima*). This concept of the singular
arises at the first contact of the intelligence with that outside
it, and is formed simultaneously with the sense knowledge of
an object. Is it not in harmony with the logic of the system
that this intuitive contact of the mind should precede the
reflective contact ? There is in the individual being perceived
by our senses an internal wealth of distinct *entities* apart from
the work of the mind. Our concepts adapt themselves to these,
and are intuitive resemblances of the real. Thanks to this
concept of the singular, the understanding enters into direct
relation with the extramental world, and perceives as existing
in their particular state those elements of reality represented
in a universal state by " distinct " knowledge. Thus the
objectivity of intellectual knowledge is accentuated, and linked
up with the existing and actual world even more than in St.
Thomas, but we must not forget that this existing world
differs in its constitution in the two theories. Furthermore,
since there is no real distinction between the faculties of the
soul, the understanding acts in close union with sense knowledge (cf. the *colligantia of* Olivi, **251**) ; the two naturally
collaborate.

G

The presence of intuitive intellectual knowledge does not in any way affect our universal knowledge, which remains the most important from the point of view of science, and which Scotus treats in the same way as St. Thomas.

Scotus enlarges the scope of the intellect in another way. Although, in the actual state of our earthly life, the essences of sensible things are the only proper object of our understanding, their intelligibility does not exhaust the representative power of which this faculty is capable, considered absolutely as a cognitive faculty. Everything which possesses being can come within the scope of the human intellect, the suprasensible as well as the sensible. We must bear in mind, moreover, that the idea of being applies univocally to all things, including God. The human intellect is *capax Dei* ; it can be elevated to the vision of the Being Who will beatify it.

For the rest, the most elevated knowledge, like the lowliest, has its origin in the same genetic process, and Scotus addresses severe but justifiable reproaches to the special illumination theory taught by Henry of Ghent and the Augustinians.[1] Unlike Godfrey of Fontaines, he stresses the active part played by the mind, and declines to look upon knowledge as the purely *passive* reception of a " species." Here again he is in agreement with the Thomist theory.

All these doctrines are linked up with the metaphysical theory that every being possesses in its natural resources the immediate principle of its proper activities, and they already suffice to show that Scotus may be called a typical representative of intellectualism for the same reason as St. Thomas.[2]

Still, it is commonly said that he teaches the primacy of the will. In what sense is this the case ?

(ii) *The primacy of the will.*—It is certainly not in the Kantian sense that we here speak of the primacy of the will. The latter has not the function of establishing certitudes inaccessible to the reason. But Scotus does affirm the following :

(a) *Freedom is the essence of the voluntary act.* Like St. Thomas he distinguishes between the tendency towards the

---

[1] " Objectum primarium potentiæ assignatur illud quod adæquatur potentiæ in ratione potentiæ, non autem quod adæquatur potentiæ ut in aliquo statu." (*In I Sent.*, D. III, q. 3, n. 24 and 25). Cf. Vacant, *op. cit.* (*Ann. Phil. chrét.* 1888, pp. 450 *et seq.*).

[2] See the fine chapter on the Scotist intellectualism in Longpré, *op. cit.*, ch. VI.

good, and the actual volition of the good. The tendency is necessary, habitual, and uninterrupted ; the act is free and intermittent. But while for St. Thomas the voluntary act is determined by the intellectual presentation of the *complete* good (282), according to Scotus every voluntary act *(elicitus)* is free *per essentiam* ; the will is *simpliciter activa*. This means that no good exercises a necessitating influence upon it, for it always retains its absolute self-determination. Even in presence of the complete good, God, this power of self-determination remains, both in its *negative* form, for the will can suspend its act by diverting the attention of the mind, [1] it can act or not act *(libertas contradictionis)* ; and in its *positive* form, for in willing it is itself the total efficient cause of its activity. Again, this implies that it alone chooses between good and evil *(libertas contrarietatis)*, and between two goods *(libertas specificationis)*. Lastly, it implies that the intellectual presentation is not the *efficient* cause, but merely the *conditio sine qua non*, or at most the *final* cause, and that the internal motion is due simply to the will itself. I will *because* I will : in created agents the total cause of the voluntary act is to be found in the will itself. " Nihil creatum aliud a voluntate est causa totalis actus volendi in voluntate." [2] Therein lies the efficiency of the voluntary act.

A doctrine like this may be described as indeterminism. But it is clear that the free act of the will is still a motived and reasoned act, and that the voluntary decision although free is in no way capricious or irrational. Scotus by his attacks on Thomas Aquinas helped to spread the idea that he entertained on the psychology of the will very different conceptions to those of his illustrious rival. According to St. Thomas, " voluntas ab aliquo objecto ex necessitate movetur, ab aliquo autem non." [3] Scotus replies : " Voluntas nihil de necessitate vult." Thomas stresses the passivity of the will in presence of the complete good, Scotus the activity of every volition. There is no divergence between the two save in the way of explaining the volition of the complete good. [4]

---

[1] " In potestate voluntatis est avertere intellectum a consideratione finis [ultimi], quo facto voluntas non volet finem, quia non potest habere actum circa ignotum." (*Op. cit.*, D. I, q. 4).

[2] *Rep.*, II, d. 25, q. 1, n. 20. Longpré goes further and holds that " sometimes " knowledge acts upon the will as a partial efficient cause (*op. cit.*, pp. 222-223).

Summa Theol., Ia IIae, q. 10, a. 2.

[3] Minges, *Ist D. Scotus indeterminist ?* BGPM., V, 4, p. 112. For instance,

For the rest, when Scotus stresses the *activity* and spontaneity of volition, the opponent he has in mind is Godfrey of Fontaines rather than Thomas Aquinas. He is reacting against a psychological interpretation of volition which exaggerates its passivity towards the good known, and ends in leaving liberty very much in the background (302). The attitude of Scotus towards Godfrey is the same as that taken up by Henry of Ghent, whose voluntarism he carries on (304).

(b) *The soul's nobility rests upon willing rather than knowing.* The superiority of the will is above all manifest in its freedom or essential self-determination, and in this it differs from the intellect, which acts by a necessity of nature. The will commands the intelligence, but not *vice versa*. Certainly its orders do not affect the nature of the intellectual act itself, but they affect its exercise, *quoad exercitium actus*, which they direct up to a certain point. Accordingly its moral value is higher than that of the intellect (against Thomas).

(iii) *Soul and body.*[5]—Man is a substantial compound, and the soul is the form of the body. But in addition to the intellectual soul, there is in us an incomplete *forma corporeitatis*, preparing the body for the reception of and determination by the intellectual soul, from which it is really distinct. The intellectual soul is one with the sensible and vegetative soul : these are three " formalities " of one and the same reality. " Sensitiva et vegetativa in homine eadem anima est cum intellectiva."[6]   Scotus thus utilizes the doctrine of the plurality of forms as well as his theory of the multiplicity of formalities in one and the same form. He introduces complications into the human being, but insists on its unity and the intrinsic and immediate compenetration of all its constituent elements.

(iv) *The immortality of the soul.* This is established by moral arguments and " persuasiones probabiles," but reason cannot prove it by metaphysical arguments.[7] The nature of the soul

he criticizes the term *movere*, which has the precise meaning of acting by efficience, and which Thomas employs " quasi metaphorice," in the sense of attracting by finality. Cf. *Summa Theol.*, Ia, q. 82, a. 4, where he uses the expression " movere per modum finis." Verweyen, *op. cit.*, p. 190, goes further and says that in combating Thomas, Scotus is fighting windmills. This is an exaggeration.

[5] H. Klug, *Die Lehre d. J. D. Scotus über d. Seele*, in *Phil. Jahrb.*, 1923 and 1924.

[6] *Rep.* IV, d. 44, q. 1, n. 4.

[7] *Rep.*, IV, d. 43, q. 2. See the exposition in Klug, *Phil. Jahrb.*, 1924, v. 60-68.

does not demonstrate the absolute necessity of its immortality,[1] otherwise we should have to say that God, who cannot do what is impossible, could not allow it or any other spiritual being to relapse into nothingness. The criticism shows the weakness of the argument of Aristotle, and equally affects his system of Intelligences. Again, we cannot infer immortality from our natural desire of living without end, or from our need of happiness.

317. Moral philosophy.—As we should expect, the great directing principles of the pyschology of Scotus are reflected in his moral philosophy.

On the one hand intellectualism penetrates the whole sphere of conduct. The morality of an act depends in the first place on its object and end, in conformity with the dictates of reason.[2] Conscience or synderesis, prudence and the *recta ratio*, are explained as in Thomas Aquinas, in terms of intellectualism.[3]

On the other hand, the emphasis laid on the primacy of the will is an immediate corollary of psychological voluntarism. Morality is principally a matter of the will ; the moral virtues, *habitus electivi*, spring from the will, like all *electiones*. The corruption of the will is worse than that of the intellect ; to love God is more perfect than to know Him ; the acquisition of beatitude consists in an act of the will. In the same way moral obligation, responsibility, merit and demerit depend on the will rather than on the intelligence. Everywhere the importance of action is emphasized.

The few references to the group life suffice to show that Scotus understands the mission of civil society in the same way as does Thomas Aquinas.

318. Philosophy and Theology.—We may say that Scotus is faithful to the constitutional theses which in the thirteenth century govern the relations between theology and philosophy. Not only does he admit the distinction between the two sciences, he also holds, contrary to what is usually said on the subject, that philosophy shows the harmony between reason and the faith, and that apologetics penetrates theology.[4]

---

[1] " Quia hoc concluderet quod Deus non posset animam vel Angelum vel aliam aliquam essentiam simplicem simpliciter destruere vel annihilare, quod est falsum " (*ibid.*, n. 17).

[2] Minges, *Bedeutung von Objekt, Umständen und Zweck für die Sittlichkeit eines Aktes nach D. Scotus*, in *Phil. Jahrb.*, 1906, pp. 328-347.

[3] Longpré, *op. cit.*, pp. 209-210.

[4] Minges, *Das Verhältniss zwischen Glauben u. Wissen* p. 8. " Theologus

320. Bibliography.—The *Opus Oxoniense* was printed first in 1481 ; different *Reportata* appeared in 1478 and in 1517-1518 ; but the first complete edition was that of Lyons (1639) due to the care of Lucas Wadding, the great annalist of the order. It was reprinted at Paris after 1891, by Vivès. Mgr. Pelzer (*Le premier Livre des Reportata Parisiensia . . .* in Vol. V of the Louvain *Annales*, 1923, pp. 449-491, has shown that the text of Book I of the *Reportata Parisiensia* by L. Wadding (Lyons, 1639) does not give the *Reportatio* examined by Scotus himself, but is an arbitrary reconstruction of his course, based partly on an abridgement of the authentic *Reportatio* made by William Alnwick, and partly on a bad *Reportatio* edited at Paris in 1517. The authentic *Reportatio* of Scotus has not been published. Complementary notes by Michalski will be found in *Miscellanea Ehrle*, I, pp. 250 *et seq.*—G. Théry (*Le De Rerum principio et la condemnation de* 1277, in *R. sc. phil. theol.*, 1924, p. 173), shows that the author of this treatise (Scotus or someone else) wrote with the object of justifying the censure of Arabian theories in 1277. Père Garcia republished in 1910 the *Quæstiones disputatæ de rerum principio* and the *Tractatus de primo rerum omnium principio* (Quarrachi), with a somewhat uncritical preface on his life and works. In 1912 and 1914 were published Books I and II of the *Comm. Oxon.* By the same, *Lexicon Scholasticum Philosophico—theologicum in quo termini, distinctiones et effata seu axiomaticæ propositiones philosophiam ac theologiam spectantes a B. J. Duns Scot. exponuntur*, 6 parts, Quaracchi 1906-1910. Contains : (1) Life, works and doctrines ; (2) Edition of the *Grammatica speculativa ;* (3) *Distinctiones et effata*, forming a supplement to the Vivès edition. The index by F. de Varesio (Venice, 1690) applies only to the Books on the Sentences and the *Quodlibeta.* In any case it is very rare. P. Déodat Marie has published *Capitulia opera B. S. Duns Scoti :* (1) Preparatio philosophica ; (2) Synthesis theologica (Le Havre, 1908 and 1911, two

in a very wide sense. Scotus is himself a Peripatetician. Certainly he seems to be influenced by some theories of Augustine ; he defends the pre-eminence of the will over the intellect and the plurality of forms in things. But are these fundamental principles of Augustinism ? Are they indeed Augustinism at all, at least if viewed in the aspect given to them by the Subtle Doctor ? " Vacant's *Dictionn. Theol. cath.* under " Developpement historique de l' Augustinisme," (Vol. One, col. 2512.) Similarly De Martigné writes : The divergence begins when, with this possession in common, the two doctors seek to enlarge the domain of science and truth." (*op. cit.*, pp. 332 and 359). Cf. Pluzanski, *op. cit.*, pp. 6 *et seq.* ; Vacant, *op. cit.* (*Annales phil. chrét.*, 1888-89, p. 465) ; Longpré, *op. cit.*

volumes so far published, a collection of texts). Werner,
Duns Scotus (Wien, 1881); De Martigné, *op. cit.;* Pluzanski,
Essai sur la phil. de Duns Scot (Paris, 1887); Bertoni, *Le
Bienheureux J. D. Scot, Sa vie, sa doctrine, ses disciples* (Levanto,
600 pp., not very critical); Card. Saranno, *Conciliatio dilucida
omnium controversiarum quæ in doctrina. S. Thomæ et Joh.
Scot passim leguntur.* Pelster, *Handschriftl. zu Skotus mit
neuen Angaben ü. s. Leben,* Fr. St. 1923, 1 ; Pelzer, *J. D.
Scot et les études scotistes,* in *Revue Neo-Scolastique,* 1923,
pp. 410-420.
Siebeck, *Die Willenslehre bei Duns Scot and seinen Nach-
folgern* (Zeitschr. f. Philos. û. phil. Kritik, 1898, pp. 182 *et seq.*);
Vacant, *D'ou vient que Duns Scot ne conçoit point la volonté
comme S. Thomas d'Aquin ?* (Fourth International Catholic
Scientific Congress, Fribourg, 1898, pp. 631-645); Vacant,
*La philosophie de Duns Scot comparée à celle de S. Thomas
(Ann. Philos. chrét.* 1887-89); Seeberg, *Die Theologie des
D. Scotus* (Leipzig, 1900). P. Parthenius Minges has corrected
many erroneous opinions on Scotus. See the works mentioned
in the notes, also *Das Verhältniss zwischen Glauben u. Wissen,
Theol. u. Philos. nach D. S.* (Paderborn, 1908); *Die Scot
Literatur des* 20 *Jahrh.,* in *Franciskan. Studien,* 1917, pp. 49
and 177 ; *Zum Wiederaufblühen d. Scotismus (ibid.,* 1914);
*D. Scotus u. die thomistisch—molinistischen Kontroversen
(ibid.,* 1920); *Scotismus und Pantheismus (Philos. Jahrb.,* 1918);
Suarez und D. Scotus (ibid., 1919) ; *Zur Erkenntnisslehre d.
D. Scotus (ibid.,* 1918, pp. 52-74); *Zur Unterscheidung zw.
Wesenheit u. Dasein in den Geschöpfen (ibid.,* 1916, pp. 51-62).
A general study by the same author, *Duns Scoti doctrina
philos. et theol. quoad res præcipuas proposita, exposita et
considerata,* is announced but has not yet appeared. By the
same : *Duns Scotus,* in *Catholic Encyclopedia ; A Digest of
Scholastic Doctrines* (Cincinnati), the original was published
in Latin after the third Franciscan Conference on Questions
of Teaching.
H. Klug, *Die Lehre des Joh. Duns Scotus ueber Materie und
Form nach d. Quellen dargest. (Phil. Jahrb.* 1914); *Die Lehre
d. Joh. Duns Scotus ueber Materie und Form (ibid.,* 1917,
pp. 44-78); *Die Lehre d. sel. Joh. Duns Scotus u. die Seele (ibid.,*
1923, pp. 131-145); *Die Immaterialität d. Engel u. Menschenseelen
nach J. Duns Scotus (Franc. Stud.,* 1916, p. 397). Dr. J. Klein,
Der Gottesbegriff des Joh. D. Scotus, vor allem nach seiner

ethischen Seite betrachtet (Paderborn, 1913), excellent ; *Zur Sittenlehre des J. D. Scotus* (Franc. Stud., 1914, p. 401 ; 1915, p. 137) ; *Intellect und Wille als die nächtsten Quellen d. sittlichen Akte nach Joh. D. Scotus (ibid.,* 1916, p. 309, and 1919, pp. 108, 213 and 295) ; article by P. Raymond in *Dict. théol. cath.* Numerous studies by Belmond on God according to Duns Scotus in *R. de philos,* 1908, 1909, 1910, 1912., and *Etudes francisc.* 1910. Claverie, *L'existence de Dieu d'après D. Scot* (*R. Thomiste,* 1909) ; P. Symphorien, *La distinction formelle de Scot et les Universaux* (*Etudes francisc,* 1909) ; Desbuts, *De S. Bonaventure à D. Scot* (*Ann. Phil. Chret.,* Nov., 1910). Landry, *La Philos. de D. Scot.* (Paris, 1922), much discussed, see the important articles against him by P. Ephrem Longpré in *Etudes franc.* 1922-1924. These have been published in one volume, *La philos. du B. D. Scot* (Paris, 1924). C. Albanese, *Studio su Scoto, la teorie del conoscere* (Rome, 1923). Minges and Longpré are the best authorities. See also the Franciscan reviews.

Art. XI—A Group of Oxford Teachers.

321. Henry of Harclay.—Among the contemporaries and immediate successors of Duns Scotus at Oxford were a group of secular clerics, not belonging to either of the two great religious orders, who displayed a certain individuality. Their attitude towards the great doctors whose teachings were discussed by everybody, was very similar to that of a Henry of Ghent or a Godfrey of Fontaines at Paris : they were eclectics, and independent thinkers. We now know something of Henry of Harclay, thanks to a monograph the inadequacy of which is realized by its author.[1] The study of other writers, Robert of Winchelsea, Kykeley, Thomas Wilton, and Simon of Faversham, is being undertaken. These, together with their Dominican and Franciscan colleagues, helped to make the University of Oxford an intense centre of intellectual life at the beginning of the fourteenth century.

Henry of Harclay came from the North-West of England, where he was born about 1270. He took his degree as Master

[1] Pelster, *Henrich von Harclay und seine Quaestionen,* in *Miscellanea Ehrle,* I, 1924, pp. 307-356.

of Arts at Oxford, and possibly after passing through the
schools of Paris, became a Doctor of Theology. He was
nominated Chancellor in 1321, and was involved in the disputes
which arose between the University and the Dominicans
concerning certain teaching prerogatives which the latter
possessed. He died in 1317 at Avignon, where he defended the
cause of the University. His contemporaries, Nicholas Trivet
and William Alnwick testify to his merits. He left commentaries on the Sentences and *Quæstiones*, the doctrinal significance
of which has not yet been clearly established.

It is certain that he combats Thomas Aquinas on questions
such as that of individuation, and does not admit that real
relations have an entity distinct from the terms which serve
as their foundations, but on other important doctrines he
speaks in the same way as the *Doctor Communis* of the Dominicans. This is the case with his metaphysical and criteriological
solution of the theory of universals, in which he rejects Scotus
and rallies to Thomistic realism : the individual alone exists,
the universal is *in repræsentatione* as taught by Avicenna, to
whom the English Chancellor expressly appeals, but the
similitude of essence in really distinct beings is the foundation
for the abstract content of our ideas.[1] This refutes the principal
argument upon which Pelster basis his opinion that Henry of
Harclay is a precursor of the nominalism of William of
Ockam.[2] The same is true of Henry's theory on the Divine
ideas and on the power of the human mind to demonstrate
the existence of God : in the texts quoted there is nothing
opposed to the purest Thomism.

On the question of forms, the Oxford master adopts the
position of the older scholasticism : there is in man various
formal principles, and the intellectual soul is the perfection
of a compound in which matter is already informed by the
principles of vegetative and sense life. This is the theory
imposed at Oxford by the anti-Thomist Archbishops (291).
An energetical affirmation of the activity of every act of the

---

[1] " Est intelligendum secundum Avicennam, quod ille conceptus mentis est
in se res quædam singularis, sed est universalis in intentione." (Pelster,
op. cit. p. 337). " Ab illis, que sunt ultima distinctiva in re, que non sunt
unum in alia re, nichilominus potest abstrahi aliquod commune ab eis, quia
talia possunt esse similia vel conveniencia " (*ibid.*, p. 338).

[2] It is surprising that Pelster falls into this error, since he himself writes :
" He must still find a place among the adherents of Moderate Realism "
(p. 338). Ockam's teaching on the point does not resemble that of Henry
of Harclay.

will, which may at any time decide against the judgment on goodness formulated by the intellect,[1] establishes a link between Henry of Harclay and Duns Scotus.

From all this it follows that the Chancellor is a man who thinks for himself.[2] He does not follow either Thomas Aquinas or Duns Scotus systematically, and keeps apart from the groups in process of constitution.

Art. XII—Logicians and Grammarians.

322. Logicians.—Petrus Hispanus.—The study of logic was not involved in the great controversies. Many people specialized in it. The large place given to logical treatises in the *lectiones*, and the extension of the *sophismata* and other dialectical exercises[3] explains the distinction in a University document of 1272 between the " magistri naturalis scientiæ " and the " magistri logicalis scientiæ "[4] of the faculty of arts.

Among the best known logicians of the thirteenth century, we may mention WILLIAM SHYRESWOOD (1249), author of *Parva logicalia*; LAMBERT OF AUXERRE (about 1250); and above all PETRUS HISPANUS. In addition to works on medicine, Peter wrote *Summulæ Logicales*, a compendium of logic making use of the *Summa* of Lambert of Auxerre, and reflecting the popularity of purely dialectical exercises. The six first parts contain an exposition of the subjects treated in the *Logica vetus* and the *Logica nova*. In particular the sixth, concerned with the *Fallaciae*, deals with all the forms of dialectical combat. The following parts, or the " parva logicalia," deal with new developments, which are accordingly described as " logica modernorum." They consist of studies on the properties of logical terms and their relations with grammatical terms : " de suppositionibus,[5] de relativis, de

---

[1] " Ergo contra judicium rationis in particulari potest agere voluntas," (p. 343).
[2] In his interpretation of Aristotle, he protests against certain contemporaries " qui nituntur de Aristote heretico facere catholicum " (p. 351). Aristotle, he says, taught the eternity of matter and did not regard the intellectual soul as the substantial form of the body.
[3] Vol. One, p. 257.
[4] *Chart.*, I, 499.
[5] " Suppositio est acceptio termini substantivi pro aliquo. Differunt autem suppositio et significatio. Significatio autem fit per impositionem

ampliatione, de appellatione, de restrictione, de distributione." The *Summulæ* of Petrus Hispanus do not deal with the logical theory of science, but are a manual for dialectical debates. They were very popular, and had innumerable commentators. Georgios Scholarios (Gennadius) reproduced them almost textually in the fifteenth century in his Σύνοψις εἰς τὴν 'Αριστοτέλους λογικὴν ἐπιστήμην, and Buridan re-edited them. The *parva logicalia* helped to a great extent to deprive logic of its character as a scientific methodology and to make it instead a *sermonicalis scientia*, and as a result the taste for subtleties was revived in the middle of the fourteenth century.

323. Speculative Grammar.—With the grammarian John de Garlande († about 1252) the old way of teaching the grammar of Donatus and Priscian came to an end at Paris. It obtained a new lease of life through logic, which widened its borders, and endeavoured to find new material by justifying its rules. Speculative grammar, which triumphs at the end of the thirteenth and the beginning of the fourteenth century, is a veritable philosophy of language, which aims at including the whole series of scholastic notions. Thus it deals with the justification of the connection between the word and thought, or *significatio* : hence the title of so many works, *de modis significandi*. Nouns and pronouns have as their function the signifying of the *stable ;* verbs and participles describe *becoming* ; the undeclinable parts of speech (*syncategoremata*) do not belong to the essence of language. In the detailed treatment of each part of speech we find applications of theories such as that of matter and form, movement, genera and accidents, and the four causes.[6]

Speculative grammar was cultivated in the faculty of arts, and as this was a preparation for the other faculties, we find in consequence that the mentality of the grammarian affected the work of certain theologians or canonists.[7] This naturally led to exaggerations in the fourteenth and fifteenth centuries.

The speculative grammarians—*modistæ*, or writers of treatises *de modis significandi*—form a group in the Faculty

---

vocis ad significandam rem. Suppositio est acceptio termini jam significantis rem pro aliquo. Ut cum dicitur homo currit, ille terminus *homo* tenetur stare pro Sorte vel Platone et sic de aliis. Unde significatione prior est suppositio." (*Tract. septimus* in Antwerp edition, 1505).

[6] An interesting chapter on these logico-grammatical questions will be found in Wallerand, *Les œuvres de Siger de Courtrai*, Ch. V.

[7] Grabmann, *Die Entwicklung d. mittelalt. Sprachlogik.* in *Philos. Jahrb.*, 1922 (p. 29 of the separate reprint).

of Arts. One of the first names we meet with is that of NICHOLAS
OF PARIS, a Master of Arts about the middle of the thirteenth
century, the period immediately preceding the Aristotelian
commentaries undertaken by Thomas Aquinas. He left a
collection of treatises dealing with logic (notes on the *Isagoge*,
a great commentary on the *Isagoge*, Introduction to the
Isagoge), and dialectics (notes on the *Differentiæ topicæ* of
Boethius, commentary on the *De accentibus* of Priscian),
in which we find pure philosophy combined with dissertations
on speculative grammar. He also laboured at a classification
of the philosophical sciences, and subjected the texts to a
grouping based on the Aristotelian theory of the four causes.[1]

More important was SIGER OF COURTRAI[2] (Dean of the
Chapter of Courtrai about 1308-1330, *magister artium* in 1309,
procurator of the Sorbonne in 1315, died in 1341), author of
various treatises on logic (*Ars priorum, Fallaciæ*), a speculative
grammar (*Summa modorum significandi*) and a collection of
sophismata dealing with logical and grammatical matters,[3]
all noteworthy for their precision and clarity. Siger's logical
work is inspired by the spirit of the scholasticism of the
thirteenth century, and shows no trace of the innovations introduced by the *compendium* of Petrus Hispanus. His grammatical speculations consist in a philosophical justification of
the grammatical rules of Donatus and Priscian.

MICHAEL OF MARBAIX or of Brabant is more prolix and also
more deductive than his Belgian compatriot, and his philosophical interpretations of the ancient grammarians are often
forced and artificial.[4]

In 1322 a certain JOHANNES JOSSE DE MARVILLA composed
a *De modis significandi*.[5] Later we get a series of Danish
masters who apparently had a preference for this kind of
exercise : PETRUS or MARTINUS OF DACIA, JOHANNES OF
DACIA, SIMON OF DACIA, and also BOETHIUS OF DACIA, who
will be referred to later on. JOHANNES AURIFABER and
THOMAS OCCAM also formed part of the group.

---

[1] Grabmann, *Die logischen Schriften d. Nikolaus v. Paris* (*BGPM.*, Suppl.
Bd. 1923).

[2] The confusion between Siger of Courtrai and Siger of Brabant has now
been finally dispelled. According to Vercruysse (**324**) Siger of Courtrai was
also called Siger of Gulleghem.

[3] 1. Amo est verbum ; 2. Magistro legente pueri proficiunt ; 3. O Magister ;
4. Album potest esse nigrum.

[4] See Wallerand's study.

[5] Grabmann, *Die Entwicklung*, p. 22.

But the most perfect production in the class of speculative grammars was the *De modis significandi* or *Grammatica speculativa*, ascribed for a long time to Duns Scotus and which Grabmann, basing himself on the manuscripts, restores to THOMAS OF ERFORD.[1] This Master of Arts conducted a school of grammar and logic about 1350. Precise and sober in tone, his little work aims at justifying Donatus, and at the same time gives a personal treatment of grammatical questions. It constitutes a remarkable philosophy of grammar.[2]

The growth of speculation delayed the discredit of the classical grammarians, but could not altogether prevent it. Donatus and Priscian were banished from the University of Toulouse in 1328, and from Paris in 1366.

324. Bibliography.—Thurot, *Not. et extr. de divers mss. latins pour servir à l'hist. des doctrines grammaticales du m. âge* (Paris, 1868); Pætow, *op. cit.* (**34**). Numerous editions of the *Summulæ* of Petrus Hispanus in the fifteenth and sixteenth centuries ; Stapper, *Die Summulæ logicales des P. Hispanus und ihr Verhältniss zu Michael Psellus* (Festschrift zum elfhundertj. Jubil d. deutschen Campo Santo in Rom., pp. 130-138 Freiburg, 1897), and *Papst Johann XXI* (Kirchengesch. Studien, Sdralek, 1898); A. Niglis, *Siger von Courtrai* (Freiburg i. Br., 1903); H. Vercruysse, *Etude critique des sources relat. à personalité du Sorbonniste S. de Courtrai*, etc. (Memoir of the Cercle histor. et archeol. of Courtrai, IV, 37-85, 1910), has biographical notes. Wallerand, *Les oeuvres de S. de Courtrai*, complete text and study (Vol. VIII of the *Philosophes Belges*), an important doctrinal study ; Grabmann, works mentioned in notes. An edition (uncritical) of the *Grammatica speculativa* appeared at Quaracchi in 1902, edited by P. Garcia (**320**).

---

[1] Grabmann, *De Thoma Erfordiensi auctore Grammaticæ quæ Joanni Duns Scoto adscribitur speculativæ*, in *Arch. fr. histor.*, 1922, p. 273-277.
[2] He defines the *modus significandi activus* thus : " modus sive proprietas vocis ab intellectu sibi concessa, mediante qua vox proprietatem rei significat." (Cap. 1).

CHAPTER III

The Group of Anti-Scholastic Philosophies

During the thirteenth century, Averrhoism was the principal anti-scholastic system (§ 1), but there were also some others (§ 2).

§ 1. *Latin Averrhoism.*

325. Its anti-scholastic character.—Taken as a whole, Latin Averrhoism consists of the philosophy of Averrhoes himself **(138)**, in which are stressed certain doctrines incompatible with scholasticism.[1] It is this anti-scholastic character which gives to Averrhoism its historical interest. Siger of Brabant wrote *Contra præcipuos viros in philosophia Albertum et Thomam* ;[2] his disciples and successors made Averrhoism a controversial weapon. We shall see that this character of opposition and contradiction to Scholasticism affects organic and fundamental theories : Averrhoism denies the Infinity of God, creation, human personality, personal immortality and responsibility. These are precisely the doctrines which were the points at issue in the discussions between Scholastics and Averrhoists.

In addition to these fundamental and profound divergencies, there were disagreements on points of detail. On some other questions Averrhoists and Scholastics were agreed. This agreement resulted from their common relationship to peripateticism, and applies chiefly to those scholastics who were the most completely inspired by the peripatetic spirit. While Scholastics

---

[1] We do not think that we can affirm without reservation, as does Père Mandonnet, that "in their general lines, the doctrines of Averrhoes are contained either explicitly or implicitly in those of Aristotle." (*Siger de Brabant*, Vol. VI of *Philosophes Belges*, p. 155). Averrhoes misrepresented Aristotle's doctrine on more than one point, and Thomas Aquinas pointed this out to Siger of Brabant.

[2] *Chart.*, I, 487.

and Averrhoists subjected certain peripatetic theses to modifications so important that they resulted in opposite extremes in philosophy, they also adopted unaltered certain other theses which, taken apart from the general systems, had the same sense for both. Thus St. Thomas and Siger of Brabant held common theories on universals, and the unity of forms (which explains the insinuations of John Peckham, see p. 42), also the principle of individuation of corporeal substances.

326. Rise of Latin Averrhoism.—Averrhoes, who was called "the Commentator *par excellence*" until the close of the Middle Ages, became known to the Latin world in company with Aristotle, and was received as his liegeman. The *Commenta* of Averrhoes were forbidden at Paris at the same time as the works of the Stagirite, and authority included them in one and the same condemnation with the books of David of Dinant and of Amalric of Bènes **(146)**.

But the preventive measures of 1210 and 1215 did not close the schools to Averrhoes, any more than to Aristotle. Already during the first years of the thirteenth century his name was upon all lips. Nevertheless, the first indication of the existence of an Averrhoist movement at Paris is in 1256. In that year Pope Alexander IV charged Albert the Great to write a special treatise, *De unitate intellectus contra Averroem;* a proof that Averrhoism was well installed in Parisian centres. Later on Averrhoism declared open war against Scholasticism. Ecclesiastical condemnations checked its progress for a time but did not eradicate it, and it reappeared in the following centuries.

327. Its doctrines.—Taking as our basis the condemnations directed against it and the works of its upholders, we can draw up a list of the principal antischolastic doctrines of Latin Averrhoism. These doctrines concern metaphysics and physics (1-3), psychology and moral philosophy (4-5), and to the relations of philosophy to Catholic theology on the one hand and to the authority of Averrhoes on the other (6-7).

(1) *Only one being is produced directly by God : others are produced through intermediaries.*[1] The First Cause, immaterial and simple, can produce immediately only one being, " cum ab uno simplici non procedat nisi unum immediate." [2] This

---

[1] Condemnation of 1277, Prop. 42-44, 58-61, 63, 70-73, 198, 199, etc.
[2] *De necessitate causarum*, in Mandonnet, *Siger*, Vol. VII of *Philosophes Belges*, p. 112.

H

engendered being is less perfect than God, but like Him is intelligent in nature. The first Intelligence produces another, and so on. Each of the Intelligences contracts an intrinsic union with a heavenly sphere. As a result of the influence of the Intelligences animating the celestial spheres, terrestrial beings come into existence. God does not know these, and has no care for them ; accordingly He does not know future contingent things.

These theories are in opposition to a group of scholastic doctrines : the direct creation of things by God, the concurrence of the first cause in the activity of second causes, the conservation by God of the *esse* of other beings, and the extension of the divine knowledge to particular and terrestrial things.

(2) *All these productions are necessitated and naturally co-eternal with God.*[1] Hence there is no question of liberty in the creative act, nor of the contingent character of things. The Intelligences are as necessary and eternal as God Himself. In the same way, the types of the corporeal have always been and will always be. Their essence is indifferent to time ; they can have neither commencement nor end. By nature they are together with God.

For the scholastics, the corporeal world commenced in time (Bonaventure), and even the hypothesis of a creation *ab æterno* can be harmonized with their contingence (Thomas Aquinas) ; this contingence would disappear if the very nature of their production required the eternity of corporeal types.

(3) *Universal determinism, and reversibility of corporeal events.*—Celestial beings exercise a full efficient causality upon terrestrial bodies : the celestial phenomena and planetary conjunctions determine fatally what takes place upon this earth. The events of the individual and of the collective life are subject to their necessitating influence. Moreover, since the number of planetary conjunctions is limited, and their succession has neither commencement nor end, there is an eternal reversibility of civilizations and religions (including the Christian religion), following from the reversibility of planetary cycles. " Christianity has already appeared and disappeared an indefinite number of times, and will continue to do so according to the position and duration it occupies in

[1] Prop. 94.

the series of transformations constituting the whole religious cycle."[1]

(4) *The unity of the human intellect, or monopsychism.*[2] The Averrhoists adhered to a pluralistic metaphysics, and recognized that each human individual has his own body and sensible soul, but they attributed to the human race as such only one intelligent soul, separated from individuals, and unique. This race-soul, which does not function as a substantial form, contracts a temporary and accidental union with the sensible soul possessed by each individual, and this union suffices to explain the genesis of thought. Monopsychism is a modified form of monism.

Of all the Averrhoistic doctrines, monopsychism was the one which the scholastics attacked most strongly, because they regarded it as a manifest betrayal of the mind of Aristotle, and above all because it was contrary to their sentiment of the value of personality. They devoted special treatises to this subject. For Aristotle the divine principle in us comes from without ($\theta\acute{v}\rho\alpha\theta\epsilon\nu$) but enters into the soul ($\epsilon\nu$ $\tau\eta$ $\psi\nu\chi\eta$), but the Arabians leave it on the threshold, outside the individual soul, with which it cannot come into intimate contact. Monopsychism is a frontal attack on the scholastic ideology : it is not the human person who thinks, but the separated intellect thinks in it. Why then do not all men think the same on all things and at all times ? The purely external union of the racial intellect with the living body constituting each individual compromises the scholastic theory of personality.

The negation of personal immortality is a consequence of the preceding thesis.[3] The sensible soul perishes at the death of the individual, the racial soul alone is immortal. Hence there is no personal survival to be hoped for or feared, and no reward or punishment for our actions.

(5) *Psychological and moral determinism.*[4] Since human acts are necessitated just as are corporeal phenomena, there is

[1] Mandonnet, *op. cit.*, Vol. VI, p. 172.
[2] Prop. 123 : " Quod intellectus agens est quædam substantia separata superior ad intellectum possibilem ; et quod secundum substantiam potentiam et operationem est separatus a corpore, nec est forma corporis." Prop. 118 : " Quod intellectus agens non copulatur nostro possibili ; et quod intellectus possibilis non unitur nobiscum secundum substantiam. Et si uniretur nobis ut forma, est inseparabilis." (*Chart* I, 550).
[3] Prop. 116 : " Quod anima est inseparabilis a corpore, et quod ad corruptionem harmonie corporalis, corrumpitur anima."
[4] Prop. 168-172.

most illustrious contemporaries felt called upon to refute his teaching, and authority thought it necessary to condemn his doctrines. Siger was a Master of Arts at Paris in the Picard "nation", and was for ten years the centre of the disturbances in the University. Already in 1266 he gave trouble to the legate Simon de Brie in matters of discipline, and when the nations differed concerning the nomination of the Rector, he took a leading part. He was first proceeded against in 1270, but nevertheless continued to teach, and emphasized his anti-scholastic position. From 1272 to 1275 he was involved in another division between the two parties in the nations. He put himself at the head of those opposing the Rector Alberic of Rheims. This was a real philosophic schism. At this time his teaching had reached the height of its popularity : he numbered among his adherents an important group of students and Masters of Arts (*Scholares Golardiæ*).[6] The measures taken and decrees issued between 1270 and 1277 are directly concerned with the party of the Brabançon teacher. A second condemnation in 1277 brought his teaching to an end. Was it in connection with this condemnation that Simon Duval, the chief inquisitor for France, summoned Siger to his tribunal on the 23rd October, 1277 ? The connection between the two events seems certain. In any case Siger left Paris at this date ; he appealed from the jurisdiction of the inquisitor to that of the Roman Court. He died at Orvieto, between 1281 and 1284, assassinated by his *clericus*, who had gone mad. The Brabançon continuator of the chronicle of Martin of Troppau writes : " Qui Sygerus, natione Brabantinus, eo quod opiniones contra fidem tenuerat Parisius subsistere non valens, Romanam curiam adiit ; ibique post parvum tempus a clerico suo quasi dementi perfossus periit."[7]

The *De anima intellectiva*, the chief among the published works of Siger, is not a commentary on the work of Aristotle, but a treatise devoted to the most important questions which

of the Divine Comedy gave free play to his personal sympathies for the prominent men of his time, and was never sufficiently well versed in the controversies of the learned to take up a definite and candid position in philosophical matters. Just as he makes St. Bonaventure praise Joachim of Floris, so also he proclaims the merits of Siger of Brabant through St. Thomas. Mandonnet thinks that Dante was governed by the desire to place a peripatetic philosopher in this part of Paradise, and Siger was a celebrated teacher and one exclusively a philosopher. (*op. cit.*, p. 305).

[6] Garlande was the name of the school district.

[7] *Monumenta Germ. hist.* SS. XXIV, 236. See the account of the matter in Mandonnet VI, 277 *et seq.* Cf. Baeumker, *Arch. Gesch. Philos.*, 1899, p. 74.

are obscure in Aristotle. Mandonnet holds that this work directly inspired the *De unitate intellectus contra Averrhoistas* of Thomas Aquinas, and that the two works appeared in 1270,[1] while Chossat,[2] basing himself on a text of John of Jandun, maintains that on the contrary the *De anima* of Siger was a reply to the work of St. Thomas, and that the latter in his *De unitate* is referring to a previous work of the Brabançon teacher. A recent graduate of Louvain[3] in a thesis which will be shortly published has made a detailed comparison of the texts, and has come to the conclusion that the arguments of Siger's *De anima* are a reply to St. Thomas's *De Unitate*, that the latter, in his work *De spiritualibus creaturis* and in the *Quæstio disputata de anima* is countering and refuting a form of Averrhoism much more developed than that of the *De anima intellectiva*, and that these two works of St. Thomas constitute a reply to the treatise of Siger with which we are now dealing. According to this view, Siger adopted an anti-scholastic position previous to the *De Unitate* of St. Thomas, and this seems quite likely if we remember that already in 1270 a first decree was directed against Averrhoism by the Bishop of Paris.

To what work did the condemnation refer ? The study and publication of the works of Siger could alone throw light on this question. Mandonnet has already given us, in addition to the *De anima intellective*, various other works by the master : a question *De æternitate mundi*, two *Quæstiones naturales*, some *Quæstiones logicales*, a question *Utrum hæc sit vera* " *Homo est animal, nullo homine existente*," a collection of six *Impossibilia*, and a treatise *De necessitate et contingentia causarum*.[4] The last mentioned is certainly of Averrhoist origin, and must have been written during the discussions preceding the condemnation of 1277. Mandonnet thinks it may have been written by Siger. Baeumker had already published the six *Impossibilia*. Pelzer has called attention to the existence of *Quæstiones super 3m. lib. De Anima*.[5]

Lastly, Grabmann has recently discovered at Munich an important series of Aristotelian commentaries left by Siger

---

[1] *Op. cit.*, ch. VI *et seq.*
[2] *S. Thomas d'A. et Siger de Brabant*, in *R. de philos.*, 1914, p. 570.
[3] Fernand Van Steenberghe.
[4] Published by Mandonnet, from a manuscript full of Averrhoist works and forming part of the bequest to the Sorbonne by Godfrey of Fontaines.
[5] MS. at Merton College, Oxford.

with a vehemence to which attention has often been drawn.

329. Other Averrhoists.—Paris was the chief centre of Latin Averrhoism in the thirteenth century. In the Arts,[5] an important group of masters followed Siger, among them being Boethius of Dacia and Bernier of Nivelles.[6] Peter Dubois, who attended his lectures, was full of sympathy for the new doctrines.

BOETHIUS OF DACIA (Boetius de Dacia), a secular master of the Faculty of Arts, was a well-known Averrhoist. A Sorbonne manuscript declares that Boethius was condemned by the decree of 1277, and Raymond Lully joins his name with that of Siger. According to Peckham, Boethius came to a miserable end in Italy.[7] He wrote on speculative grammar (*De modis significandi*), logic (*Quæstiones* on the *Topics* and the two *Analytics*, *Sophismata*), and the fourth book of the *Meteorology*. The subjects treated in this group of works do not easily lend themselves to the exposition of a definite form of Averrhoism.[8] Grabmann has discovered two other works by the Danish master, *De somno et vigilia,* and the *De summo bono,* in which he thinks he can find traces of Averrhoism inasmuch as their author makes human beatitude consist in the conquest of scientific truth and says nothing of man's supernatural destiny.[9]

As for BERNIER OF NIVELLES, who, like Siger of Brabant, was a Canon of St. Martin's of Liége,[10] he also was suspected of heresy in 1277, and summoned to the tribunal of Simon Duval, but was dealt with more leniently.[11]

---

hoists were masters of arts, and that at the death of Thomas it was the Faculty of Arts and not that of Theology which sent a message of condolence to the Dominican order. (*op. cit.,* p. 23). But were they all Averrhoists in the Faculty of Arts ? It would seem that the Averrhoists were only a minority (*pars Sigeri*), and this would upset Grabmann's argument.

[5] *Chart.,* I, 556.

[6] Mandonnet mentions various anonymous works of Averrhoist tendencies, (*op. cit.,* 222).

[7] The *tabula* of Dominican works in the fourteenth century mentions a Bœthius of Dacia, whom Mandonnet identifies with the Averrhoist. He explains the inclusion of his name either as an error on the part of the compiler, or else by the fact that in order to escape the consequences of the condemnation Bœthius may have become a Dominican. (*op. cit.,* p. 225-231).

[8] Doncœur, *Notes sur les averroistes latins. Boèce le Dace,* (*R. sc. phil. theol.,* 1910) ; Hauréau, *Journal des savants,* 1886, p. 176, *In octo lib. topic.*

[9] p. 47. It does not follow from this that Boethius denied this supernatural aspect of beatitude.

[10] " It would seem that Liége provided a very special contingent for the Averrhoist masters of Paris," (Mandonnet, *ibid.,* p. 137, note).

[11] Baeumker, *op. cit.,* 65 ; Mandonnet, *op. cit.,* p. 257.

Outside the universities, Averrhoism flourished at the Court of Frederick the Second of Sicily and his son, Manfred. Frederick the Second is supposed to have said that Moses, Jesus and Mahomet were three impostors.[1] Renan's contention[2] that the Franciscan schools were hotbeds of Averrhoism is false. He has not realized that the doctrinal division between the Dominicans and the Franciscans at the time of the censures of 1277 was connected with the opposition between the older Scholasticism and Thomism, and that the two great mendicant orders joined together in combating Averrhoes.

330. Opposition to Averrhoism.—(i) *The condemnations.* The religious authorities were alarmed at the progress of Averrhoism and the dangers which its teaching presented for Catholic theology.

The first act of repression[3] was the decree of 1270, in which the Bishop of Paris, Stephen Tempier, publicly condemned Averrhoism and its followers. The following are the theses affected : " Quod intellectus omnium hominum est unus et idem numero. Quod ista est false vel impropria : Homo intelligit. Quod voluntas hominis ex necessitate vult vel eligit. Quod omnia, que hic in inferioribus aguntur, subsunt necessitate corporum celestium. Quod mundus est eternus. Quod nunquam fuit primus homo. Quod anima, que est forma hominis secundum quod homo, corrumpitur corrupto corpore. Quod anima post mortem separata non patitur ab igne corporeo. Quod liberum arbitrium est potentia passiva, non activa et quod necessitate movetur ab appetibili. Quod Deus non cognoscit singularia. Quod Deus non cognoscit alia a se. Quod humani actus non reguntur providentia Dei. Quod Deus non potest dare immortalitatem vel incorruptionem rei corruptibili vel mortali." [4] The authorities wanted to put an end to a doctrinal dispute, as we gather from the letter of Giles of Lessines to Albert the Great.[5] But the Averrhoists nevertheless continued to teach in secret places,

---

[1] We find an allusion to this saying in the compilation *De erroribus philosoph.* which attributes to Averrhoes the error " Quod nulla lex est vera, licet possit esse utilis." (Mandonnet, Vol. VII, p. 10). Cf. the decree of 1277, proposit. 174 and 175. Cf. *Ketzerphilosophies d. Mittelalters. Das Buch gennannt de tribus impostoribus, uebers. mit Anmerk.* by G. V. Glasenapp, Riga.

[2] *Averroes et l'Averroisme*, pp. 259 *et seq.*

[3] The decree of the Council of Paris in 1210 had a merely preventive force (**146**).

[4] *Chart.*, I, 486.

[5] Mandonnet, *op. cit.*, p. 105. The first thirteen theses mentioned in the letter of Giles of Lessines coincide with the theses of the 1270 decree (**295**).

as we learn from university documents and from the following remark of Thomas Aquinas in the *De unitate intellectus* : "non loquatur in angulos nec coram pueris." Between the years 1272 and 1275, the period of the opposition of Siger of Brabant to the party of Alberic, several decrees were directed against Averrhoism. The theory of the two truths seems to be referred to in a statute of the Faculty of Arts in 1272 forbidding the masters to treat of purely theological matters "which do not concern them," or to formulate propositions contrary to theology.[1] The disciplinary dispute in the Faculty of Arts was hardly terminated by the intervention of the legate in 1273 when the whole university had to prohibit teaching in secret (2nd September, 1276), and the legate was obliged to punish by excommunication various offences showing how disastrous the Averrhoist position was for the faith and religion.[2]

The conclusion of the *De unitate intellectus* of Aquinas also testifies that the Averrhoists dealt with purely theological questions. Speaking of Siger of Brabant, St. Thomas says, "Non caret etiam magna temeritate quod de his quæ ad philosophiam non pertinent, sed sunt puræ fidei, disputare præsumit, sicut quod anima patiatur ab igne inferni." All this explains why the theory of the two truths had become a screen for heresy, and why ecclesiastical authority decided to strike a great blow at it.

The 219 propositions condemned by the censure of March 7th, 1277, do not form a homogeneous doctrinal whole. They affect above all the Averrhoism of Siger of Brabant and Boethius of Dacia, in its principles and many of its applications. The Latin codex 4391 in the Bibliothèque Nationale of Paris adds at the end of the list of these propositions the words "contra Sigerum et Boetium hereticos." Apart from the propositions relating to moral and theological matters, which

---

[1] *Chart.*, I, 499. Already in 1247 a similar prohibition had been addressed to the professors of logic by the legate Odo, Bishop of Tusculum, in his condemnation of the errors of John of Brescain : " . . . ne puritas studii que hactenus Parisiis viget ex præsumptione quorumdam qui theologica logicis inserantes non intelligunt neque que loquuntur, neque de quibus affirmant." (I. 207). Cf. the oath taken by the *incipientes in artibus* (1280) (*ibid.*, p. 586). Other enactments, and sometimes the same ones, tend to modify the zeal of theologians in their use of the dialectical method. See for instance the letters of Gregory IX. to the masters and scholars of Paris, (*ibid.*, 138). The legate Odo speaks at one and the same time of the "logici theologice et theologi philosophice procedentes," (*ibid.*, 207).

[2] Mandonnet, *op. cit.*, p. 195-212. Some clerics went so far as to play games with dice on the altars of the churches.

no one dared to teach openly and which indeed seem to have
been discovered by oral inquiry, the theses censured are taken
from Averrhoist writings.[1] But other doctrines besides those
of the Averrhoists are forbidden therein, particularly doctrines
of Thomas Aquinas (291), Giles of Rome (306), Bacon (346),
as well as several neo-Platonist theories.[2] The Bishop of Paris
and his party desired to exclude from the schools everything
displeasing to them.

These repeated decrees inspired some with the idea of
drawing up a list of the condemned doctrines. We find in
these lists not only the theses censured by Stephen Tempier,
but also the Oxford condemnations (291). These *Compilationes
errorum omnium in Anglia et Parisius condemnatorum* appeared
at the end of the thirteenth and the beginning of the fourteenth
centuries.[3] Other compilations were more general in their
scope. The treatise *De erroribus philosophorum*, wrongly
ascribed to Giles of Rome, and which Mandonnet regards as
the work of a Spanish Dominican contemporary with the
formation of the Thomist school,[4] contains a collection of
errors arising out of Aristotle and his great followers Averrhoes,
Avicenna, Algazel, Alkindi and Maimonides. This work,
which is noteworthy for the extent of its information and its
understanding of doctrines, has a tendency to clear Aristotle
from responsibility.

(ii) *The polemical works*. Already the *De universo* of William
of Auvergne contained an article entitled *Destructio erroris
Aristotelis, Alfarabi et aliorum qui posuerunt omnes animas
separatas unam esse, ipsaque separatione a corporibus unam
fieri atque illis uniri*.[5] We may say that no scholastic in the
second part of the thirteenth century passed over in silence
the thesis of the unity of the human intellect, but all opposed
it. Albert the Great, Thomas Aquinas, Giles of Rome, and
Raymond Lully devoted special treatises to it. St. Thomas
calls Averrhoes a *depravator*, and uses strong language about

[1] *op. cit.*, p. 210. Mandonnet concludes : " The condemnation of 1277
accordingly has in view peripateticism in general." This judgement seems
excessive. The theories constituting peripateticism, as for instance act
and potency, matter and form, are not affected. It is the anti-Scholastic
part of Averrhoism that is condemned.
[2] Prop. 30 : creation by intermediaries ; props. 92 and 102, the intrinsic
union of the heavenly bodies to astral intelligences.
[3] *Chart.*, I, 556. One of these collections is published by D'Argentré,
Collectio Judiciorum, I, p. 184.
[4] *op. cit.*, Vol. VII, p. 27 *et seq.*
[5] Pars I, c. xi, p. 771, in 1591 edition.

the theory of the two truths.[1] " Ille maledictus Averroes,"
is the term employed by Duns Scotus, who thus comments
on his philosophical errors : " talis errans esset a communitate
hominum et naturali ratione utentium exterminandus."[2] All
combine in an offensive and defensive alliance against
Averrhoes, in spite of the philosophical differences dividing
them, a fact which well manifests their common scholasticism.

331. Influence of Averrhoism.—From the philosophical
point of view, the Averrhoism of the thirteenth century
exercised a comparatively small influence ; its followers formed
a minority in the Faculty of Arts at Paris ; and its doctrines
faded in the light of scholasticism, as Traini has depicted in
design and cólour in the " Triumph of St. Thomas."

Was this philosophical movement more than an academic
product ? Did Averrhoism penetrate into other social spheres
of society and influence the general atmosphere ? There is no
evidence that it did. Its characteristic theories—the unity of
the race intelligence, and impersonal immortality—were
opposed to the individualism of the Western mind, and the
thesis of the two truths was contrary to the most profound
religious aspirations of the time.

Was there an Averrhoist heresy among the people at large,
applying the theories of monopsychism and terminism to
morals ? William of Tocco speaks of the " heresy of Averrhoes "
which maintains that all men have only one intellect, an error
which excuses the vices of the wicked and diminishes the virtues
of the saints. He tells of a Parisian knight who was asked if
he wanted to go to confession, and replied : " If St. Peter's
soul is saved, mine will be so as well, for if we possess the same
intellect we shall have the same end."[3] The *Directorium
inquisitorum* of Nicolas Eymerici says of the same doctrine :
" From this one could infer that the cursed soul of Judas is
the same as the blessed soul of St. Peter, which is heretical."
But the existence of a special heresy, independent of Catharism,
has not been proved.[4]

---

[1] In the *De unitate intellectus*. " Adhuc gravius quod postmodum dicit
(Siger) : per rationem concludo de necessitate quod intellectus est unus
numero, firmiter tamen teneo oppositum per fidem."

[2] *In IV. lib. Sent.*, dist. 43, q. 2.

[3] *Acta SS.*, I, p. 666.

[4] Alphandéry, *Y a-t-il eu un averroisme populaire aux XIIIe et XIVe
siècles ?* in *R. hist. relig.*, 1901, p. 395.

332. Bibliography.—The standard work is that of Mandonnet, *Siger de Brabant et l'Averroisme latin* (Vol. VII of the *Philosophes Belges*), a critical study together with the texts; includes in addition to the works of Siger mentioned on p. 97, an Averrhoist work of uncertain authorship, *De necessitate et contingentia causarum*, the treatise *De quindecim problematibus* of Albert the Great, a list of the 219 propositions condemned in 1277 arranged in logical order, and the treatise *De erroribus philosophorum*. Pelzer and Grabmann will publish in the same collection some unpublished works of Siger. Baeumker, *Die Impossibilia d. Siger von Brabant*, BGPM, II, 6. He at first regarded the solutions as the work of an opponent, but has since accepted Mandonnet's view restoring the treatise to Siger and placing it among the sophistical exercises directed by the masters. Baeumker, *Zur Beurteilung S. v. B. (Philos. Jahrb.*, 1910, pp. 177-202 ; 352-366); *Um S. v. B. (ibid.,* 1911); Mandonnet, *Autour de S. de Brabant (R. Thomiste,* 1911); see important works by Grabmann on the new works of Siger and Boethius with extracts, referred to in notes ; works by Doncœur (not very important) and Chossat ; Gilson, *Etudes* etc., p. 51 ; Renan, *op. cit.,* IIe Partie, Ch. II, " L'averroisme dans la philos. scolast." contains numerous errors ; Picavet, *L'averroisme et les averroistes du XIIIe s. d'après le De unitate intell. contra averr. de S. Thomas (Revue histor. relig.,* 1902, 14), contains nothing new. Grabmann has discovered in the Ambrosian Library a second manuscript of the *Impossibilia (Theolog. Quartalschr.* 1911). Concerning the manner of Siger's death there have been numerous discussions between historians of philosophy and others. The various opinions will be found in Baeumker, *op. cit.,* p. 114 and in *Arch. f. Gesch. Philos.,* 1899 ; Mandonnet, *op. cit.,* Ch. XI ; Gaston Paris in *Romania* 1900 ; Ch. Langlois in *Revue de Paris* 1901 and *Grande Encyclopedie*.

§ 2.—*Catharism*

333. Catharism.—The principles of the dualistic philosophy underlying Catharism as a religious system continued to give rise to discussion between the Cathari and Scholastics (**117**). We possess some Catharist works of the middle of the thirteenth century, amongst others a philosophical treatise entitled *Perpendiculum scientiarum ;* [1] and we are told that in order to carry on the fight against the scholars of the Dominican order, young " perfecti " of the sect frequented the schools of Paris and Italy during the last year of the Albigensian period.[2]   The Scholastics replied in apologetic works, and carried on the controversy begun by Alan of Lille.   Among these treatises we must mention above all the *Adversus Catharos et Valdenses lib. V* by MONETA OF CREMONA (in 1240).   Moneta was a professor of philosophy at Bologna before he became a Dominican, and he has left a methodic exposition of the opinions of the Cathari and a philosophical and theological refutation of their system.[3]

Catharism continued to spread in the south of France and in Spain.   In Italy its followers were numerous.   The Albanian school, which lasted until the beginning of the fourteenth century (two parties, that of Balasinansa Bishop of Verona, and that of John of Lugio) professed an absolute metaphysical dualism opposed to the mitigated dualism of the sect of Bagnolo.[4]

[1] Broeckx, *op. cit.*, p.223.   (Cf. Vol. I, p. 195).
[2] Alphandéry, *Les idées morales chez les hétérodoxes latins du début du XIIIe s.*, p. 92.
[3] Broeckx, *op. cit.*, p. 223.
[4] Alphandéry, *op. cit.*, p. 92-98.

CHAPTER IV

Some Non-Scholastic Directions in Philosophy

§ 1—*Latin Neo-Platonism*

334. General features.—Neo-Platonism exercised a three-fold influence on mediæval philosophy (see Volume I, p. 23).

(i) The *monistic tendency* of the system acted powerfully on the anti-scholastic philosophies. We recognize it in varying degrees in the thorough-going monism of Scotus Eriugena and his successors, and in the emanative theories and monopsychism of the Latin Averrhoists.

(ii) *Particular doctrines* concerning goodness, light, the Divine transcendence, the intelligible reasons, and the independence of the soul with regard to the body, were adopted by scholasticism, given a peripatetic aspect, and absorbed in systematizations in which the Alexandrine spirit as such found no place. By St. Bonaventure and his predecessors, they were combined in a more or less intimate manner with the theories of act and potency, and matter and form. St. Thomas himself was not hostile to this group of neo-Platonist and Augustinian elements, and he adapted those he retained to the spirit of his synthesis.

(iii) A Latin Neo-Platonism, which flourished independently of and side by side with Scholasticism and Averrhoism, and took no part in their quarrels, displayed in the thirteenth century an activity compelling the historian to give it a place apart. Although this philosophy remained faithful to pluralism, it discarded the Aristotelian framework of act and potency and matter and form. In its place it put a fundamental theory of neo-Platonist origin : " God, the Perfect Being, creates only one being, less perfect than Himself ; all other beings are produced in turn by others, forming a descending series according to the progressive degradation of intelligible nature."

It goes without saying that we naturally find incorporated in a conception of this kind the particular doctrines which Scholasticism itself adopted from neo-Platonism, such as the function of the good and of light (ii). At the same time place is found for certain doctrinal elements found in the older Scholasticism and in Thomism. Certain Aristotelian theories appear, deprived of their original meaning, and also Platonist ideas. The doctrine of the substantial independence of the soul is detached from the theory of matter and form ; the human soul becomes an inferior intelligence produced by a superior one, and its union with the soul is regarded as a hindrance. Again, the soul turns towards the beings above it, and is less concerned with the lower world of bodies.

335. Doctrinal characteristics of Latin neo-Platonism.— (i) On the whole Latin neo-Platonism remained faithful to *individualism*. In this way it differed fundamentally, on the one hand, from the neo-Platonism of Proclus and Macrobius, who regard finite beings as a prolongation of the Infinite, and on the other hand, from Latin Averrhoism, which makes their production by God a necessary and fatalistic act, and equally compromises the distinction between the workman and his work. Monism is expressly combated by Witelo and Theodoric of Freiberg, who both combine the principle of the descending hierarchy of beings with that of their creation and distinction. Eckhart manifests the same desire to safeguard the distinction between the creature and the Creator, but we think that his excellent intentions did not prevent his teaching from being pantheistic.

(ii) *The deductive method in philosophy.* The idea of the descending hierarchy, with God at the summit of the scale of reality, and the series of creatures arranged according to their perfections, leads the neo-Platonists to emphasize the deductive method, and to attach all philosophy to a theory of being. The observation of facts plays no part at all in their construction of the world. This is all the more significant because among the neo-Platonists we find some noteworthy men of science devoted to mathematics and the experimental sciences.

(iii) *A taste for misleading imagery*, resulting in a lack of clearness in diction. The propagation of light and the welling forth from a living spring, are comparisons to which the neo-Platonists love to have recourse in order to describe the relations between the Infinite and the finite, and the contact of the soul with God. These comparisons denote a vagueness in thought.

By reason of the framework providing the principles of the system, its exaggeration of the deductive method, its love of imagery, and its lack of clearness, Latin neo-Platonism is a philosophy which differs from Scholasticism and yet is not directed against it. Unlike Averrhoism, it does not set out to destroy it, but rather seeks for something new, and formulæ differing from those employed by the " communiter loquentes."[1] Therein lies its interest and its originality.

It is interesting to add that the neo-Platonism of the thirteenth century is a strictly philosophical movement, and that in the majority of its representatives theology has no place. Moreover, the group of neo-Platonist doctrines varies in different philosophers.

336. The " Liber XXIV philosophorum."—This anonymous work of the beginning of the thirteenth century is composed of a series of twenty-four " sentences " followed by a commentary. It belongs to the philosophical movement under consideration, for on the one hand we find therein a number of neo-Platonist ideas borrowed from pseudo-Dionysius, Macrobius and the *Liber de causis*, and on the other hand it is one of the authorities to which Eckhart, and later on Bradwardine and Nicholas of Cusa, refer with a marked predilection. It is not known whether it is a translation or an original work, whether the " sentences " and the commentary on them are by the same author, or if they were all composed at the same time. The development of Being (*monas*) in triadic form, the transcendence of God, and His universal compenetration are the favourite theories in this *opusculum*. The author endeavours to give a pluralistic sense to bold expressions which seem to lead direct to pantheism.[2]

337. The author of the " De intelligentiis."—To the early part of the thirteenth century belongs another work, destined to have a wide circulation,[3] and inspired by the *Liber de*

---

[1] Baeumker, *Der Anteil der Elsass*, etc., speaks of the " neo-Platonist scholasticism." It seems to us that Latin neo-Platonism is very far removed from the spirit of Scholasticism.

[2] According to Baeumker, *Das Pseudo-hermetische Buch der Vierundzwanzig Meister*, in *Festgabe Von Hertling*, Freiburg B., 1913.

[3] Some texts are quoted by Thomas Aquinas (*Quodl.* VI, q. 11, a. 19 ; *De Veritate*, q. 2, a. 1), Vincent of Beauvais, Alexander of Hales, and Gerard of Abbeville.

causis and by the metaphysics of light elaborated by Robert Grosseteste. It is called *De intelligentiis*, or *Memoriale rerum difficilium*. Baeumker, who has published extracts from it, at first thought that Witelo was probably its author.[1] He has recognized since then, following Duhem,[2] that this ascription must be rejected. The *De intelligentiis* forms a well ordered whole which cannot be identified with the *De ordine entium* which Witelo says he left unfinished. There is no allusion in it to the *Elementa theologiæ* of Proclus, known since 1268 in the translation by William of Moerbeke, and accordingly we must place the composition of this work at a time previous to Witelo. Two manuscripts indicated by Baeumker[3] ascribe the work to a master of theology at Paris, ADAM, surnamed PULCHRE MULIERIS, otherwise unknown.

The philosophical doctrines of the *De intelligentiis* most worthy of mention relate to metaphysics and psychology, and manifest a characteristic combination of neo-Platonism, the dominant element, with materials from Aristotelianism and the older scholasticism.

This treatise, in which the deductive method is rigorously followed, studies in its two parts God the first cause, His nature and knowledge, the first intelligences, and their power of knowledge of movement. The starting point in this metaphysics is not being in general (Aristotle), but the infinite being. All other things are participations, according to a descending hierarchy, of the divine being, for the multiple can only arise from the One, and the simple contains all the perfections of the composite. The identity of being with light explains the *processus*. God is light ; He is also act and substance (Aristotle). Other beings are participating lights (Augustine). Although the diffusion of light serves to determine the relations between God and the world, there is no question of an emanation, and the monist conception is absent.[4] We easily recognize here the doctrines of William of Moerbeke and the fundamental theses of the *Liber de causis*.

The psychology of the *De intelligentiis* is Platonist and

[1] *BGPM*, III, 2.
[2] *Le système du monde*, V, 370.
[3] Baeumker, *Zur Frage nach Abfassungszeit u. Verfasser des irrtümlich Witelo zugeschriebenen Liber de intelligentiis*, in *Miscellanea Ehrle*, I, 1924, p. 87-102.
[4] We have already pointed out (**278**) that Thomas Aquinas combats the neo-Platonist principle, " Omne quod influit in alio est lux vel naturam lucis habens," referring expressly to texts in the *De intelligentiis*.

neo-Platonist ; but at the same time it finds room for the Aristotelian theories concerning the formation of ideas. The soul is a simple and independent substance. Light explains not only the spatial disposition of bodies and the vital force of organisms, but also the phenomenon of knowledge. Sensation and ideas are the active phenomena of the soul (*virtus activa*, Plato), and at the same time represent reality (*virtus exemplaris*). Such activity and reproduction can only belong to an immaterial substance, and as the latter is light, the active and reproductive phenomenon of knowledge is not the reception of an action from outside, but an auto-diffusion of oneself (*sui multiplicatio*). The functions of the passive and active intellects (Aristotle) are accordingly modified, and the active intellect has as its office not only the determining of the sensible image, but also the knowledge of the reality of things.

338. William of Moerbeke may be called the originator of the neo-Platonism of the thirteenth century ; his translations[1] and commentaries on neo-Platonist works introduced the Latins to the ideas of Proclus ; his sympathies for neo-Platonism were profound. Although we do not possess any work of his containing his own personal views in philosophy, we gather his ideas on metaphysics from the prologue to the *Perspectiva* of Witelo.[2] He is there described as *totius entis sedul(us) scrutator*.

The source of the Divine goodness (*fons divinæ bonitatis*) produces a series of intelligible beings : these give rise to corporeal substances and act as a channel for the Divine efficiency. God is light, *lumen*, and hence all causality issuing from him is of a luminous nature. In the case of bodies, the *lumen* becomes the mode according to which these receive the influences from above (*corporalium vero influentiarum lumen sensibile est medium);* the *lumen* gives to the corporeal substance its form, extension, and dimensions ; in addition, as it is endowed with a tendency to return towards its source, it possesses the figure (accidental form) of a straight line, by reason of which it is called a ray, *radium*.[3] We learn from Witelo that William delighted to study these principles of

---

[1] Vol. I, p. 243.
[2] Baeumker's edition, p. 126-129.
[3] " Quia fontem a quo profluit habet semper secundum suæ virtutis exordium prospicere, dimensionem distantiæ quæ est linea recta per accidens assumit, sicque sibi nomen radii coaptat, (Prol.)

dynamic philosophy in detail, and it was at his request that Witelo himself expounded them in his *Perspectiva*.

339. Witelo.—Born about 1220-1230 in Silesia, Witelo received his philosophical and scientific education at Paris. From there, after a short stay in the land of his birth, he went to Padua, where he studied law, and where he lived probably from 1262 to 1268.[1] Afterwards he dwelt at Viterbo, and there he met William of Moerbeke, who influenced him so profoundly and to whom he dedicated the *Perspectiva*. It is possible that he became a monk at Witow in Poland.[2] He died shortly after 1270.

Witelo's *Perspectiva* was published in 1535 and 1572. The translation of the *Optics* of Alhacen which has been ascribed to him seems not to have been his work. Birkenmajer has recently published the abridged text of two other works by Witelo, *De natura dæmonum* and *De primaria causa pænitentiæ*, from the Codex lat. 14796 of Paris, as well as an anonymous work, *Solutio quæstionis*, containing extracts from the former treatise.[3] The *Solutio* begins with the following declaration : " Si casus angelorum per fidem sit necessarius, tamen per rationem naturalem et ordinem universi non est possibilis,"[4] but the author goes no further.

We gather from the Prologue to the *Perspectiva* that Witelo accepts the metaphysics of William of Moerbeke and his conception of light.[5] The body of the work contains an important series of doctrines relating to experimental psychology, and mathematical explanations of the phenomenon of vision (" omnem itaque modum visionis mathematica . . . demonstratione transcurrendo "). We find described therein after Alhacen the laws of the propagation of light. The work abounds in noteworthy observations on ordinary perception (*aspectus simplex*) and attentive perception, the function of

[1] A. Birkenmajer, *Witelo e lo studio di Padova*, Acad. Polacca di Scienze e Lettere (undated).

[2] Rubczynski, *Kwartalnik hystoryczny*, XXIII, p. 574-587. Cf. Baeumker, *Zur Biographie d. Philos. und Naturforschers Witelo*, in *Zeitschr. f. Gesch. Schlesiens*, 1912, p. 241.

[3] *Studja nad Witelonem*, Krakow, 1921.

[4] p. 25.

[5] In the *Perspectiva*, Witelo solves the problem of universals after the manner of Roger Bacon. There is in everything certain individual notes (*intentiones individuales*) and specific characters (*intentiones speciales*) to which correspond sense knowledge on the one hand, and general knowledge on the other. (*ibid.*, p. 626).

spontaneous and unconscious reasoning[1] accompanying vision (" aliis actionibus animæ accidentibus "), thanks to which the perception of light and colours is completed by that of distance, size, figure, unevenness, rest, motion, beauty, etc., and also on the function of association in the visual perception of the third dimension. The study of such problems in the middle of the thirteenth century shows the habitual way of treating psychological phenomena in connection with the soul and its faculties : they are dealt with quite in the modern manner.

340. The neo-Platonist disciples of Albert the Great.— Among the disciples of Albert who followed his neo-Platonist orientation we must mention HUGH RIPELIN OF STRASBURG, author of a *Compendium theologicæ veritatis*, and above all the Dominican ULRICH OF STRASBURG or ULRIC ENGELBERTI, who, as is shown by his correspondence, was on intimate terms with his master. He attended Albert's lectures at Cologne, became lector in theology at Strasburg (after 1248), and provincial. In 1277, the very year in which certain Thomist doctrines were condemned, he went to Paris to obtain the title of *magister*, but died there without having been able to get beyond the baccalaureate.

Ulrich was the author of unpublished commentaries on the Sentences, the *Meteorologica* of Aristotle, and above all of a large theological and philosophical treatise *De summo bono* (unfinished and unpublished), which arranges the neo-Platonist doctrinal material in a personal way. He was influenced by the *Liber de causis*, the *Metaphysics* of Avicenna, and certain neo-Platonist works of Albert, the characteristic doctrines of which he reproduces (**264**). The plan adopted in the first two books, and the way in which he treats his subjects, also manifest the influence of the *De divinis nominibus* of pseudo-Dionysius, to which Ulrich was introduced at Cologne by the lectures of Albert the Great.[2]

The first product of the supreme Being (" prima et propria emanatio primi principii ") is *esse*. This is the primordial form from which are derived all others (" prima forma est esse, quia ipsa est omnium sequentium fundamentum "). This

---

[1] " Non percipit homo quod comprehensio quæ fit per rationem et distinctionem fiat per argumentum, (III, 69 in Baeumker's edition).
[2] G. Théry, *Originalité du plan de la S. de bono d' Ulrich de Strasbourg*, (Ghent 1923, p. 22).

communication of *esse* which God confers on all things is interpreted in terms of a luminous diffusion ("talis autem diffusio est formale esse omnium "), but it takes place in inferior beings with the concourse of intelligences and the movers ("motores ") of the heavenly bodies.

341. Theodoric of Frieberg (Theodoricus Teutonicus de Vriberg) was born about 1250, probably at Freiberg in Saxony. He resided at Paris, first as a student (previous to 1285) and then about 1297 as a Master of Theology.[1] He occupied several high administrative positions in the Dominican order. The last certain information concerning him dates from 1310, and it would seem that he wrote his chief works during the early years of the fourteenth century.

His writings display an astonishing fecundity and very extensive learning. The most important[2] are : *De luce et ejus origine, De coloribus, De iride et radialibus impressionibus, De miscibilibus in mixto, De intelligentiis et motoribus cœlorum, De tribus difficilibus articulis, De cognitione entium separatorum, De esse et essentia, De habitibus, De tempore*, and above all the *De intellectu et intelligibili*, in which are set forth the most original ideas of his system.

Theodoric is of interest in the history of ideas in the thirteenth century from three points of view. As a man of science he conceived a new and remarkable theory of the rainbow, which was afterwards adopted by Descartes. He tells us that when he explained it to the provincial of his order, the latter recommended him to commit it to writing. As a mystic he resembles in many ways Master Eckhart. As a philosopher, Theodoric is a bold and original thinker. He readily differs from the "communiter loquentes " or doctors of his order, and boasts of this. On the other hand, he defends the Thomist innovations on controverted questions such as the unity of substantial form, the passivity of prime matter, the intrinsic impossibility of matter existing without form, and the intrinsic non-impossibility of creation *ab æterno*. On the other hand he adopts doctrines of Augustinian origin. Lastly, he subscribes

---

[1] A. Dyroff, *Ueber Heinrich und Dietrich v. Freiberg*, (*Philos. Jahrb.*, 1915, p. 55-63), advances the hypothesis that he belonged to the family of the poet Henry of Freiberg, who introduced neo-Platonist ideas into his verse.

[2] There were altogether twenty-four treatises, four of which exist in one copy only (Birkenmajer, *Bull. de l'Acad. sc. Cracovie*, 1917. Since then the author has drawn attention to three other manuscripts, one of which contains the *De tempore, BGPM*, XX, 5, p. 70-90).

to theories such as the distinction of the two intellects, the essential difference between sensation and thought, and the composition of matter and form, all of which link him up with the scholastics.

But this collection of elements is built up into a system the neo-Platonist character of which is more evident than in Witelo. The *Elementa theologiæ* are quoted on every page, and Proclus is put on a level with St. Augustine and Aristotle. According to the Dominican philosopher, these three thinkers all teach the doctrines which he himself expounds in his treatises.

(i) *Metaphysics.* The production of beings takes place through intermediaries, and the progressive stages of the causal descent (*quadruplex manieres*) are set out as in Proclus : the One, Intelligences or intellectual hypostases, then souls, and lastly bodies.[1] The idea of emanation (*secundum modum emanationis*) which characterizes neo-Platonism is dominant here, whereas it is absent in Witelo.

Limited beings, then, are not the direct product of the Divine activity (the common theory). God creates the pure intelligences (which must not be confounded with the angels), including the active intellect ; from these intelligences are derived the spirits animating the heavenly bodies ; the latter engender the visible beings of our earth. In order to explain the nature of these descending productions, the " ordo emanationis ut scilicet unus ab alio et ab isto alius et sic deinceps fluat in esse," [2] Theodoric has recourse to the dangerous similes of transfusion (*transfusio qua aliquid fluat in aliud*),[3] ebullition (*ebullitio*), redundance (*redundans*)[4] and a flowing forth (*profluxus entium a prima causa*). But he avoids the monism suggested by these images, by means of a twofold corrective. In the first place, the primordial act of the λόγος, by virtue of which the pure intelligences receive their being, alone deserves to be called a creative act in the scholastic sense of the word.[5] Every agent in the causal hierarchy owes its being and its causality ultimately to God, and hence the

---

[1] P. 125 in Krebs' edition, *BGPM*, V, 5-6.
[2] P. 133.
[3] P. 129.
[4] P. 125.
[5] " Hoc tamen in omnibus salvo quod solus Deus creat . . . quia quicquid agit causa secunda in essentialiter ordinatis agitur a causa superiori," (p. 132). Krebs remarks that this enables him to avoid Prop. 30 condemned by Stephen Tempier, and affecting other emanative systems of philosophy.

production of the heavenly intelligences and the visible
universe are still indirectly His work. Moreover, finite beings
are not mere prolongations or forms of the Divine energy
(neo-Platonism), but substances distinct from God and from
each other. Theodoric transposes the neo-Platonist theme,
so to speak, into a pluralistic key.

It would be unreasonable to deny the possibility of an eternal
world (against Henry of Ghent, cf. Thomas Aquinas). Even
if there had been no commencement, the world would not be
co-eternal with God. God is super-eternal (*superæternitas*);
the pure intelligences, including the active intellect, are
eternal ;[1] the heavenly bodies had a beginning, but will not
have an end ; earthly substances alone exist in time.

Common principles regulate intellectual processes : every
intelligence proceeding from an anterior one receives and conserves its being from the contemplative act by which it knows
the principle whence it is derived (Proclus). The very being
of every pure intelligence consists of *thought* (against Thomas
Aquinas); it is " intellectus in actu per essentiam."

God, who, as the primordial intellectual Actuality, is the
starting point of the procession of beings (" illa superbenedicta
natura sua fecunditate redundet extra in totum ens "),[2] is
also the terminus towards which all beings direct their activities.
This is Proclus's theory of the *reversio*, interpreted in a pluralistic
and finalistic sense : " sicut omnia ab ipso intellectualiter
procedunt, ita omnia in ipsum conversa sunt." [3]

Theodoric has a solution of his own on the foundation
(*ratio*) of individuation : the " reason " of the multiplicity of
individuals in one species is the presence in each individual
of elements foreign to the specific essence. Beings are individualized because they have " partes post totum quæ non
ingrediuntur definitionem." Now these " partes post totum "
belong not only to the quantitative order (Thomas Aquinas),
but also to the qualitative, and include such things as the
natural tendency of a being to exercise its activity in a particular
direction (*respectus habitus*).

Since Theodoric differs from St. Thomas in so many points,
it is not surprising that he opposes him also on the subject

---

[1] To God he ascribes *superæternitas*, to pure intelligences *æternitas*, thus
avoiding the fifth proposition condemned in 1277 : " Quod omnia coæterna
sunt primo principio."

[2] P. 130.

[3] *ibid.*

of the real distinction between essence and existence. In doing so he quotes the very formulæ used by Aquinas. His own solution is similar to that of Henry of Ghent and Godfrey of Fontaines : between the *entitas* and the *essentia* there is only a distinction of reason, giving rise to two different ways of speaking : " totam enim essentiam rei, quam importat in sua significatione entitas in abstracto."[1]

Corporeal substances are composed of matter and form. Matter is indetermined, and as such is not capable of existing without a form (Thomas Aquinas). Each being possesses only one determining principle, and this one form is the source of all its perfections (Thomas Aquinas).

At every stage of his conception of the world, Theodoric introduces the neo-Platonist theory of light. He regards it not as a corporeal constituent (232), but as a subsequent determination of corporeity. The heavenly bodies are animated by intelligences which are not extrinsic movers (St. Thomas), but essential forms (" substantiæ separatæ intellectuales . . . uniuntur corporibus cœlestibus . . . ut formæ unione essentiali.")[2] As for spiritual substances, these are not composed of matter and form (Thomas Aquinas).

(ii) *Psychology*. The soul is the substantial form of the body (Aristotle) and identical with its faculties (Augustine), for the mysterious principle of its being is the active intellect (" abditum mentis, principium causale essentiæ animæ ") which Theodoric identifies with the " abstrusior profunditas nostræ memoriæ " of St. Augustine.[3] The active intellect is a pure intelligence, born of the divine λόγος ; it is the divine element in us, an ocean of intelligibility (" pelagus totius intellectualitatis ").[4] Since being and action are identical, the activity of the soul is differentiated only by the direction it follows in conformity with its natural inclinations (*habitus respectus*). In the soul, everything is activity. It acts as soon as the conditions are present, just as a stone falls.

Again, all knowledge is an active phenomenon. Sensation is produced, not by the causal influence of the external object, but on the occasion of its presence.

The application to the active intellect of the principles

[1] *De ente et essentia*, Krebs edition, p. 522.
[2] P. 65.
[3] P. 71, 162.
[4] P. 77.

signifies that God is pure affirmation, and that all negation is repugnant to him. It signifies again the return of His being upon Himself. It also signifies a sort of internal overflow or pouring out of his being, which takes fire, liquifies, and, so to speak, boils within itself ; [1] it is light in light, and He is so clear that He penetrates himself throughout.

Dwelling on other well chosen texts of Scripture, Eckhart develops some of the aspects of the plenary Being of God, his unity, goodness, justice, love for himself, intelligibility, and simplicity. Simplicity and intelligibility are convertible, as are being and unity. Simplicity is the ultimate and profound source of intelligibility. The simple alone can completely turn back upon itself. That is why, as is said in the *Liber de causis*, the simple knows itself and all things by essence. [2]

Again, it is in accordance with the purest doctrine of scholasticism that Eckhart establishes the *processus* of the Trinity, distinguishing the divine substance as such and this same substance in relation with the Divine persons. Considered under the first aspect, the Divine being is in no way a principle of generation, it becomes this only when we regard it in a relation of order. [3] The need for this twofold consideration arises from our imperfect way of grasping God, and there is nothing in Eckhart's language authorizing us to conclude that he teaches a real distinction between the divinity and God, as if the divine persons were the eternal manifestation or revelation of an absolute indetermination. [4] Eckhart is equally faithful to scholasticism when he develops in his German sermons the rich collection of divine attributes upon which the feeble consideration of our minds successively dwells, comparing them to vestments covering the bare substance of the Divinity. [5]

These are dangerous images, calculated to appeal to his mystical hearers, but are nevertheless capable of a satisfactory interpretation.

---

[1] " Bullicionem sive perfusionem sui in se fervens et se ipso liquescens et bulliens " (*ibid.*)

[2] P. 598.

[3] P. 568.

[4] A mistake due to Preger and reproduced by Lasson in his latest study on Eckhart, although already in 1885 (*Archiv.* pp. 453-455) Denifle had drawn his attention to this colossal misunderstanding of scholastic terminology. Lasson repeats his erroneous statements in Ueberweg-Baumgartner, *Grundriss d. Gesch. d. Phil. d. Patrist. u. Schol. Zeit*, 1915, p. 644.

[5] *Archiv.*, pp. 454 and 455.

But Eckhart's thought takes on a bold and original aspect when he enunciates the thesis that the infinite and essential existence of God is the only existence. " Ens tantum unum est et Deus est."[1] As God is all existence, it is impossible that anything should exist apart from Him. " Rursus extra deum, utpote extra esse, nihil est,"[2] for this something would be outside existence or being. " Impossibile est aliquod esse sive aliquem modum sive differentiam essendi deesse vel abesse ipsi esse. Hoc ipso enim quod deest vel abest ab esse, non est et nihil est."[3] And again, " Extra primam causam nihil est ; quod enim extra causam primam, deum scilicet, est extra esse, quia deus est esse."[4]

(ii) *God and the world.* This doctrine, which Eckhart never tires of repeating in his Latin works, becomes the corner-stone of a very original system of relations between God and the world—not the world as present in the *Verbum,* or as the Divine thought (Eckhart adopts on this point the traditional theory of the *rationes æternæ,* but gives it a personal inter-pretation), but the world as created by God and as existing side by side with Him.

In the first place, Eckhart tells us that creation takes place in the present, for the past and the future have no existence, and accordingly, creation is eternal. This is already equivocal, for the texts do not clearly say whether this eternity or eternal present affects only the Divine activity, or also the term of this activity. No scholastic ever denied that the omnipotent action calling forth imperfect beings from nothing is on God's side co-eternal with his pure activity. But the collection of imperfect beings, the real term of this act, may nevertheless appear in time. We do not know from what standpoint Eckhart is writing when he says, for instance, that God could not have created the world sooner than He did. " How could He have created sooner, *prius,* since He created the world in the same present in which He Himself is ? . . . At the same time that God engendered His Son, co-eternal and equal to Himself, He also created the world. . . . By the same *verbum* He engendered and created."[5] This Eckhart translates in his German sermons by saying : " als balde got was, do hat er

[1] P. 549.
[2] P. 541.
[3] P. 546.
[4] P. 586.
[5] P. 553.

only produce another simple being, and safeguards the scholastic doctrine that God creates the whole universe by a direct and immediate act.

II MYSTICAL PSYCHOLOGY.—On his metaphysics Eckhart builds up a psychology and a mysticism which are equally ambiguous. The human soul, existing with the very existence of God, tends to contract with Him the closest of all unions. This union is brought about in the first place by knowledge and love, which are directed not towards the external world, but towards God who becomes the guest of the soul. Knowledge has its fruits and its repose in itself, its end is to know for the sake of knowing, for it would falsify itself and become mercenary or adulterous were it to seek some external good in addition.[1] Love is greater than knowledge: it is unified by nature, for it is directed only towards one object, that which is loved, " amor ex sui proprietate unicus est."[2] Knowledge, on the other hand, extends to many things.

But the modes of knowledge and love are simple activities of the soul which flow from its substance but do not constitute it (Scholasticism). Now Eckhart's metaphysics lead him to a more intimate union between God and the soul, a union which takes place in the inmost part of our being, in our substance, or in what Eckhart calls the spark of the soul. Just as the soul thirsts after God, so also God loves the human soul, for He loves His own existence or *esse* by which this soul lives, just as do the other beings of the universe. " Amat deus omnia quæ sunt, in quantum sunt . . . deus seipsum amat in omnibus et omnia in seipso et propter seipsum solum."[3] God penetrates into this sanctuary only if the soul has previously renounced every creature, its own self, its knowledge, and its will, and is thus in a state of absolute renunciation (Abgeschiedenheit) and complete poverty. Then the miracle takes place : God reveals Himself in the unity and infinity of His nature. The soul is transported into the silent desert in which there is no more effort, doubt or faith, and where, in order to know, we no longer require images, resemblances, interpretations of scripture and dogma, or teaching by others : God loves Himself in the soul because He finds Himself there and cannot do without it. Thus is brought about the return of man into

[1] P. 565.
[2] P. 575.
[3] P. 493.

the bosom of the infinite. Together with man, all the rest of the created world returns to the bosom of the Deity, for this world was made only for man, and the latter, by knowing it, leads it all back to God its principle. God does not comprehend Himself without the soul. As I am immanent in the being of God, He accomplishes all His works by me, and I am all that is the object of His knowledge. God became man that I might become God.[1]

A mystic system of morality is based on this psychology of deification : mortifications, external acts, and the pursuit of an end have no moral value for a soul which has become indifferent to everything, and is called to the higher forms of union with the divine. Nothing from outside penetrates its interior. Never has the interior character of the mystic life been more energetically affirmed.

In the course of the examination which ended in the condemnation of twenty-eight propositions taken from his works, Eckhart drew up a defence, which Daniels has discovered and published,[2] and which constitutes an important document for the study of his personality and the understanding of his philosophy and mysticism.

From this defence it is clear that the master's intentions are beyond doubt. He wishes to remain faithful to orthodox teaching and to avoid pantheism. He recognizes that certain expressions of which he makes use sound ambiguous, and that these must not be taken literally, but given a benevolent and acceptable sense.[3] He confesses that he is excessive by temperament, and that he uses strong language. He repeats what he says in his writings : he does not want to destroy the existence of the creature, but to establish it (" hoc autem dicentes non tollimus rebus esse nec esse eorum destruimus sed statiumus "), and the comparisons to which he has recourse must be taken as implying a dualistic philosophy.

But the intentions of the pious Dominican, certain as they are, are one thing, and the intrinsic logic of his system is another. The defending document does not introduce any fundamental modification. Eckhart repeats and maintains

---

[1] Art. 10 of the condemned propositions : " Nos transformamur totaliter in deum, etc."

[2] *Eine latein. Rechtfertigungschrift d. Meister Eckart. Mit einem Geleitwort v. Cl. Baeumker, BGPM, XXIII, 5.*

[3] " Error est sicut sonat," p. 17, etc. " Si autem sane intelligantur et pie," p. 34.

that God is the *esse* of everything,[1] introducing a subtle distinction between the *esse formaliter inherens* and the *esse absolutum*, which he does not further explain.[2] He repeats and maintains his doctrine that the soul is a *castellum*, simple like God, and that God discovers himself in it.[3] And he ends by rebuking the ignorance of his inquisitors.[4] The fact that Eckhart's intentions and the logic of his system of ideas do not agree, explain the divergent judgments passed upon him by historians, some of whom regard him as an individualist (Denifle for instance),[5] and others as a pantheist (e.g., Delacroix).[6]

343. The influence of Latin neo-Platonism.—The current of Latin neo-Platonist thought traversed the thirteenth century side by side with Scholasticism, but never had the same importance.[7] The doctrines of emanation, with their obscure images, and tendency towards pantheism, were not calculated to appeal to the neo-Latin and Anglo-Saxon minds.

Of all the thirteenth century neo-Platonists, Eckhart was the one who exercised the most lasting personal ascendancy. He appeared in Western philosophy at a time when Scholasticism was strongly constituted, he witnessed the struggles against Thomism and the rapid expansion of the latter, he was acquainted with the theories of Duns Scotus and the beginnings of Ockamism. But he followed a path of his own. The neo-Platonist doctrines which he built up into a system influenced German mysticism in the first place,[8] and subsequently German philosophy as a whole.

---

[1] P. 28 and p. 45, *passim*. " Vivere meum est esse dei . . . Dicendum quod falsum est et error sicut sonat. Verum quidem est, devotum et morale quod hominis justi, in quantum justus, totum esse est ab esse dei, analogice tamen."

[2] P. 9.

[3] " In anima est quoddam castellum quod interdum vocavi custodiam anime sive castellum. Sequitur quod est valde simplex, sicut deus est unus et simplex, etc." p. 33, Cf. p. 37.

[4] " Ruditas et brevitas intellectus eorum qui talia vitiare contendunt," p. 65.

[5] *Op. cit.*

[6] *Op. cit.*, p. 135-262. See a summary of opinions on Eckhart in X. de Hornstein.

[7] " Unsere Schrift de intelligentiis zeigt wie auch die neuplatonische Strömung einen wenn auch kleinen Kreis ergriffen hat. The book, De intelligentiis, shows how small a circle was affected by the Neo-Platonist current." (Baeumker, *Witelo*, p. 188). In his study on the *Liber XXIV Philosoph.*, he speaks of a " sidestream or undercurrent," (*op. cit.*, p. 19).

[8] Ph. Strauch and Baeumker agree in saying that Eckhart is important historically above all because of his mysticism.

344. Bibliography.—Cl. Baeumker, *Der Platonismus im Mittelalter*, Munchen, 1916 (Akad. Wiss.), an excellent general study ; *Witelo* (*BGPM*, III, 2); *Der Anteil d. Elsass an d. geistigen Bewegungen d. Mittelalters* (Strasburg, 1912). Grabmann, *Die Kulturwerte d. deutschen Mystik d. Mitt.* (Munich, 1923); *Neuaufgefundene lat. Werke deutscher Mystiker* (Sitz. ber. Bayer. Akad. Wiss., 1921, 3); *Der Neuplatonismus in d. deutschen Hochscholastik* (*Phil. Jahrb.*, 1910).

On William of Moerbeke, see Vol. I, p. 243. ; Bosmans, *G. de M. et le traité des corps flottants d'Archimède* (*R. Quest. scient.*, 1922). On Witelo, see works mentioned in note, also Baeumker, *Witelo, ein Philosoph und Naturforscher des XIII. Jahrh.*, (*BGPM, III, 2*), which contains *De intelligentiis*, gives a study of his life and works, and also important monographs on the history of the arguments for the existence of God in the Middle Ages, the philosophy of light, the Platonist ideology in the Middle Ages, and the doctrine of intelligences. A. Birkenmajer, *Studja nad Witelonem*, I. (Krakow, Akad. sciences, 1921), gives a resumé of two unpublished opuscula, *De natura dæmonum* and *De prima causa pœnitentiæ*, notes on the relations between Witelo and the *Meteorology* of Nicholas of Oresme. On the Dominican Hugh and his Compendium, see L. Pfleger, in *Zeitschr f. Kath theol.* 1904, pp. 429-440 ; Grabmann, *ibid.*, 1921, pp. 147-153. On Ulrich of Strasburg, see Grabmann's work mentioned in Vol. I, p. 406, and *Gesch. schol. Meth.*, I, 60. Engelbert Krebs, *Meister Dietrich*, etc. (*BGPM*, I, 6-7, 1906), excellent, gives in extenso the *De intellectu* and the *De habitibus* ; in connection with this work see our study on Theodoric of Freiberg in *Revue Neo-Scolastique*, 1906, pp. 434-441 ; Edition of the *De ente et essentia*, by Krebs, from the Vatican MSS. in *Revue Neo-Scolastique*, 1911, pp. 519-536. Edition of *De iride et radicalibus impressionibus* of Theodoric by Würschmidt, 1914. Pfeifer, *Deutsche Mystiker d. 14 Jahrhunderts* (Leipzig, two vols., 1845 and 1875), publishes 110 sermons, 18 treatises, and 68 verses by Eckhart (in German). Other contributions by Preger in 1864. Sievers has found twenty-six other sermons (*Zeitschrift f. deutsches Altertum*, 1872). In 1880 Denifle found and published together with a study, fragments of the *Opus tripartitum*, *Meister Eckeharts lateinische Schriften* (*Arch. Litt. Kirchengesch. Mitt.* 1886). *Die Heimath M. Eckeharts* (*ibid.*, 1889). A resumé of the literary problems will be found in Xavier de Hornstein,

Les Grands mystiques allemands du XIVe. s. Eckart, Tauler, Suso (Lucerne, 1922). Philipp Strauch, *Meister Eckhart problemen* (Halle, 1912), an authoritative work ; Daniels, *BGPM*, XXIII, 5.

§ 2—*Roger Bacon and the Experimental School*

345. The forerunners of Roger Bacon. Peter of Maricourt.—A group of English naturalists, Alfred of Sareshel, Alexander Neckham, Bartholomaeus Anglicus, Robert Grosseteste, Michael Scot, Adam Marsh and John Peckham, had implanted at Oxford certain scientific traditions which Roger Bacon was destined to imbibe and strengthen. They laid stress on the value of the mathematical as well as that of the experimental method, and they interpreted the phenomena of nature in quantitative terms.

PETER OF MARICOURT (Petrus Peregrinus de Maharicuria) was himself a master of experimental science, and exercised a great influence on Roger Bacon, if we are right in identifying him with the " MAGISTER PETRUS " whom Bacon calls " dominus experimentorum," and of whom he writes that he alone among the Latins was capable of understanding the " radices experimentorum." Tradition and marginal notes on manuscripts confirm this identification. We know little about his life. He himself tells us that he was at the siege of Luceria in 1269, and his name " Peregrinus " is an allusion to his career as a crusader. His two works, *Epistola de magnete* and *Nova compositio Astrolabii particularis* manifest their author's knowledge of scholastic philosophy, but are above all the work of a very remarkable observer of nature.[1]

346. Roger Bacon. Life and works.—Roger Bacon was born at Ilchester in England about 1210-1215. He studied first at Oxford under Robert Grosseteste and Adam Marsh, and then at Paris, where he taught (from before 1245 to 1250-2), and met Alexander of Hales and William of Auvergne. He then returned to Oxford, and about this time (between 1251 and 1257) entered the Friars Minor. In 1257 he was compelled to leave his chair, but he did not interrupt his study of languages and the scientific labours to which he had devoted himself from his youth, although the severity and hostility

---

[1] Schlund says that the *De magnete* is the first work produced according to the inductive method of the natural sciences (*op. cit.*, p. 437.)

of his superiors did not permit him to communicate his writings to those outside. The elevation to the papacy of a powerful friend was a decisive event in his life : Clement IV, by letter of 22nd June, 1266, commanded Bacon to send him the work which he proposed to write, and this in spite of the prohibition of his superiors. When in 1277 Tempier condemned divination by astrology,[1] Bacon felt that he was aimed at, and wrote the *Speculum astronomiæ* at once in defence of his astrological ideas and in criticism of Tempier's action. This act of Bacon's, in conjunction with the diatribes which he addressed to the highest personalities, the Pope included, had serious consequences. The Franciscan general, Jerome of Ascoli, condemned his doctrine and inflicted upon him the heaviest penalty, imprisonment.[2] His incarceration lasted until 1292, and he died shortly after.

The *Opus majus*, dedicated to Clement IV, is the chief work of Bacon, and comprises seven parts : the causes of our errors, the relations between philosophy and the sciences and theology, linguistics, mathematics, perspective, experimental science, and moral philosophy. The *Opus minus* contains in addition to much matter incorporated in the *Opus majus*, an exposition of speculative alchemy, and a study on the decadence of theological science and its causes (" septem peccata studii principalis quod est theologiæ ").[3] The *Opus tertium* has the same characteristics, and repeats things found in the other two works. We also find therein new questions in science, and much information on Bacon's life.[4] Mandonnet thinks that the *Opus majus* was finished and sent to the Pope in 1268, and therefore after the *Opus minus* and *Opus tertium*. These last two works would be summaries and supplements which were neither finished nor sent, but from which Bacon borrowed materials incorporated in the *Opus majus* (notably the letter-preface).[5] Bacon has left us the plan of a *Scriptum principale* which does not seem to differ from the *Opus majus*. He says that he deals therein with (1) grammar and language ; (2) mathematics ; (3) natural sciences ; (4) metaphysics and moral philosophy. In addition to commentaries on the various

---

[1] P. 102.
[2] Mandonnet, article referred to later on.
[3] Brewer, p. xxxiv, 322.
[4] The *Opus majus* will be quoted according to Bridges' edition, the *Opus minus* and *Opus tertium* from Brewer's edition.
[5] *Revue Neo-Scolastique*, 1913, p. 60.

books of Aristotle, composed in his youth, a *Compendium philosophiæ* (about 1271-76) in which he once more dwells on the faults in studies, a treatise *De multiplicatione specierum* (studying the efficient causality of bodies), the *Communia naturalium*, the *Speculum astronomiæ*, a *Compendium studii theologiæ* (his last work), and a number of other treatises and opuscula are ascribed to him. The chronology and order of his works has not been definitely settled.

347. The personality of Bacon.—Bacon remains an enigmatic personality in whom the man of science, the philosopher and the mystic are united in a strange way.[1]

He professes for the sciences in general a love which has rightly been regarded as one of his chief titles to fame. He was better versed in the natural and mathematical sciences such as perspective, optics, geography, astronomy, alchemy, and philology, than were any of his contemporaries. His applications of geometry to physics were superior to those of the Arabians. He made and perfected optical instruments. He was never tired of bitterly reproaching contemporary scholastics for their entire neglect of observation. Bacon was not only an observer, he also studied the value of the experimental method, its conditions and possibilities. The passages in which he deals with this subject are now well known. We shall see later on what place they occupy in his philosophy, and eventually in his mysticism. For, however remarkable may have been his work in the sphere of experiment, it can only be fully understood when put in its proper place in his complete synthesis.

This synthesis harmonizes with the dominant features of his temperament, and the latter itself rendered service to his doctrine. Bacon was an impulsive man, vain and self-sufficient. He really thought that the human race was going astray in his time, and that he was intended to put things right. That explains his attitude as a prophet come to curse, and accounts for his bitter criticisms of those he regarded as responsible for the evils of the society in which he lived.

Bacon is uncommonly frank, and his works constitute a first-rate source for the history of ideas in the thirteenth century. He gives us valuable information on the first translations of Aristotle,[2] on studies among the Franciscans, the teaching of

---

[1] Cf. Carton, *La synthèse doctrinale de R. Bacon*, 1924, pp. 117 *et seq.*
[2] See for instance the *Opus majus*, III, 66.

theology,[1] and various scholastic personalities, such as William of Auvergne,[2] Robert Grosseteste—of whom he never tires of speaking—Adam de Marisco, and many others. The history of Greek, Patristic, and Arabian philosophy has a large place,[3] and Bacon's development of this subject is character-ized by a personal attitude to which reference will be made later on. We must here point out that his judgments, mani-festing as they do a severity which sometimes amounts to injustice, must be accepted with reserve. Albert the Great[4] was especially the object of his attacks, so much so that the Dominican thought it his duty to reply in severe terms.[5] Thomas Aquinas is referred to in other passages.[6] Himself full of admiration for Aristotle, Bacon accuses his contem-poraries of not having understood him in the faulty Latin translations of which they made use. It would have been better for the Latins to know nothing of Aristotle rather than depend upon such detestable translations. " Si enim haberem potes-tatem super libros Aristotelis, ego facerem omnes cremari."[7] In point of fact, he himself did not always understand him rightly.[8]

Sometimes Bacon allows his pride as an Englishman to manifest itself in contempt for the Parisian masters. Thus in speaking of the plurality of forms maintained by the former and rejected by the latter, he contrasts the " Anglicani qui satis inter alios homines sunt et fuerunt studi-osi " and the " capiti vulgi philosophantium Parisius,"[9] or again he compares the " Anglicani " to the " vulgus medi-corum " of Paris.

Written in a lively and energetic style, Bacon's works are not arranged according to the ordinary pedagogical methods

---

[1] The seven sins of theology, according to the *Opus minus*, pp. 322 *et seq.* are : the incursions of theology into the domain of pure philosophy ; the ignorance of sciences ; the undeserved ascendency of the two principal theologians, Alexander of Hales and Albert the Great (" de aliis nulla vis est ") ; the preference accorded to the books of the Sentences over the Bible ; the corrup-tion of the text of the Vulgate ; the errors in exegesis ; and the ignorance of preachers.

[2] *Opus majus*, III, 47.

[3] *Opus majus*, I, 99, 45-54, contains an outline of the history of philosophy.

[4] *Opus tertium*, p. 30.

[5] The end of his commentary on the *Politics* of Aristotle.

[6] Carton, *op. cit.*, p. 19-21

[7] *Compendium philosopiæ*, Brewer's edition, p. 469.

[8] Thus he makes the signal mistake of holding that Aristotle taught the Trinity, and the Creation and non-eternity of the world. See Mandonnet *Siger*, VII, p. xxi.

[9] *Communia naturalium*, Steele's edition, p. 284.

of the time, but develop their subject matter in a freer manner. In fact, the freedom of their treatment reflects the undisciplined character of their author.   They abound in repetitions, and are lacking in didactic order.   We have seen that the last two *Opera* are incorporated in the *Opus majus*.   In the same way the *Communia naturalium* are a kind of summary of the preceding work ;   his treatise *De probatione fidei*[1] is but an outline of the *Metaphysica*, which in turn is re-edited in the *Opus majus*.

348.   Philosophical teaching.—A personal interpretation of corporeal being, the matter and form constituting it, and the activity it displays, give a certain amount of originality to Bacon's metaphysics and philosophy of nature.   Curious intuitionist theories, and personal ideas on the Divine illumination and internal experience, are brought to bear on his conception of reality, and help to unify the various departments of knowledge.

(i) *Metaphysics and natural philosophy.*   Bacon is a pluralist philosopher :   the individual alone exists.   " One individual has more reality than all the universals joined together." Again, he refutes all the forms of monism—that of those who regard the *materia universalis* as numerically one (*pessimus error*), and that of the Amalricians, who look upon God as the *esse formale omnium.*

Every limited being is composed of matter and form, and is created in time.[2]   Distinct from one another as to their substances, beings are involved in a network of reciprocal actions and reactions.   The higher act upon the lower, spirits on bodies, and heavenly bodies upon terrestrial (astrology). Bacon applies the name " species " to every action of one being upon another (*primus effectus agentis*),[3] and his treatise *De multiplicatione specierum* is devoted to the study of the transmission and propagation of efficient causality.[4]

Bacon is chiefly interested in corporeal individuals, as we might expect in a scientist studying philosophy.

We must note first of all his way of understanding the

---

[1] Wrongly ascribed to Nicholas of Strasburg, see Delorme, article " Bacon " in *Dict. theol. cath.*, 1903.   This Nicholas was a professional plagiarist, see Baeumker, *Der Anteil d. Elsass, etc.*, pp. 22, 40.

[2] *Opus tertium*, pp. 121 and 123.

[3] *Opus majus*, II, 149.

[4] H. Hoffmans, *Une théorie intuitioniste au XIIIe s.*, in *Revue Neo-Scol.*, 1906, pp. 382 *et seq.*

internal organization of corporeal substance : matter and form comprise various stages, and the individual (*linea individualis*) results from a progressive development of generic and specific realities (*linea universalis*), continually determining, restricting and completing the being in question.

Two peculiarities characterize matter, its specific nature and its activity. There is not only a *materia prima universalis* which, together with the most general form, constitutes the *natura universalis in quo omnia corpora conveniunt*, but also specific matters corresponding to the various forms which are superposed in a body : " forma differt a forma secundum se, et materia a materia per suas naturas proprias, ita quod diversitas materiæ non est a forma sicut nec e converso." [1] Again, matter has not only its own being (*actus essendi*) apart from form, but it has also a kind of active appetite which tends to realize the *rationes seminales* deposed in it. Together with the incomplete form (*corporeitas*) to which it is united, matter in this first stage constitutes an incomplete individual, and it is its internal tendency to better itself that leads this compound to go through the series of developments which eventually make it a particular individual being. The universal or natural matter, " materia universalis " or " naturalis " is therefore at once active and passive : active inasmuch as it has an efficacious tendency to lead the individual being towards its full development by the unfolding of its *rationes seminales* ; passive in the sense that this realization of forms comes about under the influence (*species*) of external agents, and does not consist in a sort of self-development as Bonaventure held.

To this genetic process in matter there corresponds a similar process in forms : these are superposed in genera and species up to the individual form which crowns the series, and at each stage in the process the compound of matter and form is the *principium materiale* with regard to the subsequent determinations. [2]

Various corollaries follow from and complete this view of

---

[1] *Opus tertium*, p. 126. " Et ideo asinus non differt ab equo per solam formam sed per materiam aliam specificam."

[2] " Sicut hoc materiale principium non est pura materia, sed unum compositum, sic formale non est pura forma sed compositum," in MS. quoted by Hover, *op. cit.*, XXV, p. 371. Holding as he did the plurality of forms, Bacon naturally accepted the theory of the *remissio formarum* or the permanence of the forms of the elements in the *mixtum*.

the individual : the first is that the essence or nature of a corporeal being is subjected to a real evolution, the stages of which correspond to the various concepts (generic and specific) in our minds. Moreover, the essence exists in each stage of reality; its generic or specific state in a particular individual is independent of our concepts. Lastly, the complete individuality, this particular man for instance (*hic homo*), the culmination of the process, results from the union of a particularized matter and form ; but the generic and specific realities appearing in the previous stages have an imperfect individuality, and Bacon speaks of an " individuum generis " or " speciei " (*hæc substantia, hoc animal, hoc rationale*).

The parallelism between the logical and the real order governs the whole ideology of Bacon, and since the action of the thing known upon the knower is explained in the same way as any other propagation of force, human knowledge of the corporeal world is a form of intuition.

(ii) *The intuitive character of knowledge.* All knowledge consists in a direct union of the knower with the thing known, and results from an immediate action (*species*) of the latter upon the former. Its content corresponds completely, neither more nor less, to the reality which is acting. Not only is sensation produced in this way (as in the common theory), but abstract thought also. This is the logical consequence of the bold Realism taught by Bacon : since there are in the individual being, apart from any act of thought, generic and specific strata of reality, these act (*species*) on the intelligence in as direct a way as the sensible and particular state of bodies acts upon the senses.[1] Similarly, the individual notes enveloping these universal elements give rise to the concept of the singular, " sicut rerum quædam sunt universales, quædam singulares, sic species fiunt ab his et aliis." The " universal " is outside us : why then should it not act upon us ? " Quarta (positio) est, quod universale sit solum in singularibus et non dependeat ab anima aliquo modo."[2]

Does the knowledge we possess of spiritual beings arise in the same way ? Do we receive directly the effects of their activity, or must we attain to the spiritual through the

---

[1] Although the content of generic and specific notions is abstract, it is obtained by an intuition, for this abstract aspect exists as such in the thing. Carton (*L'expérience physique* etc., p. 105 etc.) does not realize this, and hence his repeated criticism of the intuitionist interpretation of Hoffmans.

[2] Quoted by Hover, *op. cit.*, p. 49.

corporeal, as in the *sentencia communis* of the scholastics ?
We shall return to this question later on.

(iii) *God as the active intellect.* In an intuitionist ideology,
the active intellect in the Aristotelian and scholastic sense is
as unnecessary as an active sense.[1] The determinant (*species*)
comes directly from the intelligible reality. Still, Bacon accepts
the active intellect, and identifies it with God. The passive
intellect or understanding is in the soul, but the active intellect
is outside.[2] He adds that " Aristotle, St. Augustine, and all
the *sapientes antiqui experti* agree in separating the two
intellects. This is also the view held by Robert of Lincoln,
and Adam de Marisco. And on two occasions I have heard
William of Auvergne defend this doctrine."[3]

Bacon's idea of God as the active intellect has nothing
strange except its terminology. It is important to note that
it is very far removed from Averrhoism. Each individual has
his own understanding, and the thesis of the one intelligence
for all men is condemned as " error pejor et heresis nequior,
immo nequissima."[4] Bacon merely means that God is the
light of our intellects, and that the general concourse which
He gives to every creature in order that it may be able to act,

---

[1] R. Carton, *L'expérience mystique de l'illumination intérieure chez R. B.*,
1924, p. 203, writes that " while the intelligible is known by means of the
sensible, according to the ordinary rule, it is still necessary to draw it from
corporeal things, and this is the office of the active intellect . . . God."
But for Bacon there is no need to " draw it from corporeal things," it
exists there as such, in its own distinct ontological stratum.

[2] " Intellectus agens, secundum majores philosophos, non est pars animæ,
sed est substantia alia et separata per essentiam ab intellectu possibili,"
(*Opus majus*, III, p. 47).

[3] " Nam universitate convocata bis vidi et audivi venerabilem antistitem
dominum Gulielmum Parisiensem Episcopum felicis memoriæ coram omnibus
sententiare quod intellectus agens non potest esse pars animæ ; et dominus
Robertus Episcopus Lincolniensis et frater Adam de Marisco et hujusmodi
majores hoc idem firmaverunt," p. 47. With one reservation, Bacon's account
agrees with the theory of William of Auvergne (225). The incident of which
Bacon speaks is mentioned again in the *Opus tertium*, pp. 74, 75. He opposes
his theory to that of the " moderni," according to whom the active intellect
is a *pars animæ*. Speaking of Adam de Marisco, he adds : " unde quando per
tentationem et derisionem aliqui Minores præsumptuosi quæsiverunt a fratre
Adam, ' Quid est intellectus agens ? ' respondit : ' Corvus Eliæ,' volens per
hoc dicere quod fuit Deus vel angelus."

[4] *Communia naturalium*, Hover's edition, p. 302. He adds the following
on the theory of the two truths : " Palliant ergo errorem suum, quando artan-
tur, dicentes quod per philosophiam non potest aliter dici, nec per rationem
potest haberi aliud, sed per solam fidem. Sed mentiuntur tanquam vilissimi
heretici." Cf. Renan, *op. cit.*, p. 262. Renan bases himself on the text
quoted in the preceding note, and places Bacon and the older Franciscans
among the Averrhoist party. But Bacon was not an Averrhoist ; moreover,
he occupied a place apart among the Franciscans, for the latter agreed with
the Dominicans in regarding the active intellect as a *pars animæ*.

is called in the case of knowledge an illumination of truth. God, the universal agent, co-operates with the *species* of the real when they stimulate the understanding, and also with the latter when it reacts in the immanent act of knowledge. The Augustinian texts concerning the Divine illumination easily admit of such an interpretation, and Bacon makes abundant use of them.[1]

In addition to the general illumination or ordinary concourse which God gives to the act of knowledge, Bacon speaks of a special illumination.   However strange it may seem, this second illumination is connected with a theory of experience.

(iv) *Experience and the ways of knowing.*   There are three ways of knowing : *per auctoritatem et rationem et experientiam.*[2] Authority is not sufficient without reasoning, and reasoning itself does not result in the tranquil possession of the truth if its data are not confirmed by experience.[3]   Experience is accordingly the sole source of certitude.   The *argumentum* which Bacon contrasts with *experientia* is doubtless the empty argumentation examples of which were furnished by the *sophismata* of the schools, or that which starts from unexamined facts, or again that which would vainly claim to do without experience in studying the laws of nature.[4]   Bacon agrees that demonstration based on the facts of experience leads to knowledge.[5]

This is not all.   While experience is *par excellence* the method giving certitude, and the one which should be placed at the

---

[1] Carton has brought out this point very well, but we do not agree that the famous special illumination of the Augustinian school in the thirteenth century corresponds to Bacon's general illumination here referred to (*L'expérience mystique, etc.*, p. 69).   Père Delorme of Bordeaux will have it that Bacon's philosophy is in agreement with that of the other Franciscans of the thirteenth century, and ironically reproaches us with having incorrectly spoken of Bacon in the first edition of this *History*.   A new examination of the texts has confirmed us in our first opinion.   Père Delorme's study contains mistakes.   It is untrue that Peckham, Scotus and St. Thomas accepted the ideological conclusions of Bacon (p. 14) : all these regard the active intellect as a *pars animæ*.   Again, it is untrue that no scholastic has given so wide a scope to reason as Bacon (p. 22).   The contrary is the case.

[2] Brewer, p. 397.

[3] *Opus majus*, II, 177.   " Duo enim sunt modi cognoscendi, scilicet per argumentum et experimentum.   Argumentum concludit et facit nos concedere conclusionem, sed non certificat neque removet dubitationem ut quiescat animus in intuitu veritatis, nisi eam inveniat via experientiæ ; quia multi habent argumenta ad scibilia, sed quia non habent experientiam, negligunt ea, nec vitant nociva nec persequuntur bona."

[4] *ibid.*, p. 201.

[5] " Quod ergo dicit Aristoteles quod demonstratio syllogismus est faciens scire, intelligendum est si experientia comitetur, et non de nuda demonstratione." (*ibid.*, p. 168).

basis of all knowledge, we must add that there are two kinds of experience, external and internal. " Oportet ergo omnia certificari per viam experientiæ. Duplex est experientia."

External experience (*per sensus exteriores*)[1] which completes the data of the external senses by instruments, is perfect only when its acquired results are viewed in the light of mathematics. This serves to distinguish it from the experience of common people and the *inexperti*. Furthermore, it is only complete when its takes the occult influences into account.

Internal experience (*scientia interior*) is the fruit of Divine inspiration (*divinæ inspirationes*). There are seven degrees in this *scientia interior*, the first consisting of *illuminationes pure scientiales*. The others are the virtues, the seven gifts of the Holy Ghost, the beatitudes, the spiritual senses (*sensus spirituales*), the *fructus de quibus est pax Domini*, and lastly the ecstatic *raptus*.[2] It is difficult to get a clear notion of these various degrees. The first two are concerned with activities which are natural to man, and the others introduce us to the supernatural and mystical life. In the *illuminationes pure scientiales* we may see a more profound knowledge of bodies, and perhaps also a direct knowledge of spiritual beings, inasmuch as this divine illumination enables us to receive the effects (*species*, cf. p. 141) of the latter. In any case, there is question here of a special illumination from God, and Carton[3] has well shown that it is an exceptional and free gift,[4] distinct from God's co-operation as the active intellect and as the principal universal cause. God has bestowed the favours of His personal revelations generally, granting them to the faithful in the first place, and also to some of the wise men of antiquity.

In addition to all this, there is a third intervention of God in the acquisition of knowledge, a sort of primitive revelation, which Bacon links up with his personal opinions on the unity of knowledge.

(v) *The unity of knowledge and the primitive revelation.*

[1] He distinguishes in sensation between the actual sensation, the memory, and the *cogitativa*. The latter is the *domina virtutum sensitivarum, logistica*, and is found in animals as well as in man. It corresponds to the *vis æstimativa* of the scholastics. (*Opus majus*, II, pp. 70 and 127).

[2] *Opus majus*, II, p. 170-171.

[3] *L'expérience mystique*, etc., pp. 35-39 *et passim*.

[4] This illumination is necessarily supernatural for the five last degrees. Is it also supernatural for the *illuminationes pure scientiales* ? Not necessarily. We do not follow Carton here (II, 68). The special illumination of Henry of Ghent, for instance, is not supernatural.

The question of the unity of knowledge and the hierarchical relations between the various disciplines constituting it is a fundamental one in Bacon's system. It is dealt with in the second part of the *Opus majus*. Theology predominates; although distinct from it, philosophy has no value if cultivated for its own sake : " philosophia secundum se considerata nullius utilitatis est "[1]; it is only the instrument of dogma: " philosophia non est nisi sapientiæ divinæ explicatio per doctrinam et opus.[2] Philosophy and theology are deposited in the Scriptures, the content of which they have to unravel. " Una est tantum sapientia perfecta quæ in sacra scriptura totaliter continetur."[3] The particular sciences in their turn are not an end in themselves, but furnish us with practical and useful information, and ultimately serve theology. These are strange words in the mouth of one who dealt with so many questions in science and philosophy as though they possessed an independent value.

This ordered knowledge, in which everything combines to form a full and complete unity, was given as an integral whole by God to primitive humanity. He was Himself the teacher of our first parents, and charged them to transmit the sacred deposit to their descendants.

God alone, he writes, could teach men to philosophize. Without books and teachers the solution of the problem of universals would not have been found, and the same is true of all philosophy : " Revelatio necessaria est in hac parte (veritate universalium); et cum hæc sint puerilia et minima, multo fortius erit hoc in tota sapientia philosophiæ."[4] " Impossibile fuit homini ad magnalia scientiarum et artium devenire per se, sed oportet quod habuerit revelationem."[5] " Eisdem personis data est philosophiæ plenitudo quibus et lex Dei, scilicet sanctis patriarchis et prophetis a mundi principio."[6] This is a veritable traditionalism.

But although the plenitude of philosophic knowledge was contemporary with the cradle of the human race, the malice of men drew down the anger of God[7] ; He dispensed philosophic truths with a sparing hand, and allowed them to become mixed

---

[1] *Opus majus,* III, p. 69.
[2] P. 68.   This idea is constantly repeated.   Cf. pp. 52, 53, 76, etc.
[3] P. 36.
[4] *Opus majus,* p. 50.
[5] P. 53.
[6] P. 53.
[7] P. 67.

with error. We must seek in the writings of the ancient philosophers the soul of truth which the Divine revelation has deposited there, and follow up the traces of Christian doctrine in paganism, and ourselves add to the bequeathed treasure, " usque ad finem mundi, quia nihil est perfectum in humanis adinventionibus."[1]

Now, to discover this treasure contained in the philosophy of the ancients, we must interrogate history. The acquisition of languages thus becomes the first condition of knowledge.[2] To languages ought to succeed the study of mathematics, which are necessary for the various sciences interpreting nature[3] and for philosophy (" tota philosophiæ intentio non est nisi rerum naturas et proprietates evolvere ")[4] as also for the understanding of the facts of Scripture. Ethics is the culmination of philosophy, for it is more directly connected with theology.

Bacon thought that the sacred deposit of primitive knowledge had been singularly compromised by the mistakes of his predecessors and contemporaries, and he was not far from regarding himself as the leader of a revival, and the prophet of better times. This well explains his bitter humour and the tone of his diatribes.

To conclude, Bacon was an anachronism in two ways. As a man of science he was in advance of his time, but the use he made of experimental methods was better than his theory concerning them. As a philosopher, he was behind the times. His attempt to reduce philosophy to an apologetic was regrettable, and in spite of the respect he professed for Aristotle, " he remained always a stranger to the real Aristotelian spirit, and did not succeed in assimilating any of the fundamental ideas of the system."[5] He leaned towards the older scholasticism in admitting the plurality of forms, the existence of a *materia spiritualis*, the *rationes seminales* and the necessity of creation in time. He did not grasp the bearing of the Thomist innovations, and was either ignorant of or indifferent to them. His intuitionism, solution of the universals, theory of the active intellect, and traditionalism, gave a very personal colouring to his scholasticism.

[1] P. 66.
[2] Pp. 97, 98.
[3] P. IV, p. 98. " Omnis scientia requirit mathematicam."
[4] III, p. 52.
[5] Hadelin Hoffmans, *La synthèse doctrinale de R. Bacon*, p. 221.

a gratuitous gift, a supernatural strengthening of the natural powers of our minds, it is simply the actual functioning of these powers, and therefore part of our nature.[1]

Nevertheless, the English philosopher makes some reservations in order to secure for the intelligence a certain intervention in the knowledge of eternal truths. In particular, it furnishes the concepts which later on become the terms of certain judgments (*apprehensio extremorum*). And while it is true that *formaliter* the certitude of the judgment rests on the evidence which the divine light projects on the terms, the soul is nevertheless the inchoative principle (*inchoatio*) of this certitude.[2] In this sense Marston speaks even of a double active intellect, the one a part of our soul (*pars animæ*), corresponding to a simple natural predisposition in the soul to know truth, the other, separate from us, completing the *inchoatio* of nature.[3]

This is an unusual terminology. Although Marston appeals to the identity of God with the active intellect only in order to explain the knowledge of truth in the *rationes æternæ*,[4] his illumination theory differs nevertheless from that commonly defended by the scholastics.[5]

The numerous quotations from St. Anselm show Marston's dependence upon the philosopher of Bec, and the authority the latter enjoyed in the English Franciscan schools.[6]

351. Ontologism.—The ideology of Roger Marston borders upon Ontologism. This erroneous doctrine, according to which the human intellect sees directly in God the object of its ideas,

---

[1] Ad 14m, p. 216.

[2] pp. 211 and 215, ad 12m and 13m.

[3] "Intellectus enim agens, secundum quod dicitur ab actu illuminandi ipsum intellectum possibilem aliquo modo *incomplete*, dicitur esse pars animæ, sicut perspicuitas naturalis in oculo . . . Sed secundum quod intellectus agens dicitur ab actu illuminandi *complete* et *principaliter*, est substantia separata, Deus ipse." (*ibid.* p. 208. Cf. pp. 216, ad 15).

[4] In the case of knowledge " quæ per tempora variantur," there is a " lumen naturale, derivatum a luce æterna," (p. 206).

[5] The Quaracchi editors are aware of this, and note that on the question of the *rationes æternæ*, Matthew of Aquasparta and Fr. Eustachius hold a different opinion. Again, Ehrle thinks that Marston's theories must be viewed with circumspection, (*Das Stadium der Handschriften*, etc., p. 48). Daniels reproaches me with giving rise to misunderstandings concerning the doctrine of Marston. (*Anselmcitate*, etc., p. 42). I fail to see how. It cannot be denied that the theories of Marston and Bacon on the active intellect differ from the prevalent theory. Certainly St. Bonaventure and St. Thomas Aquinas incidentally allude to them, but even if they declare them orthodox they do not approve of them, and we cannot infer from this fact alone that they were widely held.

[6] Daniels, *op. cit.*, indicates various questions in metaphysics and psychology in which Marston manifests a dependance on St. Anselm.

was in fact defended in the schools, as is shown by the repeated refutations of it in the works of the chief scholastic doctors,[1] and by the mention of ontologist doctrines in the list of 219 propositions condemned in 1277. The names of these ontologists are unknown to us.

352. Bibliography.—Erhard Schlund, *Petrus Peregrinus von Maricourt, Sein Leben u. seine Schriften* (Ein Beitrag z. R. Baco-Forschung), in *Archiv. franc. histor.* 1911 and 1912, gives all the bibliography; F. Picavet, *Pierre de Maricourt le Picard et son influence sur R. Bacon* (*Revue intern. de l'enseign.*, Oct., 1907).

Editions of Bacon's *Opus majus* in 1733, and Jebb 1750. Edition by Bridges, Oxford, 3 vols., 1897-1900, full of mistakes. The third volume is a re-edition of a part of Vol. I. from a new manuscript. At the end of Vol. II is the *De multiplicatione specierum*. Under the title, *An Unpublished Fragment of a work by Roger Bacon*, Cardinal Gasquet published in the *English Historical Review* for 1897 a long letter from Bacon to Clement IV, which he believes to be the introduction to the work itself. It certainly does bear directly on it. Brewer, *Fr. R. Bacon opera hactenus inedita* (in *Rerum britannicarum medii ævi scriptores*), published in 1859, contains the *Opus tertium*, and the *Opus minus*, both incomplete, and the *Compendium philosophiæ*. Duhem, *Un fragment inédit de l'opus tertium de R. Bacon*, with a study (Quaracchi, 1909). He discovered a part of the *Opus tertium* attributed to Al Bitrogi in a manuscript in the Bibliothèque Nationale, which follows on, although not directly, to a fragment found by Brewer. Little, *The Missing Part of R. Bacon, opus tertium*, in the *English Historical Review*, 1912. He publishes another manuscript of the *Opus tertium*, with additions. For a bibliography, and the relations between the three works, see Mandonnet, *R. Bacon et les 3 opus*, in *Revue Neo-Scolastique*, 1913. Mandonnet has shown (*Revue Neo-Scolastique*, 1910) that the *Speculum astronomiæ* included in the works of Albert the Great is by Bacon. R. Steele, *Opera hactenus inedita Rogeri Baconi*, Fasc. I, *Metaphysica fr. Rogeri de viciis contractis in studio theologiæ* (London, undated). The title seems incorrect. According to Duhem, it is a part of the *Opus tertium*. Fasc.

---

[1] See the refutation of Ontologism in St. Bonaventure (*De humanæ cognit. ratione*, etc., pp. 22 et seq.), P. Olivi (*ibid.*, 245-247, Cf. Dissertatio c. 1, p. 7), and St. Thomas (*In I lib. Sent.*, d. 17, q. 1, a. 4).

II and III consist of the *Liber primus communium naturalium fr. Rogeri*, Oxford, the first undated, and the other 1911). They respectively contain parts 1-2 and 3-4 of the first book. Fasc. IV contains the second book and the *De celestibus* (1913), and Fasc. V the *Secretum Secretorum*, with two translations from the Arabic. Another part (the fourth) of the *Communia naturalium* (*De productione rerum in generali*) has been published according to the manuscripts in the Bibliothèque Mazarine of Paris (No. 3576) by Hover, *Roger Bacon's Hylemorphismus als Grundlage seiner philos. Anschauungen* (*Jahrb. Phil. u. spekul. Theol.* XXV and XXVI, 1911, and separate reprint Limburg, 1912, with a study on the notion of matter (Steele neglects this manuscript). Critique of this book by Baeumker, *R. B. Naturphilosophie ins besondere seine Lehren v. Materie u. Form, Individuation u. Universalität* (Munster, 1916), also an excellent exposition. *Fr. Rogeri Bacon Compendium studii theologiæ*, edited by Rashdall, una cum appendice de operibus Rogeri Bacon, ed. A. Little (Aberdeen, 1911). Delorme announces the publication of the *De probatione fidei, Un opuscule inédit de R. Bacon*, in *Archiv. francisc, histor.*, 1911, pp. 209-212. E. Nolan and S. A. Hirsch, *The Greek Grammar of R. B. and a fragment of his Hebrew Grammar*, with introduction and notes, Cambridge, 1902. Two works by Roger Bacon *De diebus criticis* have been edited respectively by Elfferding (Erfurn, 1913) and Palitzśch (Leipzig, 1918). Pelzer will publish in *Studi e Festi* of the Vatican Library certain texts of Roger Bacon, (in particular two unpublished opuscula, *Epistula de signis et causis ignorantiæ modernorum*, and *Epistula de ratione mixti*), the complete text of the *De vitiis contractis in studio theologiæ*, the unpublished conclusion of the *Opus majus*, and the *Opus minus* with three new fragments.

Bridges' editions are preceded by a biography of Bacon and studies on his works. Charles, *R. Bacon, sa vie, ses ouvrages, ses doctrines* (Paris, 1851). Delorme, *Bacon*, in *Dict. theol. cath.*, II, 1903. Narbey, *Roger Bacon et le mouvement scientif. du XIIIe s.* (*R. Quest. histor.*, Jan., 1894); Felder, *op. cit.*, Das Schulprogramm, pp. 380 *et seq.* ; S. Vogl., *Die Physik R. Bacon's* (Erlangen, 1906) ; Flugel, *Roger Bacon's Stellung in d. Gesch. d. Philologie* (*Philosoph. Studien* of Wundt, XIX, 1902, pp. 164 *et seq.*). A general treatment of Bacon by Hadelin Hoffmans will be found in the *Revue Neo-Scolastique* for

1906-1909. By the same : *La synthèse doctrinal de R. Bacon* (*Arch. f. Gesch. d. Philos.* 1907). Witzel, *De Fr. R. Bacon ejusque sententia de rebus biblicis* (*Archiv. francisc.*, 1910). L. Marchal, *Roger Bacon, sa méthode et ses principes*, report of the work of the Seminaire historique at Louvain for 1909-1910, Louvain, 1911. A. Pelzer, *Une source inconnue de R. B.* (referred to in Vol. I, p. 332). *R. Bacon, Essays* (Oxford, 1914) by various writers, edited by Little on the occasion of the seventh centenary of his birth. It contains in particular : Little, *On Bacon's Life and Work ;* Baur, *Der Einfluss d. Robert Grosseteste auf d. Wissenschaftl. Richtung d. B.* (the necessity for the study of languages, the use of mathematics in science, and the multiplication of species were already pointed out by Grosseteste), and a series of studies on Bacon's contribution to various sciences. J. E. Sandys, *R. Bacon* (*Proceedings* of the British Academy, 1914), a commemorative issue of the *Riv. fil. neo-Scol.* in 1914 ; Singer, *Studies in the History and Method of Science*, Vol. II, Oxford, 1921, contains one on Bacon and the state of Science in the thirteenth century. Bridges, *The Life and work of R. B., an Introduction to the Opus majus* (London, 1914). R. Carton, *L'expérience physique chez R. B. ; L'expérience mystique de l'illumination intérieure chez R. B. ; La synthèse doctrinale de R. B.* (Paris, 1924, three vols.). The second volume is the best : it studies the various types of illumination, but contains repetitions. The third volume leaves aside the metaphysics and natural philosophy, that is, an important part which ought to find a place in a doctrinal synthesis. See bibliographies on Bacon in Little, Hover and Carton. Carton is criticized by Hoffmans, in Revue Neo-Scol., May, 1925.

De Wulf, *Henri Bate de Malines*, in *Bull. Acad. Royale Belg.* Nov., 1909 ; Birkenmajer, *op. cit.* Daniels, *Anselmzitate bei dem Oxforder Franciskaner R. v. Marston*, in *Theol. Quartalschr.*, 1911, p. 35.

§ 3—Raymund Lully

353. Life and Works.—Raymund Lully was born about 1235 in the island of Majorca. After living for some years at the royal court, he devoted himself passionately to the study of Arabic and logic, renounced the world, and entered the third order of St. Francis. From this time he laboured with astonishing energy for the accomplishment of one end, the extirpation of Averrhoism and the vindication of Catholic doctrine against unbelievers. Lully did not only write a long series of works, he also became the apostle of his own ideas. He taught at Paris in 1288, without success however, and again from 1310 to 1311. On three occasions he journeyed to Saracen regions in order to combat the Averrhoist philosophy. Legend has largely distorted the life of Lully. Like Roger Bacon he laboured hard to introduce the teaching of languages into the universities.[1] He died in 1315.

Lully was a philosopher, a mystic, an artist, a linguist, and the most brilliant Catalonian writer in the Middle Ages.[2] Among his philosophical works may be mentioned : the *Ars generalis*, afterwards republished under the title *Ars magna ;* the *Liber magnus contemplationum ; Declaratio Raymundi per modum dialogi edita contra aliquorum philosophorum et eorum sequacium opiniones erroneas, damnatas a venerabili patre episcopo parisiensi,* also entitled *Liber contra errores Boetii et Segerii* (completed in 1298) ; *Sermones contra errores Averrois* (all written in 1311) ; *Liber de possibili et impossibili* (1310) ; *De divina unitate et pluralitate* (1311) ; *De modo naturali intelligendi* (1310) ; *Duodecim principia philosophiæ* (1311).

354. Philosophical teaching.—Being some years older than Duns Scotus, Lully did not come under the latter's influence. He went his own way. The original part of his philosophical work consists in the elaboration of a system of relations between philosophy and theology, and in the planning of the " Ars Magna."

Lully is the sworn enemy of Averrhoism. His *Declaratio per modum dialogi* deals with the 219 propositions condemned

---

[1] In 1298-99 he wrote in this sense to the University of Paris and to the King of France (*Chart.*, II, 83 and 84). In 1311 he set out for Vienna in order to get the Council to decree the obligatory teaching of languages (*ibid.*, p. 165).

[2] According to Groeber, in *Grundr. d. Romanischen Philologie*, II. 2 (1893), p. 105, he wrote in Catalan several works which his followers afterwards translated into Latin. The Catalonian texts of Lully are edited by Geronimo Rosello. A great number of Catalonian translations of philosophical works belong to the fourteenth century, amongst them being the *Secretum secretorum*, works by Cicero, Seneca, St. Augustine, and Boethius, the *Dragmaticon* of William of Conches, works by Hugh of St. Victor, etc. (*Ibid.*, pp. 92-101 and 102-110). The Mystical work, *L'Art de Contemplacio*, is edited by Probst in *BGPM*, XIII, 2-3.

by the decree of 1277, but in a different order. To the Averr-hoist theory of the two truths Lully opposes a rationalistic idea of the relation between philosophy and theology : since everything is rational in the faith, reason can and ought to demonstrate everything, including mysteries. There is no separation between the rational and the supra-rational, between natural and revealed truth. To convert the Mohammedans, we must prove, not that their beliefs are false, but that Catholicism is true. This is the whole office of philosophy. Lully thus perverts the scholastic system of relations between philosophy and theology, moreover he confuses the former with apologetics. To the error of Averrhoists he opposes another. True, the fundamental principle of his system is supplemented and balanced by this other, that faith is the preliminary condition for all intellectual knowledge. Faith is not an end in itself, it is only a preliminary disposition, by means of which reason is capable of deducing *a priori* all truths, whether natural or supernatural. It increases in intensity with knowledge ; to use the philosopher's favourite figure, it is like oil which ever mounts with water but never mixes with it. Various works follow out the application of these principles and undertake the detailed demonstration of dogmas.

Lully claimed to have discovered a logical method which he called the *Ars magna, scientia generalis*, and which in his opinion completed the ordinary methodology of the scholastics. The latter starts with sensible observation (*ascensus, scientia cum sensu et imaginatione*) and stops at corporeal things. Now there is another order of knowledge independent of the former, which has for its object suprasensible realities (*descensus, supra sensum et imaginationem*) : this is the divine knowledge of general principles (*principia alta et profunda*), which Lully identifies with the attributes of the Divine essence. All the errors of Averrhoism rest, in his opinion, on a confusion between these two methods of knowledge, and on the abusive appli-cation to suprasensible things of ideas taken from the world of bodies. The *Ars magna* is a combination of these general principles : it sets out general tables of ideas (*termini*), which only need to be combined according to a special method in order to attain to knowledge. At first these tables related to God (Figure A) and contingent being (Figure S), each figure consisting of a certain number of heads of ideas, the Divine

THIRD PERIOD

MEDIÆVAL PHILOSOPHY IN THE FOURTEENTH AND THE FIRST HALF OF THE FIFTEENTH CENTURY

contra Gentiles in his treatise Περί ουσίας καὶ ἐνεργείας.
GEORGIOS SCHOLARIOS, who was Patriarch of Constantinople
from 1453 to 1459 with the title of Gennadios II, translated
the *Summulæ* of Petrus Hispanus, the *De sex principiis* of
Gilbert de la Porrée, the *De ente et essentia* and the commentary
on *De anima* of St. Thomas, and in addition made an abridgement of the *Prima Secundæ* of the *Summa Theologica;*
DEMETRIUS KYDONES translated the *Summa contra gentiles*
(1335), the *Summa theologica* and various *opuscula;* PROCHORUS
made a translation of the *De mundi æternitate.*

357. Jewish Philosophy.—During the first half of the
fourteenth century, the Jews in the south of France continued
to translate Averrhoes from the Arabic into Hebrew. CALONY-
MUS OF ARLES, SAMUEL BEN JUDA BEN MESCHULLAM OF
MARSEILLES, and TODROS TODROSI OF ARLES were the chief
translators in this later school. There were also translations
from Latin into Hebrew of scholastic treatises by Albert the
Great, Thomas Aquinas, and Giles of Rome.[1]   LEVI BEN
GERSON (born about 1288) and MOSES OF NARBONNE were
the principal philosophers of this Provençal school. They
wrote commentaries on Averrhoes, and original works in
which they fostered the rationalist tendency inaugurated by
Maimonides. Thus Levi ben Gerson unhesitatingly admits
the eternity of the world.[2]

358. Western civilization.—Western civilization underwent
profound modifications, and these had their effect upon
philosophy : from the dawn of the fourteenth century the
powerful unitive organization of the preceding epoch began
to break up, and all the mental connections between the
European peoples all began to weaken.

(i) *The political situation.* In politics, the ideal of a universal
monarchy as dreamt of by Dante was manifestly unrealizable.
Instead of amorphous peoples governed by kings there were
organized nations, each of which became the spiritual home
of a temperament distinguishing it from the nations surrounding it. Europe took a nationalist appearance. The Hundred
Years' War increased the distance dividing the two ethnic
groups which hitherto had been at the head of civilization.

---

[1] Renan, *op. cit.*, pp. 190 *et seq.*
[2] Of Levi ben Gerson, Renan writes : " To some extent his glosses became
inseparable from the text of Averrhoes, just as the commentary of Averrhoes
was from the text of Aristotle " (*op. cit.*, p. 193).

It was not a mere quarrel between princes, or a family feud between rival sovereigns, but a conflict which divided the French and English peoples and accentuated their antipathies. Under the reign of the centralizing kings such as Philip the Fair and Edward III, France and England were organized interiorly, and in this respect also displayed their own peculiar tendencies. The same is true of Germany, Spain and Italy, which began progressively to play their part in the new state of things in the measure that France ceased to exercise her intellectual leadership.

Another phenomenon appeared side by side with the formation of nationalities, namely, the awakening of the popular consciousness. Parliaments lifted up their voice against the feudal monarchs, and the Conciliar movement began to oppose the Papacy. Kings and Popes were deposed, and these depositions were followed by wars or conflicts provoked by the fallen rulers. The rebellion of the German Emperor and other kings against the political sovereignty of the Popes was another manifestation of nationalism. Philip the Fair, the most Christian King of France, openly declared war on Boniface VIII. The epoch of lay claims began. Publicists and lawyers worked together to destroy the supra-national situation of the Papacy created by the canonists of the preceding age.

Lastly, a big cloud darkened the eastern horizon : the fall of Constantinople in 1453 threatened Europe with invasion on the part of the Turks and Islam.

(ii) *The religious situation.* The fourteenth century witnessed events of grave import for Christianity, and revealed the progressive weakening of religious unity. Within the Catholic Church the ravages of the Great Schism of the West (1378-1417) lowered the prestige of the Papacy. The conflict came to an end in 1415 with the vote of the Council of Constance proclaiming the superiority of a General Council over the Pope, the enforced resignation of John XXIII, the abdication of Gregory XII, and the election of one Pope, Martin V.

In this same year, 1415, John Huss was condemned, a sufficient indication of the extent to which religious questions affected people's minds. This leads us to a second fact : the first beginnings of Protestantism. Wyclif at Oxford and John Huss at Prague, who stood in the front of a doctrinal agitation, undermined the very principle of ecclesiastical authority. They desired nothing but the direct and mystical

M

relations uniting the faithful to Christ, without the intervention
of the existing hierarchy. In their theories we detect the first
rumblings of the Reform.

Moreover, mysticism, which underwent so great a development in the fourteenth century (Chapter V), helped in a certain
measure to favour the idea of the Christian life as something
quite internal, over which the Church's organization had, so
to speak, no control.

(iii) *The state of society and the arts.* The intense development of commerce in France and England, Flanders and
Italy, brought into existence a new social order, the Middle
Class, which was the seat of wealth and influence. On the
other hand, cataclysms such as the Great Plague and the
famine led to discontent and popular risings.[1]

The imitative arts lost their intellectualist tendencies and
aspired to realism and emotion ; Gothic architecture departed
from the law of parsimony and gave free scope to ornamenta-
tion.

(iv) *The state of studies.* (1) The university of Paris lost
its cosmopolitan character. It became a French university,
and the stream of foreigners going to Paris was very much
diminished.

There was also a relaxation of studies. The faculty of
theology became the seat of intrigues, and made light of
regulations. By means of recommendations, or even in return
for money, the " actus scolastici " were facilitated, the years
of study shortened, and examinations made a mere matter
of form. Students and graduates increased in number, but
many were attracted by the prospect of obtaining ecclesiastical
benefices. The faculty of arts displayed a similar laxity.
Scholastic exercises were shortened, and ignorant beardless
youths were allowed to occupy the chair. " Categorias,
perihermeneias, in cujus scriptura summus Aristoteles calamum
in corde tinxisse confingitur, infantili balbutie resonant
impuberes et imberbes."[2]

Other causes contributed to the decline of the University
of Paris. Not to mention the wars with the Flemish and
the English, and the terrible plague which raged in the middle

---

[1] In 1377 there was a revolt of English peasants ; in 1378 a revolt of dis-
enfranchised at Florence ; in 1382 the revolt of the Maillotins at Paris.

[2] Ricardus de Bury, *Philobiblon,* 1344, c. ix, p. 87 (1888 edition), quoted
in *Chart.,* II, p. viii.

of the fourteenth century,[1] there was the competition of other universities.[2] In the thirteenth century the universities of Paris, Oxford and Cambridge could alone confer the mastership in theology, but now other " studia generalia " sprang up and obtained or even usurped the power of conferring degrees in theology.

The decadence of the University of Paris was most marked at the time of the Great Schism, although at no moment of its history did the University enjoy so great an external prestige, or boast so much of its position. The intellectual hegemony of the Colleges of the Sorbonne and Navarre alone recalled the glorious past. This unfortunate situation led to some extent to the departure of many famous masters, who transferred the benefit of their fame to other universities to which they attached themselves. Thus Henry of Hesse went to Vienna, Marsilius of Inghen to Heidelberg. During the first half of the fifteenth century, the university continued to play a part in the politics of France. Finally Charles VI took away its independence, and in 1446 it became subject to Parliament. The rules of the faculties were reformed in 1452 by Cardinal d'Estouteville.

(2) The multiplication of universities.[3] Already in the thirteenth century *studia generalia* were created at Padua (1222), Naples (1224), and Salamanca. Beginning with the fourteenth century, they were instituted everywhere in German-speaking countries : at Vienna (1365), Cologne (1389), Heidelberg (1386), Erfurt (1392), Leipzig (1409), Fribourg (1456), Basle (1460), Ingolstadt (1472), Tubingen (1477), Wittenberg (1502). Prague had its university in 1348, Cracovie in 1397, Rostock in 1419, Louvain in 1425. In France centres of studies were instituted at Dol (1421-22), Poitiers (1431-32), Caen (1432), Bordeaux (1439-41). All these fourteenth and fifteenth century universities were national or even local in character.

From the fourteenth century onwards, Paris gradually lost the monopoly of philosophic training.

(3) The modifications in the regulations of the older universities, and the statutes adopted in the new institutions had their influence on the direction of theological and philosophical

[1] *Chart.*, II, p. xii.
[2] *Chart.*, III, pp. xiv, xv.
[3] Denifle, *Die Universitäten d. Mittelalters bis* 1400.

studies inasmuch as they affected the technique of teaching.[1]
Thus, as Ehrle points out, the commentators on the Lombard
henceforth treated the text with greater freedom ; they introduced new and difficult questions, changed the divisions, made
use of a complicated terminology, and seemed to address
their teaching no longer to beginners but to masters accus-
tomed to finesse and subtleties.[2] In the same way the hyper-
trophy of dialectical exercises in the faculty of arts at Paris
is directly connected with the progress of sophistry brought
into favour by the nominalists.

The fourteenth century saw the beginning of the regime
of an official philosophy in the universities. The foundation
statutes of the new universities, and the decisions taken by the
faculty of arts in the older institutions, imposed either Ockamism or Thomist or Scotist realism, and princes, kings, and
Parliaments intervened to forbid or impose some particular
philosophic position in philosophy. These statutes and decrees
gave rise to quarrels, incidents and complaints, and never had
very much result, for ideas do not lend themselves to government by decree. In spite of regulations, the masters did not
cease to teach what they pleased, and in one and the same
university the current of opinion changed from one epoch
to another.

(4) The religious orders continued to devote attention to
philosophy and theology, and remained in close relations with
the universities. It is true that they had special houses for
the study of the arts, but their theological activity was displayed in the theological faculties of the universities, in
which they naturally came under the influence of the current
ideas.

In general we may say that zeal for studies diminished in
the religious orders, and that at the same time discipline also
became relaxed.[3] The end of the fourteenth century was a
period of schools, and very few of these attained to more than
mediocrity.

359. The echo of the new situation in philosophy.—Just
as the European states shook off the yoke of the Papacy, so

---

[1] The university regulations of the fourteenth century are not sufficiently
known. Ehrle has in preparation an edition of the statutes of the Faculty
of Theology of Bologna from 1362. *Der Sentenzenkommentar P. v. Candia*,
p. 27.

[2] p. 26.

[3] *Chart.*, II, p. xi.

also philosophy manifested a tendency to loosen its connection with theology, if not to break away altogether.

On the other hand, the new political situation helped to develop the study of everything connected with the organization of the State.

The Great Schism was naturally the occasion for discussions on the Pontifical supremacy, the rights of a General Council representing the body of the faithful, and the function of such a Council in the settlement of the crisis. These discussions made themselves heard above all in the University of Paris. There it was taught that one might take refuge in the different obediences provided one were willing to submit later on to the true Pope, but the pressure of events made men more and more disposed to attribute to the faithful a part in the government of the Church, and to apply to the latter the democratic principles underlying group life. Again, the Universities of Oxford and Prague were the seat of the learned discussions of John Huss and Wyclif on the conception of the Church itself.

As commerce developed, so philosophy began to deal with questions concerning economics, such as usury, interest and money.

Even the changes in the organization of the University of Paris were not without their effect upon philosophy : Scholasticism, which had taken part in its development, suffered with its decline.

360. Division of Western philosophy.—As in the preceding period, we shall study successively :

(1) The group of scholastic philosophies (Chapter 11).

(2) The group of anti-scholastic philosophies (Chapter III).

(3) The independent systems (Chapter IV).

Mysticism underwent an extraordinary development, but strictly speaking this concerns the history of theology (Chapter V).

361. Bibliography.—See works referred to in No. **140**. The work of Gregory Palamas was re-edited by Halix in 1885. Commentaries of Sophonias in the *Commentaria in Aristotelem Græca*, XXIII, Berlin, 1883-84. Cf. Elter and Radermacher, who have edited the κατὰ τῶν λεγομένων περὶ τοῦ κριτηρίου τῆς ἀληθείας εἰ ἐστὶ παρὰ Πύρρωνος τοῦ καταράτου of Nicholas Cabasilas (Progr. Bonn, 1899). Renan, *op. cit.*, Part II, ch. i; M. Rackl, *Demetrios Kydones als Verteidiger u. Uebersetzer des*

hl. Thomas v. A. (Katholik, 1915) ; *Die ungedruckte Ver-*
teidigungsschrift des D. K. für Th. v. Aquin genen. N. Kabasilas
(*Divus Thomas*, 1920); *Die Griechische Ubersetzung d. theol.*
Summa des hl. Thom. (*Byzantinische Zeitschr.*, 1922); *Eine*
griechische Abbreviatio der la 2ae des hl. Thom. (*Divus Thomas*,
1922).

On the universities see *Chartularium Univ. Paris*, Vol. II,
et seq. ; important contributions in Ehrle, *Der Sentenzenkom-*
mentar Peters von Candia, der Pisaner Papstes Alexanders
V. Ein beitrag z. Scheidung d. Schulen in d. Scholastik d. XIVe
Jahrh. und zur Geschichte d. Wegenstreites (Munster, 1925.
Beiheft 9 Franc. Stud.). This work is also full of information
on the intellectual movement of the fourteenth century.
Huizinga, *Herbst des Mittelalter*, Studien über Lebens-u.
Geistesformen d. 14. u. 15. Jahrh (translated from Dutch),
Munich, 1924.

CHAPTER II

The Group of Scholastic Philosophical Systems

Art. I—General Notions

362. The decline of scholastic philosophy followed closely on its period of maturity. Various causes combined to undermine it and brought about a slow but uninterrupted disintegration.

(i) The *lack of originality* was a first symptom of exhaustion. It is indeed true that Nominalism or Terminism was a new scholastic system noteworthy in many respects, but it appeared at the beginning of the fourteenth century, and the men who were at its head had been nourished with the strong meat of the thirteenth century. It is also true that under the pressure of circumstances the scholasticism of the fifteenth century dealt with economic problems, and solved them in accordance with the principles of its moral teaching, and it is possible that the tremendous social movement which made itself felt in the fourteenth century helped to contribute to that revival of moral studies in university centres to which the regulations bear witness.[1] But this was only one special department, affecting a comparatively small number of personalities.

It still remains true that the great majority of those who dealt with philosophy from 1300 to 1450 lacked originality. They enrolled themselves in some school, chiefly in one of the three great schools of Terminists, Scotists or Thomists ; they were content to follow the ideas of others, or even to make

---

[1] The *Nicomachean Ethics*, which according to the decrees of Robert of Courçon (1215) was explained in extraordinary courses, because part of the ordinary and obligatory teaching by the statute of 15th June, 1366. We find the same obligatory teaching at Prague (statutes of 1366 and 1389), and at Vienna (statutes of 1390-1399). The University reform at Paris in 1452 lays down for the examination of a licentiate " quod audiverit libros morales, specialiter librum Ethicorum, quantum ad majorem partem."

a summary of the teaching of some master in a *compendium*. As schools increased in number, so individual thought became more rare. Compared to the thirteenth century, which was full of personalities, the fourteenth and fifteenth centuries were poor in men of mark. It is not without interest to note that a similar phenomenon manifested itself in the evolution of Gothic architecture, which lived henceforth on formulæ and copies.

In spite of all this, the number of those who devoted their attention to philosophy increased tremendously.[1] The multiplication of universities facilitated the study of philosophy, and whole orders threw themselves into controversies.

In connection with the multiplication and extension of schools we may mention the custom, which spread greatly, of awarding honorific titles. Up to the middle of the fourteenth century, these titles were awarded rarely, and only to eminent names. *Doctor communis* (or *sanctus*), *doctor subtilis*, *doctor solemnis*, *doctor profundus* designated Thomas Aquinas, Duns Scotus, Henry of Ghent, and Thomas Bradwardine, respectively. But in the fifteenth century the list of doctors became much longer, each philosophic group and every religious order chose its patron, while in the sixteenth century genealogies were fabricated and biographies invented.[2]

The constitution of the three principal schools, Terminism Thomism and Scotism, affected the tone of the discussions between their partisans. Controversy became bitter and aggressive, with personal allusions and strong expressions.

(ii) *The breaking up of the scholastic patrimony*. Although the new system founded by William of Ockam utilized the doctrinal heritage built up in the preceding century, it rejected important parts. The passionate quarrels between Terminists, Scotists and Thomists upset the economy of the fundamental theories. In theology as in philosophy, they introduced an imaginative, artificial, and even irrational element into discussions. We get the impression that in certain cases they argued for argument's sake, and that the opponents in question

---

[1] In 1406 the Faculty of Arts at Paris alone numbered more than a thousand *magistri* and ten thousand members (*supposita*). (*Chart.*, III, p. 604).

[2] See Ehrle and Pelster, studies mentioned in Vol. One, p. 324.

were not so far distant from each other as they said and would have us believe.[1]

Equally damaging to scholasticism was the ignorance of those who undertook to serve it. William of Ockam, and his first followers and opponents, knew the philosophic systems of the past, but the subsequent generations were increasingly ignorant of them. Among the numerous promotors of novelties we find young men who had not found time to study.

(iii) *The gradual spread of an exaggerated dialectics.* In the scholasticism of the thirteenth century, logic was a mental discipline which prepared the way for other philosophical studies. But the *Summulæ* of Petrus Hispanus introduced a great number of questions of pure dialectics the bearing of which is not apparent, but which were put in the forefront and became the fashion. At the same time the didactic method began to change. Distinctions and subdistinctions were multiplied, to the detriment of clarity. The Terminists and Scotists were mainly responsible for this increasing obscurity. The same is true of—

(iv) *The decadence of language.* The sober and precise language of the thirteenth century was abandoned. Barbarisms, which up till then had only appeared sporadically, and mainly in translations from Arabic into Latin, increased in number ; and even orthography betrayed an ignorance of Latin.[2]

363. Division.—The Thomist (Art. IV) and Scotist schools (Art. III) were already in existence at the beginning of the fourteenth century, but a third school, that of the Terminists, came into existence a few years after the death of Duns Scotus and obtained a considerable success (Art. II). Other schools, less influential, occupied an honourable place in the movement of ideas (Art. V). The development of political and social philosophy calls for special mention (Art. VI).

364. Bibliography.—Willmann, *Gesch. d. Ideal.*, II, 80-85 ; Werner, *Die Scholastik d. späteren Mittelalters*, in four volumes : I, *J. D. Scotus ;* II, *Die nachscotische Scholastik ;* III, *D. Augustinismus d. späteren Mittelalters ;* IV, *Der Endausgang*

---

[1] See for instance the discussion concerning the *esse subjectivum et objectivum*, which will be referred to later on.

[2] *Chart.*, III, Introd., p. xi. During the last quarter of the fourteenth century, there was a revival at the University of Paris. A few distinguished men, among whom we must mention above all Nicholas Poillevillain (de Clamengis), John of Montreuil (de Monsterolio), Peter d'Ailly, John Gerson and John Courtecuisse (Breviscoxae), made a vigorous effort to purify scientific Latin. Unfortunately their work did not last (*ibid.*, p. xii).

d. mittelalt. Scholastik. See also works by Ehrle (**361**) and Duhem.

Art. II—The Terminist or " Nominalist " School

§ 1—*General notions.*

365. General characteristics.—(i) *The simplification of metaphysics.* The Terminism of the fourteenth century arose out of a reaction against the formalism of Duns Scotus and the exaggerations of his disciples. The latter ascribed reality to all the content of their thought, and multiplied the apparatus of metaphysics. The terminist reaction was equally excessive. They adopted the motto : " pluralitas non est ponenda sine necessitate,"[1] and under the guise of attacking Scotism they commenced to destroy fundamental principles of metaphysics. The rejection of the metaphysical framework which had been looked upon as necessary by Thomas Aquinas and Duns Scotus resulted in a strengthening of individualism. Terminalist nominalism devoted all its attention to the singular, or individual which alone exists, and to direct experience (sensible or intellectual) which alone grasps it.

At the same time the Terminists adopted from Duns Scotus certain doctrines which the latter himself had inherited from the past, or constructed a characteristic attitude of mind out of the incidental criticisms which he directed against the demonstrative value of certain arguments. (iii).

(ii) *The encroachment of dialectics*, which characterized the scholastic output of the fourteenth and fifteenth centuries as a whole, was more manifest in the Nominalist school than anywhere else. For nominalist terminism, having robbed metaphysics, enriched logic with its spoils. That which was declared to be an illusion in the world of reality became the subject matter of dialectical combinations. Already William of Ockam made much of such logico-grammatical notions as *suppositio, significatio*, etc., but he retained a sense of measure. His disciples exploited the new material of the *Summulæ* of Petrus Hispanus, and abandoned themselves to a orgy of

---

[1] The formula was not peculiar to William of Ockam. It was in current use in the thirteenth century. Thorburn, *The Myth of Occam's Razor* (*Mind,* July, 1918), De Wulf, *Civilization and Philosophy,* p. 110.

sophistry which the Faculty of Arts at Paris in vain endeavoured to check.[1]

(iii) *Mistrust of reason.* On the one hand philosophical terminism stressed the rights of pure reason and gave it an ascendancy over authority. But on the other hand it took pleasure in emphasizing the weakness of reason, and in contesting the demonstrative value of the arguments on which were based the fundamental theories of the moral and religious order. The number of theories said to be incapable of demonstration increased, and the circle of truths of pure faith was correspondingly enlarged. The result was a sort of humiliation and mistrust of reason. Subsequent generations exploited this mistrust, and were increasingly disposed to hold that everything in scholasticism was unsound.

(iv) The Terminists freely cultivated the experimental sciences, and in this they were consistent, for experience brings us into contact with the singular, and the singular alone matters. (i). The forerunners of modern science are found in their group.[2]

(v) We may add that Nominalism exercised equally important influences on the *development of theology.* It relegated the method of authority to the background, and subjected all dogmatic data to the speculations of reason. The application of new sophistic methods, the love of subtleties, the search for the bizarre and the study of the strangest possibilities, opened the door to all kinds of abuses.[3]

366. Division.—William of Ockam was the real founder of Terminism as a system, although he had precursors (§ 2). It was he who opened up the *via moderna,* and the extraordinary success of the new philosophy was really due to him (§ 4 and § 5).

§ 2—Durandus of St. Pourçain and Peter Aureolus.

Terminism had forerunners in Durandus of St. Pourçain and Peter Aureolus who deserted, the one from the Thomist, and the other from the Scotist camp.

---

[1] Prantl, *op. cit.,* IV, pp. 1 *et seq.*
[2] See works by Duhem.
[3] Ehrle, *op. cit.,* p. 111. Gerson, himself affected by Nominalism, complained in 1400 of the abuses introduced into theological studies. He wrote a letter, *De reformatione theologiæ,* published by Ehrle, p. 246 (see later on).

367. Durandus of St. Pourçain obtained the *licentia docendi* in 1312 at the Parisian convent of St. James, and there drew up in its first form the Commentary on the Sentences which was to lead to difficulties with his order. In this work he did not conceal his sympathies for Duns Scotus, and abandoned Thomism on several points, after the General Chapter of Saragossa had in 1309 declared the latter to be the official doctrine of the order. James of Metz seems to have acted in similar opposition to the chapter's decision, and his doctrinal connection with Durandus is very manifest.[1] Durandus left Paris in 1313 for the Papal Court of Avignon, where he was the *lector curiæ* for four years, but in this same year 1313, the Dominican Chapter held at Metz plainly referred to him in its decree that works spread abroad outside the order would be subject to censorship and revision. In point of fact a commission of censors presided over by Hervæus of Nedellec, drew up a list of 93 articles taken from the work of Durandus.[2] We do not know whether the Dominican chapter at Bologna (1315) which dealt with an over-daring *disputatio* by Ubertus Guidi, also discussed the case of Durandus, but the Chapter of Montepellier (1316) seems to have decided that his writings were not to be circulated without a list of points in which he abandons Thomism. Durandus then made a second version of his Commentary, which he completed at the latest in 1317. It contains *additiones* and *correctiones*, and in certain points obeyed the decision of his superiors.[3] From 1317 he took up administrative work, and became successively Bishop of Limoux (1317), Puy (1318), and Meaux (1326). He died in 1332.[4]

Among his other works we may mention, besides the *addiciones* to the first Commentary, the *Quodlibeta* delivered at Paris and Avignon, and a treatise *De habitibus* in which he defends the thesis that the faculties of sensitive life alone, to the exclusion of the intellect and will, are capable of *habitus*.

The *doctor resolutissimus*—such is the honorific title given to Durandus—was resolutely attacked by his brethren in religion, and notably by Hervæus of Nedellec (*Defensio doctrinæ D.*

---

[1] J. Koch, *Die Jahre 1312-1317 im Leben des Durandus de S. Porciano*, in *Miscellanea Ehrle*, 1924, Vol. I, p. 274.

[2] *Op. cit.*, pp. 277-284.

[3] On this double redaction see Michalski, *Die Vielfachen Redaktionen einiger Kommentäre zu P. Lombardus*, in *Miscellanea Ehrle*, I, p. 220.

[4] *Chart.*, II, pp. 225 and 718.

Thomæ, and treatises against Durandus's commentary on the
first and fourth books of the Sentences in its first redaction);
Peter of Palude (whose Commentary on the Sentences quotes
a great deal from Durandus), James of Lausanne (*Super
Sententias lectura thomasina*), John of Naples (*Quodlibet.,
Quæstiones ordinariæ*), Bernardus Lombardi, and Durandellus
(*Evidenciæ contra Durandum*). The Carmelites, Guy Terrien
and Gerard of Bologna attacked his teaching with equal
vigour.

In his Commentaries on the Sentences, Durandus teaches
conceptualism very clearly : he stresses the individuality of
things to the point of denying to the abstract concepts formed
by the mind any correspondence with extramental reality.[1]
The universal corresponds to nothing at all, and is reduced to
a thought-content, fabricated by the concept. It would be
puerile (*frivolum*) to ascribe to it a value in a realm in which
everything is marked with individuality.[2] Again, the understanding of the singular is the primordial form of intellectual
knowledge (" primum cognitum ab intellectu non est universale
sed singulare ").[3]

The intentional *species*, which Durandus seems to have confused with the *id quod cognoscitur*, is declared to be superfluous
for sensation as for thought,[4] and hence the active intellect is a
needless fiction.[5] Since there are only individuals and it is
idle to ask how a form can be multiplied, there is no reason for
regarding quantified matter as the foundation of individuation.
It is the union of the two constituent principles, *hæc materia*
and *hæc forma*, that constitutes the corporeal individual.[6]
The question of individuation vanishes, and that of individuality alone remains.[7]

Durandus, as we see, did not hesitate to attack Thomism
openly, and in fact his motto was to prefer reason to the
authority " cujuscunque doctoris quantumcumque celebris vel
solemnis."[8] He was an independent thinker who became the

---

[1] Vol. I, p. 101.
[2] " Frivolum est dicere quod universalitas fiat in rebus quia universalitas
non potest esse in rebus, sed solum singularitas." (*In II Sent.*, d. 3, q. 7, 8,
in Lyons edition, 1595).
[3] *Ibid.*
[4] *Ibid.*, d. 3, q. 6. 11-13.
[5] " Fictitium est intellectum agentem ponere," q. 7, 8.
[6] Q. 2, 14-16.
[7] Vol. I, p. 279, n. 1.
[8] Prologue.

head of a school for the time being, and lived to see his teaching followed at Paris and at Salamanca.

368. Peter Aureoli, of French origin, was the author of Commentaries on the Sentences (in two editions), *Quodlibeta*, and treatises *De paupertate et usu paupere*, and *De principiis*. About 1304 he attended the lectures of Duns Scotus at Paris, and then became successively lector at Bologna (1312) and at Toulouse (1314), bachelor (1316) and master of theology at Paris (1318), Franciscan minister for Aquitaine (end of 1320), and Bishop of Aix in 1321 until his death (before the 23rd January, 1322).[1]

Aureoli endeavoured to construct a personal system of philosophy based directly on St. Augustine, Averrhoes and Aristotle, and to improve on the ideas of the *doctores moderni* or contemporary scholastics. The theory of universals constitutes one of the fundamental points in his system. General concepts of specific differences and genera differ from one another only in their degree of clearness, they do not refer to irreducible determinations in a being, but to one and the same individual reality. As for the notion of *species*, this has no other content than the qualitative resemblances between various beings (" conceptus qualitativi et similitudinarii "). In a system like this the problem of the multiplicity of individuals (*coindividua*) in one and the same species is meaningless.

Aureoli's conceptualism was directed both against the moderate realism of Thomists and the *formalitates* of Duns Scotus, which Aureoli regards with contempt (*illud refugium*) and which he condemns in the name of the principle of parcimony.[2]

Not only does he deny any extramental value to abstract and general knowledge : even in the intuitive knowledge which he contrasts with the former he introduces a measure of phenomenalism. Normally intuitive knowledge, sensible or intellectual, presents us with a real and existing object ; but God could, in the absence of real beings, create in sensation and intellectual intuition a content which would give us the illusion of its existence.

---

[1] *Chart.*, II, 225, 718. See R. Dreiling, *Der Konceptualismus in der Universalienlehre des Franziskanererzbischof Petrus Aureoli* (*Pierre d' Auriole*) *nebst biograph.-bibliograph. Einleitung, BGPM*, XI, 6.

[2] " Multitudo ponenda non est, nisi ratio evidens necessaria illud probet, aliter per pauciora salvari non posse." (*In II Sent.*, 189 a. Cf. C. Dreiling, *op. cit.*, p. 205).

The ideology of the *doctor facundus* sacrifices the *species*, or rather identifies it completely with the psychological act of knowing ; whence it follows that a distinction between the *species impressa* (the action of the object upon the subject) and *expressa* (the reaction of the subject) has no meaning. At the same time, this psychological act of knowledge (*esse subjectivum*) has a representative content, an *object* in the etymological sense of the word, *id quod objicitur*. Aureoli calls it an *esse objectivum*. This *esse objectivum* is characterized by a stability and a uniformity which contrasts with the changing and multiple aspects of the successive and numerous psychological acts which attain to it. Some contemporaries of Peter Aureoli [1] did not admit this distinction between an act of knowledge and its content, for the latter, in their view, has no reality apart from this act itself. The controversy was an empty one, and turned on shades of meaning, [2] but the authors of the early fourteenth century found it a pleasant theme, and it provides an example of the subtleties in which scholasticism wandered and lost itself.

Like Durandus, Peter Aureoli denied the distinction between essence and existence. He went further by refusing any demonstrative value to the proofs advanced for the thesis that the soul is the form of the body. [3]

The scattered elements of Terminism in Peter Aureoli and Durandus were built up into an organized system by William

---

[1] C. Michalski, *Les sources du criticisme et du scepticisme dans la philosophie du XIVe siècle* (extract from La Pologne au Congres international de Bruxelles, Cracovie, 1924), p. 11-15, shows that on this point Peter Aureoli follows James of Esculo.

[2] Michalski attaches great importance to this controversy. He denotes as " logical conceptualism " and " psychological conceptualism " the thesis of those who distinguished or identified the *esse objectivum* and *subjectivum*. This discussion seems to us to be of secondary importance. In the first place it has no criteriological bearing, for it does not in any way deal with the value of a representation, or the correspondence between the object conceived and the real object (Michalski himself admits this on p. 24, and so abandons the foundation for his appellation of conceptualism). In the next place, even those who identify the *esse objectivum* with the *esse subjectivum* do not deny that knowledge has a content (for otherwise it would cease to be knowledge), but they wish to identify the content with the psychological event. Hervæus of Nedellec, mentioned by Michalski as upholding " logical conceptualism," clearly teaches the *esse objectivum* in these words : " intellectum existens *in prospectu* intellectus." This is the very meaning of *ob-jectum* (*id quod menti objicitur*, content of representation). On the other hand, the *species* is " *subjective in intellectu.*" (*Op. cit.*, p. 11).

[3] Together with Peter Aureoli we may mention William Farinier, the minister-general of the Franciscans (1348-1357) and Cardinal, author of *Quæstiones de ente* dealing with metaphysics and psychology. See E. Longpré, *Melanges histor. de théol. franciscaine*, in *La France francisc.*, 1922, p. 436.

of Ockam. He knew the works of Peter Aureoli, but tells us
that he gave them only a hasty reading, and that at the time
when he had himself almost completed the redaction of his
first book of Sentences.[1]

369. Bibliography.—The second redaction of the Commentary on the Sentences and the *Quodlibet* of Aureoli were
published at Rome in 1596 and 1605 ; the commentaries of
Durandus appeared in numerous editions in the sixteenth
century. On Durandus, Aureoli and William of Ockam, see
Werner, *Die nachscot. Scholastik,* each chapter of which examines
a group of doctrines. N. Valois, *P. Aureol, frère mineur* (*Hist.
Litt. France,* Vol. 33, 1901), deals with life and works, super-
ficial judgments on his doctrine. See also works mentioned
in notes ; Dreiling, *op. cit.* (good), and Michalski.

§ 3—*William of Ockam.*

370. Life and works.—William the Franciscan, was born
about 1300 at Ockam in Surrey, studied at Oxford from
1312 to 1318, and taught there as a bachelor until 1324.
The bachelors at Oxford who did not go on to the mastership
were known as *inceptors,* and this explains the title *venerabilis
inceptor* given to Ockam by his admirers.[2] His progress to the
doctorate was perhaps barred by the boldness of his views,
for already in 1324 he was summoned to the Court of Avignon
to give an account of his philosophy, and consigned to the
convent of his order. From this time the Papacy took alarm
at the theories he put forward in his commentaries on the
Sentences,[3] and Cardinal James of Furno seems to have been
instructed to examine them.[4] Moreover, we possess a report
in 1326 of the masters of theology to whom John XXII entrusted

---

[1] Ockam, *In I Sent.,* d. 27, q. 3. " Pauca vidi de dictis illius doctoris . . .
Quam materiam tractavi et fere omnes alias de primo libro."
[2] Ehrle, *Die Sentenzenkommentar P. von Candie,* p. 82. He mentions other
inceptores, and in particular Cowton, Chatton, William of Alnwick, and
Olivi (p. 83). J. Hofer, *Biographische Studien ueber W. von Ockham* (*Archiv.
franc. histor.,* 1913, p. 209, 439, 654) destroys many legends concerning his
life. In particular he shows that Ockam was not a disciple of Scotus, did not
obtain the degree of master in theology, and did not teach at Paris.
[3] In 1329, John XXII wrote of him : " Contra quem . . . pendebat
inquisitio auctoritate nostra jam erat diu in eadem curia inchoata." (Ehrle,
op. cit., p. 84, n. 1). This process had nothing to do with the case of the
Spirituals and the quarrel over evangelical poverty. (*Ibid.*).
[4] *Ibid.,* p. 88 *et seq.*

the task of judging a series of 51 articles taken from the works of the Franciscan master. The " pestilential teaching " referred to the judgment of the Holy See concerns not only theology but also logic, natural philosophy, psychology and metaphysics. Pelzer has identified in the master's works the passages referred to.[1] The case dragged on but did not end in a condemnation. The subtle theories of the English bachelor were elusive and difficult to make clear, and this is perhaps the reason why he did not share the fate of so many other theologians and philosophers before and after his time. In the fifteenth century the Parisian Ockamists made the most of this abortive inquiry.[2]

In 1328 William championed the cause of the Spirituals against John XXII ; and in May of the same year, together with Michael of Cesena, General of his order, and Bonagratia of Bergamo, he left Avignon and went to the Emperor Louis of Bavaria at Pisa, where two years previously other malcontents, John of Jandun and Marsilius of Padua had taken refuge. William and his friends were excommunicated in June, 1328. He accompanied the Emperor Louis of Bavaria to Munich and stayed there. About 1334 his antipapal activity reached its climax. After the death of Louis of Bavaria he tried to be reconciled with his order and with the Church. He died in 1348 or shortly after.

His career was a scientific, political, and religious one. He wrote his great work *Super lib. IV sententiarum* at Oxford, and therefore before 1324. This, together with the *Quodlibeta*, Aristotelian commentaries (*Expositio aurea super totam artem veterem*) and the *Summa totius logicæ*[3] contains his original theories. In conformity with the custom of the fourteenth century of which Gerson complained, the first book of the Sentences was the principal subject of the commentaries of William.[4] Some works on Physics are ascribed to him, and in

---

[1] A. Pelzer, *Les 51 articles de Guillaume d'Occam censurés à Avignon en 1326 (R. hist. eccles.*, 1922, pp. 240-269).

[2] Ehrle, p. 91. Thomas Claxton similarly writes : " Hockam vitat multoties suam exprimere opinonem," p. 79, n.

[3] The prologue tells us that this work was written at the invitation of his disciple Adam de Anglia (Adam Wodeham ?) The prologue of the latter is joined to that of William of Ockam in the edition of 1508 (Venice), the text of which was somewhat modified by the nominalist humanist Mark of Benevento. Ehrle, *op. cit.*, p. 99 *et seq.*, reproduces the two prologues.

[4] It was the custom of the " nominalists " of the fourteenth century to neglect the third and fourth books. Ehrle, *op. cit.*, pp. 77 and 92.

N

particular *Quæstiones super physicam* (unpublished).   The chronology of these various works is not definitely established.[1]

In the latter part of his career, William opposed the temporal rights and political supremacy of the Popes.   All historians record his salute to the haughty German emperor : " Tu me defendas gladio, ego te defendam calamo."   When Louis of Bavaria wanted to have the adulterous marriage of his son declared lawful in spite of the Church's decrees, William defended the absolute omnipotence of the State in political matters. From 1330 onwards he openly published work after work, the *Dialogus*, the *Opus nonaginta dierum*, the *Compendium errorum Joannis papæ XXII*, the *Quæstiones octo de auctoritate summi pontificis*, and *De Imperatorum et Pontificum potestate*.   The philosophy of William of Ockam forms a consistent whole, the framework of which is provided by psychology and metaphysics.

371. Psychology.—(i) Three theories sum up the ideological and criteriological position of William of Ockam : the intuitive knowledge of individuals, the theory of signs and terminism, and the suppression of the intentional species and the active intellect.

(*a*) William of Ockam like all other scholastics establishes a fundamental distinction between two orders of knowledge : sensation, which consists in the apprehension of phenomenal states by the senses and depends upon the corporeal organs ; and thought, which attains to the fixed and constituent element in things.   Sensation is intuitive ; thought is either intuitive or abstractive.   Ockam, then, adopts the Scotist doctrine of an intuitive intellectual knowledge having as its object the existence or non-existence of individual things, the inherence or non-inherence of qualities, and also the existence of internal subjective states such as joy and sorrow.[2]   But he

---

[1] In the Fourth Book of the Sentences, William identifies quantity with physical substance, a theory which led to his being accused of heresy, while in the *Summa logicæ* he sets forth this identification not as his own opinion but as that of Aristotle.   From this change of attitude Michalski infers that the *Summa* is later.   (*Les sources*, etc., p. 8.) Cf. F. Federhofer, *Ein Beitrag z. Bibliographie und Biographie W. von Ockams*, in *Philos. Jahrb.*, 1925, pp. 26-48).   P. of Candia also mentions treatises by William, *De principiis theologiæ* (taken perhaps from the Commentary on the prologue to the Sentences) and *De successivis*.   (Ehrle, *op. cit.*, p. 95).

[2] " Singulare . . . est primo cognitum . . . quia res extra animam quæ non est signum tali cognitione primo intelligitur." (Quodl. I, q. 3). " Notitia intuitiva est talis, quod . . . si Socrates in rei veritate sit albus . . . potest evidenter cognosci quod Socrates est albus." (*Sent.*, Prol. q. 1).

comes to very different conclusions when there is question of referring this collection of experimental and concrete facts to extramental reality. Moulded in these judgements, intuitive knowledge forms the basis of contingent truths, for instance, that Socrates is white, or that one feels sad. The abstract and universal concept is subsequent to intuitive knowledge, " notitia abstractiva præsupponit intuitivam," and either perceives a note attributable to a great number of things, or else represents some determination without adverting to the question of its existence.[1]

(b) All knowledge (intuitive sensible knowledge, and intuitive or abstract intellectual knowledge) is a sign (*signum*) which as such takes the place (*supponere*)[2] of the object signified. This sign, which is also called a term (*terminus*) is natural[3] in contrast with the artificial signs (*secundum institutionem voluntariam*) of language and writing.

What is the value of these signs ? What is their relation to the things signified and the beings to which they apply ? Here we must make a distinction : all intuitive knowledge, whether sensible or intellectual, attains to reality, as experienced. We must bear in mind this declaration : it will serve to defend the master against an exaggerated suspicion of subjectivism, although from another point of view it leads to this. For on the one hand it maintains an objective contact

---

[1] " Notitia abstractiva potest accipi dupliciter : uno modo quod sit respectu alicujus abstracti a multis singularibus . . . aliter . . . secundum quod abstrahit ab existentia et non-existentia." (*Sent.*, Prol. q. 1). " Notitia intuitiva est talis notitia virtute cujus potest sciri utrum res sit vel non sit. . . . Similiter notitia intuitiva est talis qua, quum aliqua cognoscuntur quorum unum inhæret alteri, vel unum distat ab altero loco . . . statim virtute illius notitiæ incomplexæ illarum rerum sciret, si res inhæreat vel non inhæreat, distet vel non distet, et sic de aliis veritatibus contingentibus." (*Quodl.* VI. q. 6.). " Propositio contingens potest cognosci evidenter ab intellectu, puta hec albedo est, et non per cognitionem abstractivam, quia illa abstrahit ab existentia per intuitivam. Ergo realiter differunt." (*Quod.*, V. q. 5.).

[2] The *suppositio personalis* is the substitute for an individual object thought of : the *suppositio simplex* takes the place of an object conceived abstractly. " Signum accipitur pro illo quod aliquid facit in cognitionem venire et natum est pro ipso supponere." (*Log.*, l.c., I, 1).

[3] " Intentio est quoddam in anima quod est signum naturaliter significans aliquid, pro quo potest supponere." (*Ibid.*, c. 12). " Quodlibet universale est intentio animæ, quæ secundum unam probabilem opinionem ab actu intelligendi non distinguitur ; unde dicunt, quod intentio qua intelligo homines est signum naturale significans hominem, ita naturale, sicut gemitus est signum infirmitatis vel doloris ; et est tale signum quod potest stare pro hominibus in propositionibus mentalibus." (*Summa tot. log.*, I, c. 15). Again : " intentio animæ dicitur universalis quia est signum prædicabile de multis." (*ibid.*, I, c. 14).

with existential being, and on the other, it introduces between this existential being and the knowing subject an intervening curtain (sign) which threatens accordingly to diminish the objectivity of knowledge.

Have abstract concepts the same value as intuitive concepts ? No, they apply to the object *as thought of*, not to the *real* object in itself, for the abstract does not exist *in any way* outside the mind. These internal representations do not correspond to anything outside : they are fabricated and combined together entirely by the understanding.[1]

But what then is their function ? Why have recourse to these artificial forms ? Ockam replies that they take the place (*supponere*) in the mind of the multitude of individual beings. They are symbols or mental labels which enable us to catalogue our views of real individuals, and to arrange them according to genera and species. Everything happens *as if* these notions applied to the individuals themselves, but in point of fact they do not attain to them.

It was objected to Ockam that according to his system knowledge is illusory, since it deals with universals which are nothing at all. In reply he admits that it is illusory in the sense that the object of science is not the chimera called the universal *reality*, but the universal term. Certainly the term is capable of application to a number more or less great of individual beings independent of each other ; but the object of thought behind the abstract term does not belong to the beings to which it is applied. Science is only extrinsically related with the real.

An epistemology like this contains all the germs of agnosticism. The abstract notion of being ceases to be univocal (Scotus) or analogical (St. Thomas), and hence God becomes inaccessible. The ideas of law, cause, and end are mental fabrications and hence do not affect either the world of bodies or that of our conduct. Such a doctrine destroys not only the reality of the *formalitates* with which the Scotists encumbered individual things, and which Ockam never tired of ridiculing (" hæc

---

[1] " Illud quod prædicatur de pluribus differentibus specie, *non est aliqua res quæ sit de esse illorum* de quibus prædicatur, sed est una intentio in anima naturaliter significans omnes illas res de quibus prædicatur." (*Expos. aur.*, Prædicab. de genere, quoted by Prantl, III, n. 789). " Et ideo genus non est commune pluribus per identitatem in eis, sed per quamdam communitatem signi, quomodo idem signum est commune ad plura signata." (*Expos. aurea.*, Prædic. de genere). " Et ideo non est universale nisi per significationam, quia est signum plurium." (*Log.*, I, 1, c. 14).

opinio videtur irrationalis ")[1] but also the reality of every abstract element to which the Thomists ascribe a foundation in the individual thing apart from the work of generalization to which it is subjected.

How should this series of doctrines be designated? The appellation " terministæ " appeared with Gerson, and about the end of the fourteenth century P. Nigri spoke of the " conceptistæ " whom he identified with the " nominales."[2] This latter designation prevailed at Cologne, where we meet with it from 1425, and at Paris, where it figured in official documents. The doctrine which we have just outlined combines the affirmations of conceptualism in the sense in which we have defined this (48, 49), and as elevated by Kant into a law of thought. We may keep the historic appellation of " nominalism " provided we remember the precise meaning the term had in the fourteenth century. To identify Ockam's nominalism with that of the eleventh century[3] or with modern nominalism would be to mispresent his system. His protests against those who regard the universal as a " hollow sound," *flatus vocis*, a *vox* without content[4] separates the system of the Franciscan master from that of the verbalists of the eleventh century (56). We should greatly err if we were to put him in the same category with the contemporary empiricists of every kind who reduced thought to sensation.[5] Although they are devoid of real value, abstract concepts retain their ideal value for Ockam, and the royal prerogative of the mind consists in building them up hierarchically into mental constructions.

It is worthy of note that the denominations " terminism," " conceptualism "[6] and " nominalism " refer only to one

[1] *Logica*, I, c. 16.

[2] Prantl, *Gesch. d. Logic*, IV, 146, 222. In the editions of P. Nigri (1494 and 1498, Bononiæ), William of Ockam is called " nominalium inceptor."

[3] The designation " nominales " was accordingly employed in two different periods and with two different meanings : in the eleventh and in the fourteenth centuries, and it is clear that fourteenth century writers were no longer thinking of Roscelin's party. We cannot admit with Ueberweg-Baumgartner (*op. cit.*, p. 599) that Ockam's teaching adopts—with the exception of the theory of the *suppositio*—the theories of Roscelin and Abelard. These are separated by an abyss. Ehrle holds the same opinion. (*op. cit.*, p. 107).

[4] " Quarta posset esse opinio quod nihil est universale ex natura sua, sed tantum ex institutione, illo modo quo vox est universalis . . . sed hæc opinio non videtur vera." (*In I. Sent.*, 1, dist. 2, q. 8).

[5] Empirical sensualism is foreign to the genius of scholasticism and to mediæval philosophy as a whole.

[6] Ehrle speaks of the conceptualism of Durandus and Aureoli, and of the terminism of William of Ockam ; the two former insist on the value of the general concept, and the third on its verbal expression. (*Op cit.*, p.

doctrine in Ockam's philosophy, namely, his epistemology. " Ockamism " is a much more comprehensive term.

(c) In Ockam's ideology, the collaboration between sensation and thought which is so close in the systems of the other scholastics becomes purely external : while the intuitive concept arises out of a direct contact with the real experienced, the abstract concept is a purely mental product which does not involve the causal intervention of sensation. What then could be the use of an *intellectus agens* ? Ockam crosses it out with a stroke of the pen.

At the same time he makes a bitter criticism of the intentional species which was utilized later on by the enemies of scholasticism. Understanding "species" in the peculiar and erroneous sense given to it by Henry of Ghent for example, he declines to account for the genesis of knowledge by the reception of an image issuing from the object.[7] Knowledge, he writes, is an immanent activity (*actus intelligendi*), and the act of knowing (*esse subjectivum*) is ultimately identical with its content (*esse objectivum*) inasmuch as the latter is that which constitutes the former.[8]

(ii) Following Scotus, William of Ockam professes an absolute voluntarism, but in a different sense. The will is independent of the intellectual presentation of the good. How could our real conduct be affected by combinations of concepts concerning ends, means, and morality, or in other words by the play of symbols created by the mind ? The will is invested with an absolute power of self-determination, decisions are independent of rational motives, and the spontaneous act is confused with the free act. Since the will is the very essence of the soul, and the essence of a thing does not admit of increase or diminution of itself, all variation in the degree of freedom is impossible : the question of the primacy of the will over knowledge becomes an idle one.

From another point of view, the will as the autocrat of mental life intervenes even in the discursive operations of the understanding, with which moreover it is identical, in accordance with the general theory of faculties.

(iii) As abstract knowledge is independent of sensations in the way indicated, Ockam is able to weaken the bonds uniting

108).   It goes without saying that in Ockam we find together with terminism as thus defined all the conceptualism of his predecessors.

[7] Vol. I, p. 293.

[8] *Quodl.*, V, q. 13.   Cf. Michalski, *Les sources*, etc., p. 17-20.

soul and body. Thus he finds place for three substantial forms : a form of corporeity, a sensitive soul, and an intellectual one. Hence " hominis est tantum unum esse totale," comprising " plura esse partialia." [1]

Moreover, the purely symbolical and subjective nature of our abstract and universal ideas cannot reveal the immaterial nature of the soul, and so the principal proof of its spirituality collapses. Furthermore, one could not prove that such an immaterial soul could be the form of a body. All these theses are to be accepted on faith. [2]

372. Metaphysics.—The fundamental principle of Ockam's metaphysics is that of a pronounced pluralism and individualism. Everything is individual. There is nothing similar or common between one individual and another. The universal does not exist in any way in nature, " nullum universale est extra animam existens realiter in substantiis individuis, nec est de substantia vel esse earum." [3] It is banished from metaphysics and transported into psychology and logic. Consequently the problem of individuation is meaningless, and it is not surprising that the states of individuality constitute the proper object of the human mind (against Thomism).

Having established this, Ockam proceeds to make a ruthless destruction of entities within each individual substance. In the first place, accidents are not distinct realities in the substance, but concepts or aspects of this substance. This is the case with quantity and extension. [4] For if quantity were other than prime matter, God could make this matter exist without quantity, and as such matter would still possess within itself parts situated outside each other, we should be forced to the contradictory concept of matter quantified and non-quantified at the same time. *A fortiori*, in quantity itself there can be no question of regarding with Walter Burleigh (Art. III) points, lines and surfaces as separate entities. [5]

Qualities in their turn are confounded with substances. Applied to man, the thesis leads to the absolute identification of the soul with its faculties. In the same way, the activities

---

[1] *Quodl.*, II, q. 10.
[2] *Quodl.*, I, 10. " Ista tria solum fide tenemus."
[3] *Expos. aurea prædicab.* Præmium. " Nullo modo est extra animam quodcumque universale." (*Quodl.* V, q. 12).
[4] These accordingly become identical with the essence of bodies, as in the system of Descartes.
[5] Doncœur, *R. sc. phil. et théol.*, 1921, p. 33 *et seq.*

structed in the thirteenth century. But he showed by what methods these could be attacked, and called forth the spirit of agnosticism.

377. Bibliography.—Ockam's Commentaries on the Sentences were published in 1483 and 1495 (Lyons); the *Quodlibet* in 1487 (Paris) and 1491 (Strasburg); the logical treatises appeared in several editions at Paris, Bologna, and Venice (fifteenth and sixteenth centuries). Biographical study by Hover. On the works on physics attributed to him, see Baur, *BGPM*, XVIII, 4-6. Detailed tables of the Commentaries on the Sentences in *Etudes franc.*, June, 1914. Pelzer *op. cit.* Political writings : edition of *Monarchia* II by Goldast, and R. Scholz, *Unbekannte Kirchenpol. Schriften aus d. Zeit Ludwig des Bayern*, II (Rome, 1914). Separate editions of the *Dialogus*. W. Mulder, *G. Ockham tractatus de Imper. et Pontificum potestate*, in *Arch. franc. hist.* 1924, pp. 72-97 and 469-492, publishes the last part of the treatise from a manuscript recently discovered.

On Ockam see general work of Stöckl, II, pp. 976 *et seq.*, and Prantl, III, pp. 331 *et seq.* Siebeck, *Occam's Erkenntnisslehre in ihrer historischen Stellung* (*Arch. Gesch. Phil.*, 1897, pp. 317 *et seq.*). Muschiotti, *Breve saggio sulla filos. di G. d'Ockam* Fribourg in Switzerland, 1908), A. Kühtmann, *Zur Gesch. d. Terminismus* (Leipzig, 1911), comparison between Ockam, Condillac, Helmholtz and Mauthner. F. Bruckmüller, *Die Gotteslehre W. v. O.* (Munchen, 1911), a dissertation ; L. Kugler, *Der Begriff d. Erkenntniss bei W. v. O.* (Breslau, 1913), a dissertation ; excellent study in Maréchal, *op. cit.* (see p. 35) ; P. Doncœur, *Le mouvement, temps et lieu d'après O.* (*R. de phil.*, May, 1921); *La relation chez O.* (*R. Neo-Scolastique*, 1921, p. 5); *La théorie de la matière et de la forme chez G. O.* (*R. sc. phil. theol.*, 1921, pp. 21-52). C. Michalski, *Les courants philosoph. à Oxford et à Paris pendant le XIVe. siècle* (Bull. acad. polon. sc. et lettres., Cl. hist., 1920) ; *Les source du criticisme* etc. (referred to in notes). Ehrle, *Die Sentenzenkommentar P. von Candie*, pp. 78-95, full of learned details.

§ 4—The *Via Moderna* at Oxford and Paris.

378. Strength and expansion of Ockamism.—The philosophy of William of Ockam had the success of a novelty and a reaction. It naturally appealed to doubting minds, and to all those who liked to find reason in default in presence of certain dogmas. It represented a new method, that of subtleties and dialectical *finesse*. It welcomed witticisms, tolerated irony, and allowed a common and even trivial phraseology—all liberties which rendered discussion more lively and attractive to young minds. Mental gymnastics became a kind of sport which the disciples of the *venerabilis inceptor* practised with more virtuosity than the master himself.

The Ockamists,[1] called by Peter of Candia *filii, sequaces, sequentes, imitatores Ockam*[2] formed a numerous group, representing the *via moderna* in contrast to the *via antiqua*. They were also known as *nominales* to distinguish them from the *reales*, a term which, as used by them, signified the Thomists as well as the Scotists. The whole doctrinal history of the universities in the fourteenth and fifteenth centuries consists of the conflict between the ancients (*reales*) and the moderns (*nominales*). In these centuries one was either for or against Ockamism : nobody overlooked it, and we may say that it represents the chief scholastic tendency of the time.

In the old universities of Oxford and Paris, the Faculty of Arts increased in importance, and the adherents of the new philosophy were above all drawn from the ranks of the artists. The same is true of the numerous universities of Central Europe, the organization of which was modelled on that of Paris. The Faculty of Arts was the principal seat of the quarrels between the two *viæ*, and these quarrels were clearly philosophical in character. Theologians were in general more circumspect. The intellectual members of the great mendicant orders, educated in the Arts in their religious houses but allowed to teach in the faculties of Theology, were generally speaking opposed to the innovations. Nevertheless we see prominent regulars passing over to Ockamism or preparing the way for it. Furthermore, even among the opponents of Ockamism there were men who, on one point or another, were affected by its sceptical spirit : suspicion became an element

---

[1] The term " Occhaniste " appears for the first time in 1341, in *Reg. procur. nat. Angl.* at Paris. " . . . Statutum facultatis contra novas opinione. quorundam, qui vocantur Occhaniste." (*Chart.*, II, 607 n., *Auctarium*, I. 44)

[2] Ehrle, *Die Sentenzenkommentar Peters v. Candia* etc., Munsters 1925, pp 78, 79.

in the intellectual atmosphere of many different circles of thought.[1]

The Ockamists of the fourteenth century were not all to the same extent disciples of the *venerabilis inceptor*. They appealed to his name but did not always follow his doctrine. Ockam had introduced a germ of dissolution into scholasticism, and stood for all sorts of critical and negative philosophies. Among these there were some which the Paris Faculty of Arts thought it its duty to forbid, but did not succeed in extirpating. Again, certain Ockamists were opposed by others.

379. Ockamism at Oxford.—Originating as it did at Oxford, Ockamism predominated there but did not obtain a monopoly.[2] Certain " artists " greatly developed logic and its subtleties. Among their number, WILLIAM OF HEYTESBURY and RICHARD BILLINGHAM (about 1344-1414) enjoyed a certain celebrity, and their logical treatises were adopted as classical manuals in several German universities.[3] About 1350 CLYMETON LANGLEY wrote *Sophismata*, and JOHN DUMBLETON of Merton College two treatises on Logic. These works well merit the qualification " subtilitates anglicanæ " found in Richard of Bury.[4] The love of sophistry and subtleties was so much the speciality of Oxford men that the university boasted of its superiority in this respect over every other rival institution.[5]

The Faculty of Theology, and in particular the regular masters, remained faithful to the cause of Duns Scotus, and St. Thomas. But even there the new ideas were welcomed.

ADAM WODEHAM (Voddam, Goddam) was one of the first disciples of Ockam.[6] After teaching at London, he commented on the Sentences at Oxford in 1332, shortly after the master's departure, became a doctor of theology, and died in 1358. His commentaries were abridged by HENRY OF OYTA (about

---

[1] William of Ware holds that reason cannot conclusively prove the Divine unity (255) ; John Reading allows that God could create illusions in our faculties ; Thomas Sutton does not think that one can demonstrate the Divine Omnipotence ; Thomas Claxton suspects the probative force of the arguments for the Divine unity and omnipotence. William de Rubione and John of Bassols show the weakness of the rational arguments for the existence of God, his unity, the incommunicability of his creative power, his omnipotence, the immortality of the soul, and free will.

[2] *Ibid.*, p. 241.

[3] *Ibid.*, p. 202, 205, 241.

[4] Ricardus de Bury, *op cit.*, under the year 1344, writes thus of the Parisian masters : "Anglicanas subtilitates, quibus palam detrahunt, vigiliis addiscunt." (*Ibid.*, p. 590, n.)

[5] " Mira scientiæ logicalis subtilitas qua præfata mater nostra super cætera mundi studia dignoscitur hactenus claruisse. (Ehrle, *op. cit.*, p. 241).

[6] " Imitator," says Peter of Candia, (Ehrle, *op, cit.*, p. 79, n. Cf. p. 96-103).

1370-1378) and this shortened form was published at Paris by John Major in 1512. This abridgement ought to be compared with the original redaction, which is still unpublished, in order to get a clear idea of Adam's teaching.[1] The rational proofs for the existence of God are regarded as unsatisfactory ; the soul is identified with its faculties, and the act of willing is not distinguished from that of thought.

ROBERT HOLCOT (died 1349) who taught at Cambridge and wrote on the Sentences, lays down the thesis that formulated judgements, and not real things, are the object of science ; he outlines the theological determinism afterwards developed by Bradwardine (414), and holds that God in virtue of His *potentia absoluta* could command man to hate Him.

Ehrle also mentions BRINKEL, an English Franciscan of the second half of the fourteenth century, who commented on the Sentences from an Ockamist point of view, and also wrote a *Logica*.[2]

It is hardly necessary to add that the theologians who, like Bradwardine and Baconthorp, opposed Scholasticism as a whole, found in Ockamism a good reason for their extreme doctrines.

380. Ockamism at Paris in the fourteenth century.—Paris was the second home of Ockamism, and, even more than Oxford, the place in which it took deepest root. This is shown by the number and character of the personalities occupying the history of the university in the fourteenth century.

The Faculty of Arts, ever increasing in importance, was in general favourable to Ockamism, and was quite ready to be influenced by it. As at Oxford, the realist reaction chiefly affected the theologians, who as we shall see were careful to repel the untimely incursions of philosophers into their domain. The theologians of the mendicant orders were best able to escape the Ockamist influence, for the seculars, who were in addition more numerous, were inclined to favour doctrines which they had learned to admire when studying the arts.

At Paris as elsewhere, Ockamism had its changes of fortune. Already in the beginning of the fourteenth century it encountered some resistance, and in the first place, on the part

---

[1] On these redactions see Michalski in *Miscellanea Ehrle*, I, 239, and above all Ehrle, *op. cit.*, p. 96. The identification with Adam de Anglia referred to in the Prologue to Ockam's *Logica* is doubtful. See above, p. 177.
[2] *Op. cit.*, p. 278.

of the Papacy. On the 8th May, 1317 Pope John XXII complained to the university of the tendency of many theologians
to devote themselves to philosophical subtleties.[1]   His actual
intervention, as well as his later action against Ockam himself,
was inspired by the preoccupation of maintaining the teaching
of Theology in all its purity in conformity with the " university
politics " of the Papacy.[2]   The same concern for theological
orthodoxy led Clement VI, in a letter addressed to the University in May, 1346, to renew the complaints of John XXII,
and to denounce the " extraneæ doctrinæ sophisticæ " which
led theologians astray into vain and doubtful discussions.
The Pope clearly alludes to the English origin of Ockamism,
and notices with regret that this sophistical teaching is welcomed in other Universities.[3]   The vagaries of Gregory of
Rimini (1344) justified these complaints, which were followed
by condemnations in 1347 when Nicholas of Autrecourt and
John of Mirecourt converted their Ockamism into antischolastic philosophy.

We are concerned still more with the steps taken by the
Faculty of Arts to prevent the spread of Ockamism. In 1339
it was decreed " quod doctrina Ockannica non dogmatizetur." [4]
It was forbidden to teach in public or private (occulte) the
philosophy of William " dicti Okam," and this for disciplinary
reasons, for no one is authorized to explain (legere) works other
than those which have been officially designated, and in the
order laid down (certa ordinatio) ; the masters have sworn
to conform to these decisions. This time the reference was to
philosophical works, and those chiefly logical, which alone
concerned the teaching in the Arts. Fourteen months later
there were new decrees. But now the Faculty changed its
tone and gave a cry of alarm : the new teaching is full of
danger, and is calculated to compromise theology as well as
philosophy. The statute of December, 1340, mentions the
principal doctrines which are to be banished from the schools,
and from this point of view is of great interest. It tells us
that the Ockamists have especially inherited the dialectical
spirit of the master, and that they have a predilection for the

---

[1] "Curiosis, inutilibus et supervacuis philosophicis questionibus et sub-
tilitatibus se immiscent." (Chart., II. 200).
[2] Vol. One, p. 251.
[3] Chart., II, 588, " que (doctrine sophistice) in quibusdam aliis doceri
dicuntur studiis."
[4] Chart., II, 485.

logical and grammatical subjects treated by Petrus Hispanus. If separated in the least from the *real* content of philosophy, this formal logic must of necessity lead to verbal discussions and plays upon words which are worthy of sophists and not of philosophers. The masters aimed at by the statute admit only the *suppositio personalis* (" Quod nullus dicat simpliciter vel de virtute sermonis omnem propositionem esse falsam, que esset falsa secundum suppositionem personalem terminorum . . . actores enim sepe utuntur aliis suppositionibus ") and the literal interpretation (" Quod nullis dicat quod nulla propositio sit distinguenda. Quod nullus dicat propositionem nullam esse concedendam, si non sit vera in ejus sensu proprio . . . quia Biblia et actores non semper sermonibus utuntur secundum proprios sensus eorum "). They reduce science to a study of concepts and words instead of things (" Quod nullus dicat scientiam nullam esse de rebus que non sunt signa, id est, que non sunt termini vel orationes.") [1]

These prohibitions of the Faculty of Arts remained without effect, although they were never withdrawn. Indeed, they were contemporaneous with the vigorous development of Ockamism from 1328 to 1358 under the direction of a prominent personage, John Buridan. It is true that the latter stood for a moderate form of Ockamism, and was hostile to extreme theories. Anxiety was aroused only by an exaggerated Ockamism ending in subjectivism in philosophy and absurdities in theology.

381. John Buridan, born at Bethune, was the leader of Ockamism at Paris during the first half of the fourteenth century. He was Rector in 1328 and 1340, taught during twenty-five years, and died shortly after 1358.[2] Among his works, which were exclusively philosophical, we may mention an elaboration of Ockam's logic under the title *Scriptum super summulas* (later on commented on by John Dorp), the commentaries on the *Physics*, *Metaphysics*,[3] and *Politics* of Aristotle. Of the Commentary on the *Nichomachean Ethics* there exists a *reportatio* dated 1372.[4]

---

[1] *Chart.*, II, 506. The statute of the faculty was published and became obligatory in the following month (January, 1341) in a document in which we find the term *Occaniste*.
[2] It is accordingly untrue that he went to Vienna, which University was not founded until 1365. It is equally untrue that he was in communication with Joan of Navarre. (*Chart.* II, p. 646, n.)
[3] Edited by Jodocus Badius of Assche in 1518.
[4] Mentioned by Michalski in *Philos. Jahrb.* 1916, p. 311. Duhem contested

Buridan took no part in the exaggerations of the Parisian terminists, and indeed reproved them.   He was against abusive interpretations of the *suppositio personalis*, and maintained that the letter of a text, whether in a sacred or a profane author, is less important than the spirit.   In the same way he defended the value of the principle of causality against the attacks of Nicholas of Autrecourt, and used this principle as a foundation for his proof for the existence of God.

Buridan devoted his best attention to the problem of liberty, in which he sided with psychological determinism.   Every good set before us by the intellect exercises on the will, which is undetermined of itself, a natural attraction, and if we were to abandon ourselves to this *complacentia*, of two good things we should necessarily chose that which appears to us to be the better.   But the liberty possessed by the will enables it to suspend its choice and to impose upon reason a fresh examination of the alternatives present.   Our determination will be in accordance with morality if in this comparison we take as our guide the end of our nature (*ordinatio finalis*).   It belongs to the will to prolong its deliberation, but once the moment of decision has come, it necessarily chooses the good which it judges to be the best.[5]   This conclusion reminds us of Leibniz' balance and its stability when equal weights are placed in it.   Everyone knows the story of the donkey dying of hunger in the presence of two bundles of hay equal in quantity and quality.   This is not found in the writings of Buridan, and it was doubtless invented by contemporaries in order to ridicule the theory.   Perhaps Buridan made use of it in his oral teaching to show the difference between man and beast[6] : while an animal necessarily obeys the strongest inclination, man by reflection has the means of discovering the best good.   In any case, Buridan could scarcely object to it, for his determinism is unquestionable.   The only objection which could be brought against it, he writes with a sceptical tone, is that it ill agrees with the Catholic faith.[7]

the authenticity of these commentaries (*Etudes sur Leonard de Vinci*, 2nd Series, p. 438), but he was not aware of this manuscript.

[5] We do not speak of the necessary volition of the good in general, which Buridan explains like the Thomists.

[6] Explanation of Siebeck, *op. cit.*, p. 204.

[7] " Et ad hujusmodi opinionis . . . reprobationem . . . nullas rationes habemus nisi ex fide nostra catholica et quia sic essemus in omnibus nostris actibus necessarie predeterminati." (*Quæst. in Ethic.*, X, q. 2 ; cf. Michalski, *op. cit.*, p. 28).

A convinced Ockamist, Buridan denies any distinction between the various faculties of the soul. "Voluntas est intellectus et intellectus est voluntas." [1] Nevertheless, the cognitive operation precedes the exercise of the will, and plays the principal part in our moral life.

Duhem has pointed out in the commentaries on Aristotle's *Physics* (Book VIII q. 12) the difficulties which Buridan opposes to the mechanics of Aristotle, and the theory of the *impetus* which he would put in its place. The moving body impresses upon the body put in motion a certain power which the latter conserves after the mover has ceased to act, and this is progressively neutralized by the resistances of the air and gravitation. The Aristotelian theory of place vanishes, together with the hypothesis of intelligences moving the heavenly bodies, for the stars obey the same laws as terrestrial bodies. These new opinions, which were later adopted and developed by a group of nominalist scientists, carry back the origins of modern physics to the fourteenth century. [2]

382. Marsilius of Inghen was a disciple of Buridan, whom he succeeded in the Faculty of Arts as the champion of Ockamism during the second half of the fourteenth century. The university documents relate that while he was *magister regens* the Faculty had to take steps to secure sufficient accommodation for all those who wished to hear him. [3] He was Rector in 1367 and 1371, and was for twenty-three years one of the most prominent men in the University. The difficult situation created by the Great Schism caused him to leave Paris. About 1383 he went to the young University of Heidelberg, became its first Rector (1386), and there introduced Ockamism. The departure of Marsilius from Paris was not an isolated case. From 1378 to 1383 there was a veritable exodus of Parisian masters to the new German Universities in order to avoid the difficulties resulting from the Schism ; Gerard of Calcar, Henry of Langenstein, Henry of Oyta, and Henry of Odendorp were among the number.

The *Quæstiones supra IV lib. Sent.* constitute the chief theological work of Marsilius, but he also left explanations of the

---

[1] *In Eth. Arist.*, Book X, q. 1, fol. 204, Paris edition, 1513.
[2] Duhem, *Etudes sur Léonard de Vinci*, 3rd series, 1913. The progress of mechanics was due " to this idea, that the motion of a projectile cannot be explained as in Aristotle's view, by the motion of the surrounding air, but that it is conserved by an *impetus* impressed upon the moving body." (*Dominique Soto et la scolastique parisienne* in *Bulletin Hispanique*, 1910, p. 275-276).
[3] *Chart.*, III, 93, 555 ; *Auctarium Chart.*, I. p. xxxiii.

Prior Analytics, a *Dialectics*, *Quæstiones in lib. de generatione*, and an abridgement of the *Physics*. Marsilius reproduces the psychological determinism of Buridan, and like the latter takes refuge in the faith in order to avoid the inconvenient consequences of his determinism. On the other hand, while declaring himself an Ockamist he makes an important modification in the master's conceptualism, for he endeavours to link up the general concept with the external reality. The universal is not only in the mind ; it has its connections with reality, inasmuch as the latter is similar in different beings.[1]   Is this a concession to realism ?

HENRY HAINBUCH OF LANGENSTEIN (1325-1397) a contemporary of Marsilius, taught at Paris from 1363 onwards, and in 1384 went to Vienna. His scientific activity was concerned chiefly with mathematics and astronomy, and after his departure he took up problems in theology and social economy.

383. Gregory of Rimini and the Augustinians.—The artists were not the only ones influenced by Ockamism. Secular theologians and members of various orders were also led astray by its novelties. The Dominicans ARMAND OF BELLOVISU, master of the sacred palace (died 1334-40),[2] and PETER DE PALUDE accepted the new teaching, and it was against these and Holcot at Oxford that the general chapters of the Dominicans multiplied their pressing injunctions from 1340 onwards.

A Servite and a Cistercian were among those summoned to Avignon in 1340, and another Cistercian, John of Mirecourt, who will be dealt with later on, burnt his boats and went to extremes. In the person of Gregory of Rimini, Ockamism had a powerful protagonist amongst the Augustinians, who up till then had faithfully followed the traditions of Giles of Rome, and a doctrinal division broke out within the order.

GREGORY NOVELLI DE RIMINI taught at Bologna, Padua and at Pérouse, after having obtained the baccalaureate at Paris. He subsequently returned to the French metropolis and became a master in theology in 1345. For four years he lectured on the

---

[1] G. Ritter, *Studien z. Spätscholastik*, I, *Marsilius v. Inghen u. die Okkamistische Schule in Deutschland*, II, *Via antiqua u. via moderna auf d. deutschen Univ. des* XV. *Jahrh.* (Heidelberg, 1921 and 1922).

[2] Author of a commentary on the *De ente et essentia* of St. Thomas, and also a dictionary, *Declaratio difficilium terminorum tam theologiæ quam philosophiæ*. Both have been printed.

Sentences. Later on he succeeded Thomas of Strasburg as general of the order (1357) and occupied this position until his death at Vienna in the following year. His numerous works are almost all unpublished. Of his great treatise on the Sentences (1344) the first two books alone have been printed, and that in a very rare edition.[1] Gregory's philosophy breathes the atmosphere of terminism, which was at its height in Paris at the time of his first stay there (1324). True, he opposes the plurality of forms in man, and accepts the demonstrative value of the arguments for the spirituality of the soul. But like Ockam he denies any distinction between the soul and its faculties, and his ideological and criteriological theories are clearly terministic. Not only the senses, but the intellect also has a direct knowledge of the individual which is prior to the abstract concept. The *species*—and by this we must understand the *imago rei cognitæ*—is required only to explain the knowledge of absent objects. The abstract and universal concept does not correspond to anything *extra animam*, and is but a psychological fabrication, a substitute or sign of many individual beings (Ockam). Again, science, which is built up from such concepts, has as its object a content of representations joined together by syllogistic methods (" significatum totale conclusionis est objectum scientiæ ") [2] and not at all the world of realities.

Nominalism made other converts in the Augustinian Order in the persons of HUGOLIN MALABRANCA OF ORVIETO, Bonsembiante of Padua, and John of Basle. The first mentioned. who became general of the order, was the author of statutes of the university of Bologna, and it is interesting to note that in order to guard the Italian university from the errors which had affected Paris (" ne nostram Bononia universitatem inficiant ") he reproduces in an appendix the official list of propositions condemned in 1347 and taken from the writings of John of Mirecourt and others).[3] This is yet another proof that Ockamists like Hugolin did not aim at making the new philosophy serve for antischolastic ends.

The ideas of BONSEMBIANTE, born in 1327, a Doctor of Theology of Paris, of whom we possess four *principia* dating

---

[1] J. Wursdörfer, *Erkennen u. Wissen nach Gregor von Rimini*, p. vii.
[2] *I Sent.* Prol., q. 1, a. 1. (*op. cit.*, p. 118).
[3] See texts in Ehrle, *op. cit.*, p. 105 and 273. Ehrle announces the publication of the Statutes of Bologna, Cf. Birkenmajer, *BGPM*, XX, p. 235.

from 1363, resemble those of Gregory of Rimini rather than the philosophy of Giles of Rome or Thomas of Strasburg. In spite of this, fourteenth century manuscripts calls him " doctor nostri ordinis." He takes a sophistical pleasure in dwelling at length on the *significabile complexe*, and devotes his time to the search for paradoxical formulæ.[1]

JOHN OF BASLE, doctor of theology at Paris in 1371, then Provincial of his native province, and finally general (died 1392) has left Commentaries on the Sentences (about 1370), the Ockamist inspiration of which is equally evident. Ehrle has pointed out therein a defence of the articles of Ockam incriminated in 1324 and subjected to examination by Cardinal James of Furno.[2] On the other hand, John also reproves the excesses of his namesake of Mirecourt, and the determinism of Bradwardine which leads to regarding God as the author of sin : " in hac parte plus confusus quam profundus "[3]

384. The Franciscans. Peter of Candia.—Ehrle has recently given us much new information on two Franciscans of the second half of the fourteenth century who adopted the *via moderna* at Paris, Johannes Ripa and Peter of Candia.[4] The former, who was connected with John of Mirecourt, will be dealt with later on (418).

As for PETER OF CANDIA, he was a most remarkable personality, standing out in great relief. He was born at Candia about 1340 of Greek stock, and passed his baccalaureate at Oxford. We know that in 1378 he held his first *principium* at Paris, and that in 1380 he finished the explanation of the Sentences. Accordingly, he cannot have obtained the mastership before the autumn of 1381. From 1386 onwards he filled the office of a bishop, until the Council of Pisa, convoked in order to put an end to the Great Schism, elected him Pope. He took the name of Alexander V (1409-1410). His election was designed to put an end to the double obedience, but in point of fact only increased the confusion. The Schism was brought to an end only at the Council of Constance.

Peter has left Commentaries on the Sentences (especially on the first two books) which exist in numerous manuscripts,

---

[1] Ehrle, *op. cit.*, p. 51-55.
[2] *Ibid.*, p. 56.
[3] *Ibid.*, p. 273.
[4] He adds Francis of Perouse but gives no details. (*Op. cit.*, p. 87).

disciple of St. Thomas (of whom he says in his Prologue, " *quem omnibus propono* "), applies the principles laid down by the master to new domains. He studies in turn the production of wealth, its distribution, and utilization. Man is not an instrument for the service of production,[1] but the latter is a means for the service of man and his end (scholastic individualism.[2] Hence wealth is good and commerce takes on a moral aspect, provided they are controlled by reason. Speaking of the burning question of interest and usury, he considers that money is of itself unproductive, that it is immoral to profit by the activity of others, but that the merchant has a right to make use of his own capital by means of his work and to derive therefrom a moderate profit.[3] Furthermore, in virtue of a fiction which henceforth becomes general, Antoninus authorizes the person lending money to retain on this head a part of the recompense which it would have procured for him if he had himself devoted it to commerce. The interest on a loan becomes a compensation due to the lender, whether the latter be a private person or the State. Antoninus thus takes a great step forward in a problem in presence of which Thomas Aquinas remained undecided.

Wealth ought to serve for all, for " the poor man is not made of earth and the rich of precious metal." There may be poor, but there should be none unhappy. Let the State, which ought to provide for the well-being of its members[4] see that the community is provided with corn ; let it organize charitable institutions. Although private property is of the natural law, the State can control the possessions of the rich.[5]

Antoninus condemns luxury and extravagance, but he imposes upon all the duty of using their goods for the upkeep of the family, the progress of the State, and the improvement of the city. Like a true Florentine, he extols the virtue of magnificence.

Other questions are treated by the episcopal moralist, such as the contract of labour, which in fixing the wages must take account of the worker's ability, needs, dangers, established customs—also the education of the family, and the characteristics of government, which ought to be inspired by the *pru-*

[1] IV, 5, 17.
[2] Cf. Vol. I, p. 305.
[3] III, 1, 6, II, 1, 16.
[4] II, i, 11.
[5] IV, 12, 8.

dentia regnativa and observe justice in the declaration and conduct of wars.

410. Bibliography.—General works : Janet, Carlyle, mentioned in Vol. I, p. 35 ; Dunning, *A History of Political Theories Ancient and Mediæval* (New York, 1921) ; Mertz, *History of Political Philosophy.* R. Scholz, *Unbekannte Kirchenpolit. Streitschr. aus d. Zeit Ludwigs d. Bayern*, 1327-1354. Marsilius of Padua : edition of *Defensor Pacis* in Goldast, *Monarchiæ s. Romani imperii*, Vol. II, 1614. New edition by Cartellieri (Leipzig, 1913), and Scholtz (1914). A. Hurant, *Etude sur M. de P.* (Montauban, 1892) ; L. Stieglitz, *Die Staatstheorie des M. von P.* Dissert. (Leipzig, 1914) ; J. Sullivan, *The Manuscripts and date of M. of P.'s Defensor Pacis*, in *English Historical Review*, 1905, p. 293 ; Previte Orton, *M. of Padua* (ibid. 1923) ; Janet and Poole, *op. cit.* study by N. Valois, in *Hist. Litt. de la France*, Vol. 33.

On Nicholas of Cusa, see the excellent work by Van Steenberghe. Cf. J. Vilmain, *Les principes de droit public du Card. N. de C.* (1922, a thesis) ; E. Zack, *Der publicist Pierre Dubois, seine Bedeutung in Rahmen der Politik Philipp IV des Schönen, u. seine literarische Denk.—u. Arbeitsweise im Traktat De recuperatione Terre Sancte* (Berlin, 1911).

On Wyclif, see Poole, *op. cit.* (Vol. I, p. 34), ch. x ; H. O. Taylor, *Thought and Expression in the Sixteenth Century*, Ch. I.

Numerous editions of the *Summa theologica* of Antoninus of Florence (Venice 1477, Verona 1740, etc.). C. Ilgner, *Die volkswirtschaftlichen Anschauungen A. v. F.* (Paderborn, 1904), good ; Bede Jarrett, *St. Antonino and Mediæval Economics* (Herder, 1914), based on the preceding work. Edition of the *De recuperatione terre sancti* by Ch. Langlois (Paris, 1891).

CHAPTER III

The Group of anti-Scholastic philosophies

Averrhoism still remained the great rival of scholasticism (§ 1). The Divine Determinism inaugurated by Bradwardine (§ 2) and the subjectivism resulting from the terminist philosophy (§ 3) both helped to create an atmosphere of scepticism, and an ever-increasing mistrust of the scholastic systematizations hitherto held in honour.

§ 1—*Latin Averrhoism*

411. Averrhoism at Paris. John of Jandun.—In spite of the prohibitions directed against it, and although scholastics of all parties joined together to oppose its doctrinal position, Parisian Averrhoism expanded anew at the beginning of the fourteenth century. Certain disciples of William of Ockam went over to its camp. They were attracted by the theory of the two truths, towards which they were inclined by the Ockamist idea of watertight compartments in thought.[1]

The recognized leader of Parisian Averrhoism was JOHN OF JANDUN (*de Genduno, de Ganduno, de Janduno*),[2] master of arts at the College of Navarre. We have mentioned above that while at Paris he was a colleague of Marsilius of Padua,

---

[1] Karl Wenck, (*War Bonifaz VIII ein Ketzer?* in *Histor. Zeitschrift*, Bd. 94, 1) shows that the accusations directed against the memory of Boniface VIII. at the process at Avignon constitute a charge of Averrhoism. " I am very sceptical," writes Mandonnet, " about the Averrhoism of Boniface VIII, but I am less sceptical about that of the *entourage* of the King of France. I quite think that it was the agents of Philip the Fair who foisted their own Averrhoism on the memory of the hated and no longer living Pope." (*Siger*, etc., VI, 188, note).

[2] For a long time confused with John of Ghent (de Gandavo), a peaceable theologian at Paris and curé of Kieldrecht. He taught in 1303, while in 1316 John of Jandun had not yet obtained the mastership in arts. He wrote commentaries on the Sentences and *Quodlibeta* wrongly attributed to John of Jandun.

himself a convert to Averrhoism, and that his political and anti-papal theories as developed in the *Defensor pacis* com pelled him to seek refuge at the court of Louis of Bavaria These political theories formed a chapter apart in the teaching of John of Jandun, and had no logical connection with the rest of his philosophy, which consisted of Averrhoism. They served as a personal bond between himself and malcontents who did not share his views in psychology and metaphysics.

In 1315 John commented at Paris on the *Expositio problematum Aristotelis* by Pietro di Abano, the physician-philosopher of Padua. A copy of the work had been procured for him by Marsilius. In addition he commented on the *De anima* (two redactions) the *De cœlo et mundo*, the *Metaphysics*, *Physics*, and the *Parva naturalia* of Aristotle, and the *Expositio* and commentary on the *Sermo de substantia orbis* of Averrhoes.[1] All these works are parts of one edifice, the style of which is definitely Averrhoist. John of Jandun says of himself that he is the ape of Aristotle and Averrhoes,[2] and that he imperfectly copies the perfect work left by these two men of genius ; he blames any who should dare to suggest that there are contradictions in the Commentator. Again, he commented at great length on the chief doctrines of Latin Averrhoism (**327**), the eternity of the world and of motion,[3] the necessary realization of the possibles,[4] the absence of any evil in the eternal beings,[5] the impossibility that God should create beings or know anything other than Himself.[6] In psychology he professes the isolation, unity and eternity of the human intellect : " Unus substantialiter est omnium intellectus, non plurificabilis seu multiplicabilis ad corporum multiplicationem."[7] Hence the intellectual soul cannot be the sole form of the human compound : it is really distinct from the sensible soul ;[8] and

---

[1] In the commentary on the *De anima*, he incidentally refers the reader to several other writings from his pen : *Quæstiones de formatione fœtus, Quæstiones de gradibus et pluralitate formarum, Tractatus de specie intelligibili, Duo tractatus de sensu agente*. He likewise informs us that one of these treatises *De sensu agente* was his first work.

[2] Commentary on the *Metaphysics* (Venice, 1525, f. 84).

[3] " Totum mundum ingenitum secundum totum necesse est esse " (*De cœlo et mundo*, I, q. 29 ; *Phys*., VIII, q. 3).

[4] *Metaph*., VII, q. 5 : " Utrum aliquid sit possibile in rerum natura quod nunquam erit." He replies in the negative.

[5] *Ibid*., IX, q. 12.

[6] *Ibid*., f, 142, c. 3.

[7] *De anima*, III, q. 7.

[8] " Anima sensitiva et intellectiva sunt diversæ substantiæ et formæ," (*ibid*., III, q. 12).

although this way of explaining the constitution of our being leads to numerous difficulties in philosophy, he declares that his doctrine is more satisfying than the scholastic theory.[1] In ethics John of Jandun confuses the free act with the voluntary act in order the better to defend psychological determinism: " Liberum arbitrium est quod est gratia sui . . . ergo liberum habet illud quod est gratia sui, licet ex necessitate agat."[2] Here we certainly have anti-scholasticism. No less significant is his attitude as a Christian seeking to save his threatened faith. Although he holds as true for his reason all the doctrines of Averrhoism, he explains that nevertheless he considers them false in presence of his religion. In the words of St. Augustine, it is therein that the merit of faith lies. " Ibi cessat meritum, ubi ratio præbet experimentum." And to crown it all, we are told that the miraculous omnipotence of God knows no limits, not even the impossible. " Responderem breviter concedendo tanquam possibilia apud Deum omnia ad quae illæ rationes deducunt tanquam impossibilia."[3] This discovery puts him at ease and gives him the illusion of reconciling two irreconcilable things.[4]

Although John of Jandun is never tired of repeating that the contradictions between reason and faith ought to be solved by the theory of the two truths, and that accordingly dogma is as true as the philosophic thesis which destroys it, we get a definite impression that for his part he sacrifices the faith. The little ironical phrases which he uses and the tone of his reasoning leave no doubt as to his mental attitude.[5]

After this, it is not surprising to find that John of Jandun did all in his power to lessen the reputation which St. Thomas enjoyed in the University of Paris. He contemptuously belittled the commentaries of this exegete " qui putatur fuisse melior inter latinos," and concludes " Sed re vera salva

---

[1] " Quamvis igitur difficile sit intelligere quomodo ex materia et forma subsistente, non inhærente, fiat unum, tamen multo difficilius est hoc intelligere de anima intellectiva et humano corpore secundum positionem catholicam quam secundum positionem commentatoris," (*ibid.*, f. 65).

[2] *De cælo et mundo*, f. 22.

[3] *De anima*, fol. 66, c. 1.

[4] " Quod si alicui primo adspectu non videretur sufficere ad solutiones rationum, non tamen propter hoc debet conturbari, quia certum est quod auctoritas divina majorem fidem debet facere quæcumque ratio humanitus inventa " (*De anima*, f. 60, c. 1). Again in the *Metaph.*, f. c. 1 : " Credo melius esse quoad salutem animarum nostrarum assentire et simpliciter credere, quam rationibus sophisticis ea probare et rationes ex sensibus electas debiliter minus evidenter annotare."

[5] Cf. Gilson, *Etudes de philos. médiévale*, pp. 63 *et seq.*

reverentia hujus hominis, ipse inaniter laborat contra commen-
tatorem sicut et in aliis philosophicis in quibus ei objicit . . .
Dico quod ego non credo ei in hoc, sicut nec in aliis conclusion-
ibus philosophicis in quibus contradicit commentatori."[1]

John of Jandun was one of the leading lights of the school,
and he himself quotes in many places of his books, various
monographs of his *socii* on special questions of Averrhoist
doctrine.[2]

412. John of Baconthorp (Johannes Baco, died in 1346),
a Carmelite religious and an intimate friend of Thomas Bradwardine, adopted with regard to Averrhoism a peculiar
position which is not yet quite clear.[3] In his commentary on
the Sentences, so rich in information concerning his contemporaries, he rejects the doctrine of monopsychism, but considers that the arguments of Thomas Aquinas and Hervæus
of Nedellec against Averrhoes are not conclusive. The
doctrine in question would apparently, in his view, be a fiction
in the system of the Arabian philosopher, a theme proposed
for discussion.[4] John himself ascribes to man a *forma corporeitatis* besides the *anima intellectiva.* Wherever he can, he
excuses Averrhoes, and follows him in doctrines which can be
reconciled with the faith. The long series of his commentaries
on Aristotle (unpublished) are inspired by Averrhoes.

413. Italian Averrhoism.—From the middle of the fourteenth century, and up till the seventeenth, Northern Italy
was an intense centre of Averrhoism. At Bologna, the Servite
URBAN OF BOLOGNA (died 1405) who commented on Averrhoes'
Commentary on the Physics, adopted a rather reserved attitude,
very similar to that of John of Baconthorp ; while at Venice,
PAUL OF VENICE (died 1429) boldly followed John of Jandun.

The University of Padua was the stronghold of Averrhoism.
It is wrong to say that the physician and naturalist PIETRO
OF ABANO (1250-1315 is his probable date) was the founder

---

[1] *Physics,* f. 96, c. 4 ; 97, c. 2.
[2] The particular features of the Averrhoism of John of Jandun have been
communicated to us by Pelzer. Edition of his Commentaries at Venice,
1522.
[3] We suspect that his Averrhoism has been exaggerated, especially by
Renan, who gives the name of Averrhoism to " exhausted Scholasticism "
and puts on the same footing Baconthorp and Gabriel Biel. Cf. Werner,
Der Averroismus in d. christl. peripat. Psych.
[4] " Non reputat nisi fictionem et solum ponit eam propter exercitium ut
veritas completius inquiratur." (*In II. Sent.,* d. 21, q. 1, a. 3. Venice
edition, 1526).

of the school of Padua.[1] Among its principal representatives we may mention CAJETAN OF THIENE (Cajetanus Thienæus) (died 1465), who abandoned Averrhoism on some doctrines clearly irreconcilable with the Catholic faith ; NICOLETTA VERNIAS, a Professor at Padua from 1471 to 1499 who closely followed the characteristic doctrines of Averrhoism. The *Summulæ Logicæ* of PAUL OF VENICE were adopted as a standard work by a decree in 1496.

Padua was in the sixteenth century the scene of a keen combat between Averrhoists and Alexandrians.

§ 2—*Divine Determinism*

414. Thomas Bradwardine.—The theory that the infinite and all-powerful God extends his determining influence to the very depths of human volition is a new subject of discussion linked up with doctrines of Ockamist origin. It forms the centre of a system of determinism first set forth by Thomas Bradwardine.

Born about 1290, Bradwardine was an illustrious member of Merton College[2] and the University of Oxford, in which he was professor and procurator (1325). Afterwards he became chaplain to Edward III ; in 1346 he accompanied the king in his triumphal journey in France, and became Archbishop of Canterbury in 1349, holding this office until his death in the same year. In addition to his chief and important work *De causa Dei contra Pelagium et de virtute causarum ad suos Mertonenses* (between 1338 and 1346), Bradwardine wrote

[1] The Averrhoism of Peter of Abano has been defended by Sante Ferrari, *I tempi, la vita, le dottrine di P. d'Abano* (Genoa, 1900), and in a note in *Mem. Acad. Lincei* 1916, S. V, vol. 15, fasc. 7. His thesis has been attacked by Bruno Nardi, *La teoria dell' anima e la generazione delle forme secondo Pietro d'Abano* (*Riv. di filos. neo-scolastica*, 1912, p. 723, (Peter of Abano is not an Averrhoist in psychology) ; and *Intorno alle dottrine filosofiche di P. d'Abano*, Milan, 1921, (Nuova Rivista Storica). P. of Albano went to Constantinople, and returned to Paris about 1300, and there commenced or wrote his chief work, *Conciliator differentiarum philosophorum et præcipue medicorum* (Venice, 1483). From 1307 onwards he taught medicine and natural philosophy at Padua. He translated medical works from the Greek, and wrote a commentary on the *Problems* of Aristotle (*Expositio problematum Aristotelis*). The *Conciliator* accepts many Thomist theories, for instance in the question of universals, abstraction, and the unity of forms (Ueberweg-Baumgartner, *op. cit.*, p. 546). On other questions such as the eternity of matter and the unity of the intellect, the interpretation of the texts is doubtful. Cf. Nardi, *Intorno*, etc., IV. A. Dyroff, *Dante u. P. d'A. (Philos. Jahrb.*, 1920, pp. 253-271).
[2] Founded at Maldon in 1264, transferred to Oxford in 1274.

Commentaries on the Sentences, and a *Summa theologica* or *Summa scientiarum*. In addition, he wrote treatises on mathematics, and so carried on the Oxford tradition.

The *doctor profundus* was a theologian and a philosopher—*magnus logicus* is the description applied to him by Peter of Candia. Although he attacked certain Nominalist theses, he was dependent on William of Ockam, and it is with doctrines of Ockamist origin that he built up the system of natural theology and ethics to which his name remains attached. The Pelagianism which he sets out to combat in its contemporary forms gives rise to the important problem of human liberty and its relations with God. The question is a burning one (" sciens in flammam terribilem manum mitto ").[1] In order to solve it, Bradwardine inaugurates a Divine determinism of which the following are the main ideas :

God, whose existence can be proved by the idea which we have of a perfect being (Anselm), is infinite knowledge and will. His free will is the sovereign master of essences and existences in the contingent world (Ockamism), it is the arbiter of human nature and of the morality of its acts. " Non est ratio nec ulla lex necessaria in Deo prior ejus voluntate."[2] From this it follows, according to the English philosopher, that the Divine will is the necessitating cause, *necessitas antecedens*, of all contingent activity, and therefore also of our volitions. Man is free only in the measure in which his act is independent of everything other than God : and in particular, independent of intelligence and the conditions of sensibility (*libertas a necessitate naturali ;* Bradwardine refutes the psychological determinism of the Averrhoists), external agents, the heavenly bodies (*libertas a necessitate fatali*), and of any external violence (*libertas a necessitate violenta*). Liberty is thus reduced to a spontaneous act of will.[3]

Certainly Bradwardine's restrictions weaken human liberty, and with it the whole scholastic ethics. They lead by another way to the Averrhoist theories which he wishes to avoid.

---

[1] Bradwardine's *Præfatio*.
[2] *Causa Dei*, I, 21, p. 233 A.
[3] " Sufficiat homini ut sit liber respectu omnum citra Deum et tantummodo servus Dei, servus inquam spontaneus, non coactus " (*ibid*, III, 9, p. 667 E). " Nihil ergo est in potestate nostra, nisi secundum quid tantummodo, scilicet subactiva, subexecutiva et subserviente necessario, necessitate scilicet naturaliter præcedente respectu voluntatis divinæ : quod ideo dicitur in nostra potestate, quia cum volumus, illud facimus voluntarii, non inviti," p. 675. C. In our exposition we follow Hahn, see later on.

The Archbishop vainly strives to safeguard responsibility and moral merit. His principles compel him to declare that God is the whole cause of cosmic evil and of sin, but he is alarmed at the consequences of this and has recourse to subterfuges.

The *Causa Dei* had a very great influence at Oxford and Paris. Chaucer in his Canterbury Tales[1] gives a summary of his ideas, a proof that they attracted the attention of intellectual circles outside the universities. Very soon there arose disciples and opponents. An Oxford master of the name of BUCKINGHAM endeavoured to combat Bradwardine's determinism by attributing to the will the power to suspend its acts, but he admits that God concurs with all human volitions, sin included.[2] PETER PLAOUL is mentioned among his opponents. On the other hand, JOHN WYCLIF and JOHN OF MIRECOURT adopted and developed his doctrines.

415. The Pantheism of Guido.—The suppression of the activity of second causes logically leads to pantheism. It is not surprising that some adherents of Bradwardine accepted this other consequence of his ideas. Among them was a certain GUIDO, whom the authors of the *Chartularium* identify with Ægidius of Medonta. In the act of revocation of his errors (1354) we see that after having denied moral liberty[3] he plainly enunciated the principle of pantheism.[4]

§ 3—*Ockamist Subjectivism.*

416. Origin.—The system of William of Ockam was after all a scholastic one. It retained the essential features of the patrimony constituted by the generations of the twelfth and thirteenth centuries. But hardly had the master disappeared from the scene when the artists and theologians began to extend in the direction of phenomenism the doctrine in which they had been formed.

Three doctrinal elements in Ockamism favoured this ten-

---

[1] Nun's priest's tale.

[2] According to Michalski, *Les courants philos. à Oxford*, etc., pp. 12-13.

[3] " Dixi quod bonum meritum est a Deo, ita quod nichil est a voluntate." (*Chart.* III, p. 22, no. 5. Cf. no. 6).

[4] " Dixi et scripsi quod nulla creatura rationalis specialiter est in se, nisi quia Deus est sibi inesse. Ex hoc intuli in eodem scripto, quod in omni eo quod non est Deus, essentialius est non-esse, quam ipsum esse " (*ibid.*, no. 8).

dency towards subjectivism : the theory of signs, the purely ideal value of the notion of causality and the logico-grammatical method.   People argued that if knowledge is merely a sign of the thing, it attains to the sign only, not to the thing signified. If the abstract concept of cause has no connection with reality, the principle of causality is powerless to demonstrate not only the existence of the external world, but also that of God.   As for the subtle rules concerning the *proprietates terminorum*, the *consequentiæ*, *obligatoria*, and *insolubilia*,[1] their application led to paradoxical and false theories of which we shall give some examples later on.   Applied to theological subjects, these three Ockamist doctrines led to the ruin or at least to the ridicule of all dogma.   Thus the censures of 1340 to 1346 coincided with the appearance of extreme doctrines.

Exaggerated Ockamism became allied to the Divine Determinism of Bradwardine, which it inspired, and which in return provided it with doctrinal elements.   It also freely embraced incoherent theories the very strangeness of which constituted an unhealthy attraction, and which seem to have been accepted simply for the pleasure of giving scandal.

417. Nicholas of Autrecourt.—Nicholas of Autrecourt (born at Autrecourt on the Meuse), was the centre of an anti-Scholastic movement at Paris.   In 1340, when he was a master of arts and a bachelor of theology, he was cited by Benedict XII before the Roman curia, together with six other students of theology[2] to answer for various errors.   He alone was severely censured and obliged to retract (1342).   Seven years later, the curia censured a series of 65 propositions extracted from his works, ordered his writings to be burnt, deprived him of his mastership of arts, and forbade him to become a master of theology.   The condemnation is dated 1347, which shows that the letter of sympathy and warning addressed by Clement VI to the University of Paris in May, 1346, had remained without effect.   Before his condemnation, Nicholas took refuge at the court of Louis of Bavaria, the rallying point of innovators and malcontents, and retracted in 1347.[3]

We learn from the condemnations of Nicholas of Autrecourt that he wrote nine letters against one of his opponents, the

---

[1] See Prantl, *op. cit.*, p. 1 *et seq.*
[2] John the Servite, Elie of Courson, Guido of Veeli, Peter of Monteregali, and Henry the Englishman.
[3] *Chart.*, II, 505.

Franciscan BERNARD OF AREZZO, and a pamphlet of which we know only the first words, " Exigit ordo executionis." If we are to accept literally the propositions singled out by the curia, Nicholas allowed it to be understood that he was inspired by God, and charged with the renewal of science.[1] " When Master Bernard and I," he says, " engaged in a controversy, we both decided that the principle of contradiction alone ought to serve as a basis in the interchange of our arguments."[2] Having laid this down, Nicholas puts forward with the aid of subtleties a number of anti-scholastic theories. They are thrown together anyhow in the documents relating to his condemnation, but we can reconstitute the logical connection between a certain number of them, thanks to a reply made to the first two letters of Nicholas of Autrecourt.[3] This reply was written, not by Bernard—who did not seem to have been very strong in philosophy—but by a certain master Giles. Nicholas reasoned thus : since the principle of contradiction is alone evident and certain, no truth can be certain unless it can be reduced to this primordial affirmation of the mind. Certitude does not admit of degrees, it exists or does not exist [4] Now, in order that a truth may be reduced to the principle of contradiction, it is necessary that the antecedent and the consequent, and in the last analysis, the predicate and subject of the certain proposition should be identical. The mind, then, cannot pass from the knowledge of one thing to that of another, for if the latter is really another, it is not capable of being identified with the first, and the judgement attributing a predicate to a subject which is different from it would not admit of reduction to the principle of contradiction.[5] From this it follows that the

---

[1] *Chart.*, II, pp. 580 and 581. We must add that according to Peter d'Ailly, " multa fuerunt condemnata contra eum causæ invidiæ." (Prantl, *op cit.*, IV, 112).

[2] " Quando magister Bernardus predictus et ego debuissemus disputare, concordavimus ad invicem disputando conferre de primo consensu omnium principio, posito a philosopho IVe *Metaphisice*, quod est : Impossibile est aliquid eidem rei inesse et non inesse, loquendo de gradu evidentie qui est in lumine naturali strictissimus. Istis suppositis dixi in predictis epistolis eo (sic) quod tales conclusiones nec explicite continebant contradictionem nec explicite." Further on he reduces this first principle to the principle of identity : " Item, quod hoc est primum principium et non aliud : si aliquid est, aliquid est," p. 583 (53).

[3] Published by Hauréau, *op. cit.*, p. 332.

[4] *Chart.*, II, p. 576 (9).

[5] " Ex his infertis talem conclusionem : quod ex eo quod una res est cognita non potest evidenter, evidentia reductibili in certitudinem primi principii, inferri quod alia res sit." (Hauréau, *op. cit.*, 333. Cf. *Chart.*, II, p. 576, 5, 6, 7).

principle of causality is devoid of value,[1] and that the observation of our mental acts does not enable us to affirm the
existence of faculties[2]; that God could arouse in us the sensible
impressions which we think we receive from the external world,
and that the existence of this external world cannot be demon-
strated.[3] Similarly, to infer from the presence of phenomena
that of a substance or permanent foundation supporting them
would be to infer one thing from another, a procedure condemned by logic.[4] The only substance which a man can know
with certitude is that of his own soul, and Aristotle himself
did not know more than this.[5] Accordingly Nicholas criticizes
the philosophy of Aristotle, which scarcely contains one or
two certitudes.[6] Knowledge is reduced to a series of intuitive
acts, sensible and intellectual, without order or relation
of dependence. We must abolish the abstractions of Aristotle and Averrhoes, and keep in direct contact with the
singular.[7]

This phenomenism constitutes the clearest feature of the
sophistical theory of Nicholas of Autrecourt. Elsewhere he
shows that it is almost the same to say that God is and that He

[1] *Chart.*, p. 576 (5); 577. " Hec consequentia : *a* est et prius non fuit,
igitur alia res ab *a* est, non est evidens evidentia deducta ex primo principio."
Cf. pp. 578 (29) and 580 (2). The argument is well developed by Master Giles,
p. 334.

[2] " Iste consequentie non sunt evidentes : actus intelligendi est ergo
intellectus est. Actus volendi est ; igitur voluntas est," p. 578 (30).

[3] " Quod in lumine naturali intellectus viatoris non potest habere notitiam
evidentie de existentia rerum evidentia reducta seu reducibili ad evidentiam
seu certitudinem primi principii," p. 583.

[4] " Ex his conamini probare quod Aristoteles non habuit evidentiam
notitiam de aliqua substantia, etc., quia de tali vel habuisset notitiam ante omnem discursum, quod non potest esse, quia non apparent intuitive et etiam
rustici scirent tales substantias esse, nec per discursum, inferendo ex perceptis
esse ante omnem discursum, nam probatum est quod ex una re non potest
evidenter inferri alia. Item, demonstrato ligno vel lapide, arguitur sic :
cum omnibus apparentibus ante omnem discursem, potest esse per aliquam
potentiam, puta divinam, quod substantia non sit ibi, igitur in lumine naturali
non infertur evidenter quod substantia sit ibi." (p. 333).

[5] " Item dixi epistola secunda ad Bernardum quod de substantia materiali
alia ab anima nostra non habemus certitudinem evidentie." (*Chart.*, p. 577,
10.) This somewhat obscure statement is explained by Master Giles, who
summarizes this second letter previous to refuting it : " Aristoteles nunquam
habuit notitiam evidentiæ de aliqua substantia alia ab anima sua, intelligendo
per substantiam quamdam rem aliam ab objectis quinque sensuum exteriorum,
et a formalibus experientiis nostris." (p. 333).

[6] *Ibid.*, p. 334.

[7] " Quod de rebus per apparentia naturalia nulla certitudo potest haberi ;
illa tamen modica potest in brevi haberi tempore, si homines convertant
intellectum suum ad res et non ad intellectum Aristotelis et commentatoris."
p. 580 (1).

is not,[1] that God and creatures " non sunt aliquid,"[2] that the acts of the soul are eternal[3] and that we end by obtaining all that we desire.[4] But these are possibly just rhetorical exaggerations. It is more interesting to note that Nicholas of Autrecourt denies substantial transformation, and that in conformity with the atomist theory he explains the generation and corruption of natural things by the agglutination or disintegration of atomic particles.[5] Lastly, he is anti-scholastic in his doctrine concerning God : the traditional arguments for the existence of God, based as they are on the principle of causality, are of no value ; a holy and inviolable necessity obliges God to realize from all eternity the order of the world (Averrhoism),[6] and all activities are due to the immediate action of the first cause (Bradwardine).[7] The application of these principles to the act of sin concerns theology rather than philosophy.[8]

418. John of Mirecourt, a Cistercian, known in documents as *monachus albus*,[9] explained the Sentences as a bachelor at the College of St. Bernard at Paris. Besides his *Principium*, Birkenmajer has discovered commentaries by him on the four books of Sentences, in a twofold redaction, one long and the other short, the former of which is certainly and the second possibly his work. His doctrines were attacked by a Benedictine JOHANNES NORMANNUS (*monachus nigrus*) against whom the *monachus albus* drew up a *declaratio*[10] in his own defence.

---

[1] " Item quod propositiones : Deus est, Deus non est, penitus idem significant, licet alio modo," p. 580 (3). Cf. p. 578 (33) : " Item dixi in quadam disputatione quod contradictoria ad invicem idem significant."

[2] P. 578 (32). This thesis of Nicholas of Autrecourt is expressly recalled in the prohibition of the Faculty of Arts in 1340 : " Item quod nullus asseret sine distinctione vel expositione quod Socrates et Plato, vel Deus et creatura nichil sunt." (*Chart.*, II, p. 506).

[3] P. 582 (45 and 47).

[4] P. 583.

[5] P. 581 (37). " In rebus naturalibus non est nisi motus localis, scilicet congregationis et disgregationis, ita quod quando ad talem motum sequitur congregatio corporum athomalium naturalium, colliguntur ad invicem et sortiuntur naturam unius suppositi dicitur generatio ; quando segregantur, dicitur corruptio ; et quando per motum localem athomalia sunt cum aliquo supposito, que fiant talia, quod nec adventus illorum facere videtur ad motum suppositi vel ad id quod dicitur operatio naturalis ejus, tunc dicetur alteratio."

[6] *Chart.*, II, p. 581 (39).

[7] *Chart.*, p. 577 (14).

[8] *Ibid.*, p. 584 (58) and (59).

[9] Also in the edict of Louis XI. against Nominalism (1473).

[10] *Ein Rechtfertigungsschreiben J's von Mirecourt, BGPM*, XX, 5, pp. 91-128, publishes the text of this *declaratio*. Cf. Michalski, *Les sources du criticisme et du scepticisme dans phil. XIVe s.* (extract from La Pologne au Congres intern. de Bruxelles, Cracow 1924, p. 2 of the separate reprint. On the twofold redaction of his commentaries, see Michalski in *Miscellanea Ehrle*, I, 226.

In spite of this, however, the Chancellor of the University, together with the Faculty of Theology, condemned shortly after 1347 a group of forty propositions extracted from the writings of John of Mirecourt, which the latter endeavoured once again to justify.

As presented in his chief work and in the accusations against him, the philosophy of John of Mirecourt is tainted with the same subjectivism which we found in Nicholas of Autrecourt, and at the same time it adopts and develops the terminism of Bradwardine. Our primordial knowledge, endowed with absolute certitude, comprises in addition to a series of analytical judgements reducible to the principle of contradiction, an immediate intuition of our own existence. To doubt this would be implicitly to allow the psychological reality of the doubt and the existence of the doubter (Augustine). The second type of knowledge (*experientia*), which puts us in contact with the external world, does not present the same guarantees of certitude, for God or some other agent could play the part of an evil genius and give us the illusion of the existence of things outside us although nothing really existed. Activities immanent to each being would explain equally well the modifications which we ascribe to their causal interaction. Hence it follows that causality is indemonstrable (Nicholas of Autrecourt), and so the argument for the existence of God as prime mover collapses.[1]

The accusers of John of Mirecourt condemned the extreme consequences which he inferred from the determinism of Bradwardine. If it is God who acts in us and who gives rise to our volitions, there is no free will,[2] and sin itself becomes the work of God, and we cannot do wrong in committing it. " Quod Deus est causa peccati ut peccatum est."[3] With John of Mirecourt, the evolution of exaggerated Ockamism reaches its culminating point.

The Franciscan JOHN DE RIPA (de Marchia), who taught at

[1] According to Michalski, who was the first to give an analysis of the Commentaries on the Sentences, pp. 21-24.

[2] *Chart.*, II, p. 612, no. 35. " Quod voluntas creata qualitercunque causat aliquid seu aliqualiter agit, illud agit seu taliter agit virtute prime cause moventis et sic causantis." No. 9 : " Quod qualitercunque sit, Deus vult efficaciter sic esse, et quod voluntas divina cujuslibet rei ad extra, qualitercunque ipsa sit vel fiat ab aliquo, est efficiens prima causa."

[3] See nos. 9-18, 27-34, etc. We possess an account of the theory of the principle of causality in Nicholas of Autrecourt, by John of Autrecourt, (Lappe, *op. cit.*, p. 4).

Paris in 1357 and was much thought of by Peter of Candia and Gerson, seems to be closely connected with this destructive philosophy of John of Mirecourt. He was a personal writer who departed from Scotism in order to follow his own path. The Augustinian John of Basle reproached him for making God the author of sin inasmuch as God is the author of human actions, and connected his doctrine with the articles condemned in 1347.[1] The condemnations of 1346 and 1347 were the only measures of repression against Parisian Ockamism in the fourteenth century. They were aimed at theological doctrines, but indirectly affected the philosophical doctrines upon which these were based.

419. Bibliography.—The *Causa Dei* of Bradwardine was published in London in 1618, edited by Savile of Merton College, Oxford, with a bibliography. The mathematical treatises (*De proportionibus velocitatem, De arithmetica speculativa, De geometrica speculativa*) were published at Venice in 1502 (?) and 1505. Dr. S. Hahn, *Thomas Bradwardinus und seine Lehre v. d. menschlichen willensfreiheit* (*BGPM*, V, 2), good. Werner has studied Bradwardine in *Der Augustin. d. späteren Mittel.*, pp. 234 *et seq.*, but Hahn justly points out (p. 12) that Werner is difficult to understand. The reply of Giles to Nicholas of Autrecourt is published by Hauréau, *Notices et extr. de ms. lat. de Bibl. nat.*, Vol. XXXIV, Part II, p. 332 (1895). Dr. Hastings Rashdall, *Nicolas de Ultricuria, a mediæval Hume* (Proceedings of the Aristotelian Society, 1907) ; J. Lappe, *Nicolaus v. Autrecourt, Sein Leben, seine Philosophie, seine Schriften* (*BGPM*, VI, 2), a study, publishes the letters of Nicholas to Bernard, those of Giles to Nicholas, an extract from the letter of Nicholas to Giles, the account of the process, and the text of the condemnation. Manser, *Drei Zweifler am Kausalprincip im XIV Jahrh.* (*Jahrb. f. Phil. u spek. Theol.* 1913, p. 405). The three referred to are William of Ockam, Nicholas of Autrecourt and Peter d'Ailly. On John of Jandun, see study by N. Valois in *Hist. litt. de la France*, Vol. 33.

---

[1] Ehrle, *op. cit.*, p. 272. He gives other information concerning the doctrine of John de Ripa.

of knowledge which governs all Nicholas's teaching and is the foundation of the whole system.

(i) *Theory of knowledge*. In addition to the senses, which attain to corporeal things in a gross and confused manner, man possesses a " reasoning reason " which expresses reality in abstract concepts according to the principle of contradiction. The knowledge we obtain from this reason is limited and relative, for there are no two things alike ; the beings which reason grasps are separated and incommensurable. Hence human science is composed of conjectures. The integral truth of things is hidden in God from Whom things spring, and in Whom they lie beyond our reach. Nevertheless, above the rational mode of knowledge there exists an intellectual intuition in which the principle of contradiction has no place, and which with a synthetic glance, grasps the coincidence of the contraries which reason regarded as incompatible. The Nominalist and Aristotelian dialectics had no place for this spiritual vision, upon which Nicholas of Cusa endeavoured to found a new metaphysics, and for this reason he was not on good terms with the Aristotelians. JOHN WENCK of Herrenberg, a professor at Heidelberg, in the *De ignota litteratura* which he wrote against him, criticized this negation of the principle of contradiction, showing that it destroys both science and faith.[1] Nicholas defended his position in the *Apologia doctæ ignorantiæ* which he wrote in reply, and in which he strives to show that " the admission of contraries, which is regarded as heresy by the Aristotelian sect, is the starting point of the mystical ascent."[2] The recognition of the incurable ignorance to which we are condemned so long as we take reason for our guide, is the way to raise ourselves to these higher intuitions. The reality which we then attain to, and in which all contradictions vanish, is God himself.

(ii) *God*, the greatest possible being (Anselm), is not only the Absolute Maximum, but at the same time He is identical with the lowest possible or minimum. In Him, to exist and not to exist coincide, and the same is true of all contraries : they coincide in God. What is the meaning of these statements,

---

[1] *De ignota litteratura*, pp. 21-2, quoted by Van Steenberghe, *op. cit.*, p. 283.
[2] " Unde, cum nunc Aristotelica secta prævaleat, quæ heresim putat esse oppositorum coincidentiam, in cujus admissione est initium ascensus in mysticam Theologiam . . ." *Apologia doctæ ignorantiæ*, pl. 64, in *Opera omnia*, Basle edition, 1565.

at first sight so paradoxical ? Nicholas wants to point out that there is no comparison between the transcendent Divinity and finite being ; only finite greatness admits of more or less ; the existence of the finite is as nothing compared with the Divine existence ; hence, if we bear in mind His transcendence, the Divine Being is placed above the contradictions which affect our knowledge of created being. To bring out this doctrine of the coincidence of opposed attributes, Nicholas has recourse to mathematical imagery. He observes that a curved line becomes identical with a straight line when its curvature is infinitely diminished, and that the hypotenuse of a triangle coincides with the two other sides when the angle becomes infinitely great.

Thus our knowledge of God is a mixture of ideas which tell us what He is not (negative theology) and what He is (positive theology). His transcendence renders Him unknowable by us ; His relations with the created world allow us to reason imperfectly and make conjectures concerning Him.

(iii) *God and the world.* God, being the Infinite, is all that can be. He is the " enfolding " of everything in the sense that everything is in Him. He is also the " unfolding " of everything inasmuch as everything is in Him and He in everything.[1] Nicholas adds : " Tolle Deum a creatura et remanet nihil."[2] These are bold expressions, which have a pantheistic sound. They would lead to heresy, as Wenck maintained, if taken literally. But the theories of the divine transcendence and the coincidence of contradictories enabled Nicholas to evade the objection : enfolding and unfolding are human words. God is above them both, in a way which surpasses reason. Hence God is not confounded with the world, and the principle of the identity of contraries, which is valid for God, does not apply when we are dealing with the Creator in relation to the creature. For the things of the universe are to God what multiple images are to their model or prototype. God calls them into existence by an " intention "—which excludes any community of being between the created and the uncreated.

Created things have within themselves a certain " concord-

---

[1] " Deus ergo est omnia complicans, in hoc quod omnia in eo ; est omnia explicans, in hoc quia ipse in omnibus." (*Docta ignor.*, II, ch. 3). Duhem shows by comparing texts, that the unitive theory of Nicholas of Cusa, based on the consideration of unity and equality and the connection between them, was borrowed from the *De opere sex dierum* of Theodoric of Chartres.
[2] *Ibid.*

ance," i.e., a common nature or element. They are divided into three classes, for some are more sensible, others more rational, and the third more intellectual. No single thing possesses in a pure state the element which is dominant in it. That is why the inorganic world consists only of compounds, and why no two bodies are alike. The spiritual nature which is shared in by all animated things, comprises the degrees of the vegetative, sensible, rational and intellectual life. Throughout there is a mixture of vegetative darkness and spiritual nature.[1]

Man, who is the centre of creation and the most perfect image of God, sums up in himself the various kinds of being. " The senses are as it were the streams which unite in the river of reason, and by means of the latter end in the sea of intelligence."[2] Humanity, of which each man is a participation, is a " contracted " unity, which " enfolds " all. Man is a microcosm, comprising a human God and a human world. The soul is immortal, and is united to the body by the intermediary of a *spiritus* or very ethereal breath which it sends all through the body.

(iv) *The mystical ascent.* The whole world is in process of returning to God. The movements which take place have no other origin than the love of unity, that is, God. Each being strives to perfect its type, and in the case of man, the mode of union is brought about by way of assimilation or knowledge. His intellectual nature allows of a more intimate approach to God, for knowledge is a passing backward from the multiple to unity. Very imperfect in sensible knowledge, this reduction to unity is more accentuated in the abstractive knowledge of genera and species. It attains its summit of perfection in intellectual intuition, in which the principle of contradiction ceases to exercise its rule, everything is a vision of the creative thought, and mathematical symbolism takes the place of dialectics. At this point there is a fusion between philosophy and theology : Christ is the way which elevates us to God.

423. General characteristics.—(i) The thought of Nicholas of Cusa presents manifold aspects, for it was developed side by side with his religious and political activities. We may say that the *desire of harmony* and synthesis is the basic principle :

---

[1] E. van Steenberghe, *op. cit.*, Ch. VIII.
[2] P. 346.

harmony of faith with reason, harmony of the world with God in one vast unity.

Did Nicholas of Cusa go so far as to be a pantheist ? He expressly repudiated this, and his explanations on the meaning of the identity of contraries and the divine " enfolding " leave no doubt as to his intentions. But ought we not to say of his system what we have already had to point out in the case of Master Eckhart, who was, together with pseudo-Dionysius, John Scotus Eriugena, Lully, Apuleius, and Proclus, one of the sources from which he derived his ideas ?[1] John Wenck (Venchus) was not mistaken in linking up the doctrine of the *Docta Ignorantia* with the monism of Master Eckhart Can we exclude the principle of contradiction from the theory of the Infinite ? If we banish it, how are we to control these visions of the spirit, and how can God be distinct from the world? " If at the summit of thought and at the summit of things, to exist and not to exist coincide, we abandon spiritual visions of the spirit, and how can God be distinct from the world ? If at the summit of thought and at the summit of things, to exist and not to exist coincide, we abandon the domain of speculation and enter into that of dreams."[2]

(ii) Nicholas wished to show the *weakness of dialectics* as understood by the disciples of William of Ockam ; in order to save metaphysics from the ruin caused by Nominalism, he wanted to bring about a return to neo-Platonism. This is the explanation of his opposition to the "Aristotelians." From this point of view he belonged to a period of transition, and voiced a battle-cry that was soon to be heard throughout Europe : " Down with the Aristotelians ! " In other respects he belonged to the Renaissance movement : by his love of classical Latin, his cult of the humanism then beginning to spread, and his passion for antiquity, the study of which he vainly endeavoured to direct towards Christ.

424. Influence of Nicholas of Cusa.—A small Cusian school sprang up in Italy about 1450, but did not last long. Leonardo da Vinci was an admirer of his mathematical works. James le Fèvre of Etables (J. Faber Stapulensis, 1456-1537) edited his works and made them known in France, together with those of pseudo-Dionysius. Charles Bouillée (Bovillus, about 1470-

---

[1] He mentions many other mediæval philosophers, and is in fact a " living encyclopædia." (*Op. cit.*, p. 439).
[2] *Op cit.*, p. 446.

1553) applied his mysticism to original ideas; Rudolph Agricola continued his tendencies and imitated him in endeavouring to put humanism to the service of Christianity. But people's minds were too full of feverish ideas to allow Nicholas of Cusa's work to prevail. The enthusiasm of the Renaissance for antiquity confused their minds, and they did not worry about the temperament which the pious bishop endeavoured to introduce into humanism. On the other hand, the monks of Tegernsee who from 1450 to 1456 were greatly influenced by the *Docta ignorantia*, very soon returned to the traditional mysticism, and we find their prior, Bernard of Waging, commenting in his *Tractatus de cognoscendo Deo* on the last chapter of the *Itinerarium* of St. Bonaventure.[1] Moreover, mysticism was everywhere snuffed out by the breath of the Renaissance, and thus disappeared the circles in which Nicholas of Cusa might have found admirers. The only thing that survived was a dry and cold scholasticism, exposed to the combined attacks of the movements resulting from the Renaissance.

425. Bibliography.—Editions of the *Theologia naturalis* of Raymund of Sabunde in 1488, 1496, 1507, 1509, 1852. Cf. Cl. Webb, *Studies in Mediæval Theology*, etc. Editions of Nicholas of Cusa in 1484 (Strasburg) and 1514 (Paris, 3 vols., more complete). Studies by E. van Steenberghe in *BGPM*, VIII, 6; XIV, 2-4, and above all his splendid work, *Le Cardinal N. de C.* (1401-1464), *L'action*, *La Pensée*, in *Bibl. du XVe. s.* (Paris, 1920). Ranft. *Schöpfer u. Geschöpf nach Kard. N. v. Cusa* (Wurzbourg, 1924).

Duhem, *N. de C. et Leonard de Vinci* (Etudes sur Leonard, 2nd series, Paris, 1909, pp. 97-279, pp. 424-441), *Thierry de Chartres et N. de Cuse* (*R. sc. phil. theol.*, July, 1909).

---

[1] Grabmann, *Die Erklärung d. Bernard v. Waging zum Schlusskapitel v. Bonaventuras Itinerarium*, in *Franc. Stud.*, 1921, pp. 125-135, with the text.

The Platonists of the Renaissance went to Plato to be delighted rather than instructed. Their Platonism was akin to neo-Platonism, and their claim to reduce Plato to Plotinus shows that they misunderstood the real thought of both. The same must be said of the other thesis, advanced by Cardinal Bessarion, concerning the fundamental agreement of Plato with Aristotle. Similar fantasies had been entertained by some Alexandrine writers of the Grecian decadence who display a like sterility of thought and ignorance of history.

The Aristotelianism of the Renaissance opposed to Platonism manifested equally serious faults.

440. Aristotelianism.—Averrhoes and Averrhoists and Alexandrines.—According to the Aristotelians of the Renaissance, Scholasticism had disfigured Aristotle, and this was in their opinion a primary reason for returning to the real Aristotle. The honour paid to Plato was looked upon as a second reason for championing the doctrines of the Stagirite, and in the fifteenth century there were fierce quarrels in Italy concerning the respective merits of these two great Greek thinkers.[2]

These disciples of Aristotle, however, were not in agreement as to his teaching. Some, continuing the anti-scholastic traditions of the fourteenth century, knew only the Aristotle

various dialogues of Plato into French, and De Serres (1510-1597) made a new Latin translation of all his works.

[2] The quarrels concerning the pre-eminence of Plato over Aristotle or *vice versa* began at Byzantium, where Gennadius argued in favour of Aristotle ; they then spread to Italy and Rome, where Michael Apostolius, Andreas Contrarius and Bessarion sided with Plato ; Theodore Gaza, George of Trebizond (1396-1484), and Andronicus Callistus sided with Aristotle. About 1463-64 there was a war of pamphlets in which too often personal invective took the place of argument. Among the Aristotelians, Theodore Gaza (died 1478), was a personality who might be compared to Bessarion, with whom he was on terms of friendship. He was born at Salonica at the beginning of the fifteenth century, spent some time at Constantinople, and then left for Italy shortly before the capture of the city. At the pontifical court, which had under Nicholas V. become the rival of that of the Medici, Theodore Gaza translated all the works of Aristotle. This was his chief work, and was more highly valued than the similar task of George of Trebizond, his rival in the pontifical favour. In addition, there were other translators of Aristotle. Thus the Byzantine Joh. Argyropulus, who died at Rome in 1486, translated at the Court of the Medici the *Organon*, the *Ascult. Phys.*, the *De cœlo, De anima*, and *Eth. Nic.* (L. Stein, *Der Humanist Theodor Gaza als Philosoph*, in *Arch. f. Gesch. d. Philos.*, 1889, p. 426). A. Gaspary, *Zur Chronologie de Streites d. Griechen über Plato u. Aristoteles im 15 Jahrh. (ibid).* " In this great quarrel between the admirers of Plato and those of Aristotle . . . the philosophical works of St. Thomas were thrown into the balance by the Byzantine Aristotelians," (Bouvy, *op. cit.*, p. 406, *Revue Augustin*, 1910) Georgios Scholarios translated his commentary on the *De anima*, and part of the commentaries on the *Metaphysics* ; J. Argyropulus translated the *De ente et essentia.* There were also anonymous translations of the commentaries on the *Physics* and the *De fallaciis (ibid.)*

of the Commentaries by Averrhoes; others interpreted him after the manner of Alexander of Aphrodisius. Thus there arose Averrhoists and Alexandrians,[1] whose controversies during the fifteenth and sixteenth centuries sum up the history of philosophic thought in the two centres of Aristotelianism in Italy, Padua and Bologna.

The immortality of the soul was the chief subject of their discussions. For the Averrhoists, immortality is impersonal; for the Alexandrians, the human soul perishes altogether with the body as a form disappears at the dissolution of a compound. Both parties agreed that there is neither Providence nor liberty. Those who wished to retain dogma—and they were in a minority—had recourse to the theory of the two truths. In 1513, the Fifth Council of the Lateran condemned this theory as heretical, together with that of the unity of the human intellect and the mortality of the human soul.[2]

ALEXANDER ACHILLINUS (1463-1518, *De intelligentiis, De orbibus, De universalibus*), AUGUSTINUS NIPHUS (1473-1546), and ZIMARA (died 1532) were the best known Averrhoists at Padua at the beginning of the sixteenth century,[3] not to mention the crowd of *literati* of whom Petrarch speaks and who thought it good taste to declare themselves Averrhoists. Achillinus was called " the second Aristotle " by reason of his commentaries on the Stagirite. Niphus was not so thorough-going. After having taught pure monopsychism (*De intellectu et dæmonibus*) like his master NICOLETTO VERNIAS, and editing the works of Averrhoes (1495-1497), he modified his teaching in order to harmonize it with Catholicism. And when his rival Pomponatius began to lecture in opposition to him, he was unable to defend the authority of Averrhoes against his attacks. The *De immortalitate animæ* (1518), in which Niphus replied to the similar work by Pomponatius (1516) was conceived in the spirit of the Council of the Lateran, and borrowed from Thomism its best arguments in favour of the immortality of the soul. As for ZIMARA, he was more frankly Averrhoist. He wrote commentaries on Averrhoes, and edited the works of John of Jandun.[4]

Averrhoism entered upon a polemical phase when PETRUS

---

[1] Here and there other Greek commentators were revived.
[2] Werner, *Sitzungsberichte*, etc., 1881, p. 209.
[3] The first edition of Averrhoes appeared at Padua in 1472.
[4] On the Averrhoism of the school of Padua, see Renan, *op. cit.*, IIe Partie, Ch. III.

POMPONATIUS (Pomponazzi, 1462-1525) opposed the Aristotelianism of Alexander of Aphrodisius to that of Averrhoes. After studying at Padua, Pomponatius taught at Ferrara and at Bologna. In his *Tractatus de immortalitate animæ* (1516) and in the *Defensorium* which contains his reply to Niphus, he maintains that the substantial information of the body by the soul, the materiality and mortality of the latter, and the disappearance of personality at death constitute the genuine teaching of Aristotle. He adopts the Stoic view of Providence and human liberty, and holds that reason teaches the same as revelation (*De fato, libero arbitrio et prædestinatione*). Lastly, in a third work, *De incantationibus*, he denies miracles, angels and demons, and attempts to explain by the natural influence of the stars all the extraordinary phenomena that foster superstitions.[1]

Pomponatius was followed by others, among them being SIMON PORTA of Naples (1555) and the Spaniard SEPULVEDA (died 1572).

441. Stoicism and Atomism.—JUSTUS LIPSIUS (1547-1606), a scholar rather than a philosopher, was a professor at the University of Louvain, and undertook the defence of Roman Stoicism (*Manuductio ad stoicam philosophiam*). In spite of his great reputation, he did not succeed in founding a school,[2] but the doctrines of the Porch influenced a number of Renaissance systems. We find them in ERASMUS, ZWINGLI, LEONARDI BRUNI, MELANCHTHON, and various representatives of Natural Theism.

Atomism as taught by Democritus and Epicureus reappeared in DANIEL SENNERT (1572-1637), ERYCIUS PUTEANUS (1574-1646) the successor of Justus Lipsius at Louvain, and others. The most celebrated atomist of this time was PETER GASSEND or GASSENDI (1592-1655 ; *Exercitationes paradoxicæ adversus Aristotelicos ; De vita, moribus et doctrina Epicuri*.)[3] All these philosophers, and especially those last mentioned, waged a relentless war against Aristotelianism ; they joined forces

---

[1] A. Douglas, *The philosophy and psychology of Pietro Pomponazzi*, (Cambridge, 1910). The author says that Pomponazzi's characteristic consists in not being influenced by the parallel movements to which the Renaissance gave rise around him, and in simply following an authentic interpretation of Aristotle (p. 1). Cf. Cl. Webb, *Studies in Natural Theology*, Ch. VI.

[2] See De Wulf, *Histoire de la philos. en Belgique*, pp. 159 *et seq.*

[3] Pendzig, *Pierre Gassendis Metaphysik u. ihr Verhältniss zur scholast. Philosophie*, (Bonn 1908, Collection Dyrhoff).

with men of science in order to cast discredit on the antiquated
physics of the Stagirite, and in consequence on the whole of
his philosophy.

§ 3.   The Philosophy of Nature.

442.   Forms of Naturalism.—Simultaneously with the revival of the chief doctrines of Greek philosophy, an earnest study
of nature gave rise to more original systems.

The Renaissance was greatly impressed by the beauties of
the created world and fascinated by its mysteries, and gave
to nature a cult which reminds one of the enthusiasm of the
Alexandrians.   This was the starting point for observations
and researches which afterwards led to the great discoveries
in physics and astronomy in the seventeenth century.

But these elementary experiments were insufficient in themselves and could not satisfy the great longing to penetrate
the mysteries of nature, and so recourse was had to hidden
forces, concerning which information was sought in the Cabala,
magic, and astrology.   Physicians especially revelled in occult
arts, in the hope of thereby discovering the philosophical
stone of health or elixir of life.

Lastly, the majority of naturalist systems of this time were
pantheist in tendency.   In extolling nature they deified it :
is it not easier to explain the beauty of the world if we regard
it as a living revelation of God ?

Observation, the practice of the occult sciences, and the tendency towards Pantheism are the principal characteristics
found in varying degrees in the naturalists of the Renaissance.
Hence we shall accordingly divide them into three groups,
according to the predominance of one or other of these three
traits :   (i) empirical naturalism ;   (ii) occult naturalism ;
(iii) pantheistic naturalism.   To Leonardo da Vinci belongs
a place apart.

443.   Leonardo da Vinci.—A genial artist and scholar,
LEONARDO DA VINCI (1452-1519) was one of the originators
of modern mechanics and physics.   Some of his scientific
doctrines were inspired by Albert of Saxony ; his ideas on the
infinitely great and the infinitely little and on the plurality
of worlds were based on scholasticism ; his metaphysical
doctrines came from Nicholas of Cusa, so that " the science

of Leonardo was nourished by the milk of scholasticism."[1]
In addition, Leonardo was a philosopher, but he did not systematize his ideas in this domain, and indeed only touched upon
them incidentally.

444. Empirical naturalism.—We find empirical naturalism
in its most original form in the writings of two other Italians,
Telesius and Campanella. BERNARDINUS TELESIUS (1508-1588),
the founder of the naturalism of the Renaissance, devoted
himself entirely to the study of the natural sciences, and ranks
among the bitterest detractors of Aristotelian physics. He
founded at Naples an Academia Telesiana for the development
of the natural sciences. His chief work, *De natura rerum juxta
propria principia*[2] is the work of a naïf but logical physicist,
in which he endeavours to explain nature by a restricted
number of physical forces.

In the inert and passive mass of matter, God has created
two active principles, heat and cold, the one principle of movement, and the other characterized by absolute immobility.
These two forces are incorporeal and mutually exclusive, and
share between them the quantum of matter. Thus we get a
division of the created world into a centre of heat, the heavens,
and a centre of cold, the earth. Each principle, being endowed
with a tendency towards self-preservation, possesses the faculty
of *feeling* the destructive action of its opposite. This over-
throws the Aristotelian theory of the four elements ; and makes
the phenomenon of sensation a universal fact. Particular
things come into existence as a result of the contact of the
celestial heat with the icy surface of the earth. One and the
same law presides over the genesis of minerals and the formation
of living beings.

On these physical bases Telesius constructs a new form of
vitalism, which we may outline as follows. The principle of
animal life is a *spiritus*, a modicum of heat circulating in the
body and presiding over organic functions : this theory of
animal spirits, a revival of the ancient doctrine of the πνεῦμα
was to become the starting point of the physiology of Bacon

---

[1] Duhem, *Léonard de Vinci*, 1st series, p. 3. On the origins of dynamics,
see by the same, *J. Buridan et Léonard de Vinci* (Bulletin Italien, Vol. X,
1909) ; *La tradition de J. Buridan et la science italienne au XVIe s.*, (Vol. X,
1910) ; *Dominique Soto et la Scolast. Parisienne* (Bulletin Hispan., 1910, pp.
275, 276).
[2] This appeared in 1911 as the first volume of the *Classici della filosofia
italiana* (commenced under the direction of G. Tocco). Five volumes will
probably be devoted to Telesius.

and Descartes. The *spiritus* is not, as in the scholastic system, an emanation from the informing principle, it takes the place of the substantial form, which Telesius never tires of ridiculing. Sensation and appetition are modes of action of the *spiritus* ; cognitive phenomena are reduced to transformations of sensation ; and moral acts arise from the instinct of conservation. The human *spiritus* is more refined and subtle than that of the brute, but is of the same nature.

It is true that Telesius modifies this exaggerated naturalism, just as did Cardanus and Paracelsus, by admitting in addition in man, a *forma superaddita,* immaterial and immortal, which enables us to know God. But he only deals with it in a secondary way, and this theory, destined to save appearances, introduces into the psychology of Telesius a dualism similar to that which St. Thomas condemned in the upholders of the plurality of forms.[1]

The Physics of Telesius were adopted by CAMPANELLA (1568-1639), who added a Metaphysics and a Politics.[2] Campanella lays down the thesis that all knowledge comes from sensation, and that the latter is a purely passive act which does not require the intervention of intentional species. What we call a general concept is but a weakened form or schematic *résumé* of sensation. Observation is accordingly the foundation of knowledge, but as it is limited, we must also study the resemblance of things with each other and with God. This writer, who ridicules the scholastic ideas, makes use of all the phantasmagoria of the imagination and the chimera of astrology in order to explain the analogies of beings.[3]

Since the universe is an image of God, the explanation of created reality must be sought in the study of God. He alone possesses in the pure state and in an infinite degree the three " primalities " (*primalitates*) which constitute the essence (*essentialiter*) of being, namely, the power by which it is able to be and to act (*potentia*), the knowledge which reveals it to itself (*sapientia*), and the love which inclines it to will its good

---

[1] V. Troilo, *Bernardino Telesio* (Modane, 1911) ; Gentile, *B. Telesio,* Bari, 1911.

[2] Among his numerous works, re-edited in 1854 by A. d'Ancona, we may mention : *Prodromus philosophiæ instaurandæ, Realis philosophiæ partes quattuor, Philosophiæ rationalis partes quinque, Universalis philosophiæ seu metaphysicarum rerum juxta propria principia partes tres.*—See a recent work by Blanchet, *Campanella,* (Paris, 1920), and a study by Gilson in *Etudes de philos. médiévale.*

[3] E. Gilson, *Le raisonnement par analogie chez T. Campanella,* in *Etudes de philos. médiév.,* pp. 125-145.

(*amor*). Conversely, pure non-being comprises *impotentia*, *insipientia* and *odium*. Every creature distinct from God is a mixture of being and non-being (traces of scholasticism) ; it possesses the essential " primalities " in the measure in which it shares reality. Telesius had already attributed to physical forces the power of feeling. Campanella gives to this cosmic pan-psychism a metaphysical interpretation.

Campanella's Politics is based on man's love for himself and for society as the prolongation of himself. His *Civitas solis*, like the *Utopia* of Thomas More by which it was to some extent inspired, is a fantastic description of an ideal state in which individual liberty is regulated to the smallest details for the good of the community.

445. Naturalism and the occult sciences.—The naturalists who wanted to substitute for the old physics a new philosophy, based partly on observation and partly on the data of the Cabala, astrology, magic and alchemy, were almost all physicians. The first was PARACELSUS OF HOHENHEIM (1493-1541), who wrote a number of works in German, which were translated into Latin by his pupils. Among them we may mention the *Opus paramirum*, *Die grosse Wundarznei*, and *De natura rerum*. He wished to build up medicine on four pillars, theology, philosophy, astrology and alchemy.

We find the same medley of cabalistic doctrine with alchemy, magic and astrology in another physician, who arrived at similar conclusions, but apparently was not acquainted with the works of Paracelsus, the Italian HIERONYMUS CARDANUS (1501-1576), author of treatises *De varietate rerum* and *De subtilitate*.

446. Pantheistic naturalism deifies the cosmos and ascribes to it one unique life, of which the world-soul is the principle. It was professed by Patritius and Giordano Bruno.

PATRITIUS (PATRIZZI, 1529-1597), who belonged to the series of Renaissance Platonists, was a bitter detractor of Aristotle and Scholasticism. He accused the latter of doing ill service to the Catholic faith, and begged Gregory XIV to impose upon Christendom the new synthesis of which he was the author. This is contained in a *Nova de universis philosophia*, of which the four parts, *Panaugia*, *Panarchia*, *Panpsychia*, *Pancosmia*, are respectively devoted to light, the first principles, life, and cosmic order. The absolute One, *Unomnia*, the only reality and supreme goodness, produces the Holy Trinity within, and the invisible and visible world without. The *anima mundi* is one of the stages in this process of emanation and descent (Plotinus). It communicates life and movement to the things of nature, including man. The finite is a prolongation of the Infinite. Patritius explains physical phenomena by a theory of light (*Panaugia*), which recalls that of Telesius.

GIORDANO BRUNO (1548-1600) was another ardent champion of pantheism. He wrote numerous works in Latin and Italian : *Dialoghi della causa, principio ed uno ; Degli eroici furori ; Dell' infinito, universo e dei mondi.* God is immanent in the world. He is the *complicatio omnium*, the *coincidentia oppositorum* (Nicholas of Cusa) ; and the continual flux of phenomena is but the unfolding of one unique and eternal substance *omnibus præsentissimus*. The " accidents " of this substance arise from one unique original matter, the passive source of all possibility. One unique form—the soul of the world, the universal intelligence and active principle of all possibility—vivifies this matter (formal cause) and produces by its internal plasticity (efficient cause) the beings of the universe. The original matter and primitive form com-penetrate ; they are the two aspects of one and the same reality, God. Matter is God, as maintained by David of Dinant. Everything is good and beautiful in nature, because everything lives with a Divine life.

In his Latin works, Bruno seems to have modified this pantheism without however abandoning his fundamental principles.

§ 4—*The Philosophy of Natural and Social Law*

447. Thomas More and Hugo Grotius.—The awakening of nationalities, the study of the political forms of Greece and Rome, and the spirit of independence which animated states, led to the development of a philosophy of public law based on the study of man. The originator of these new theories was THOMAS MORE (MORUS, 1480-1535). His remarkable work, *De optimo rei publicæ statu sive de nova insula Utopia*, written before the Reformation in England, links him up with Italian Platonism. It consists of two parts. The first contains the plan of an ideal state organized according to the conceptions of Plato's Republic. But he faithfully reflects the aspirations of his age in a second part, more practical, in which he justifies the independence of Church and State, and the neutral attitude of the State towards the Churches.

These principles were expounded and synthetized better by HUGO GROTIUS. Born in Holland, where the wars of religion had led to religious indifference, Hugo de Groot (Grotius, 1583-1645, *De jure belli et pacis*) may be considered as the legislator of natural and social right for the Renaissance.

Natural law (*jus naturale*), which is derived from the individual, is the collection of imprescriptible rights revealed by the rational study of human nature. The fundamental characteristic of nature is sociability, which is innate and instinctive.

The origin of social authority is the social contract, of the free volition of the individuals, who for the sole end of better safeguarding their rights, live in common. Accordingly, the state exists only by and for the individual.

The people delegate their sovereignty, and this delegation is irrevocable according to some, revocable according to others.

Between human law, known by reason, and divine law which is revealed, there exists an impenetrable barrier. The religious indifference of the State and toleration are corollaries of the separation of Church and State, but this does not prevent Grotius from believing personally in the Christian revelation.

We readily recognize in the theories of More, and above all in those of Grotius, certain mediæval contributions: the natural law, the natural character of society, popular sovereignty, and popular delegation, are doctrines which directly descend from the thirteenth century. But the solidarity between public life and the moral life of citizens is broken, and the integral and unifying conceptions of the thirteenth century have vanished: the State is indifferent to religions and tolerates all of them. Machiavelli later on did but draw out the consequences of these new principles, and after his time it was soon maintained that an atheistic state is possible.

448. The divine right of kings.—The theory of the divine right of kings is foreign to the mediæval spirit. For the theorists of the thirteenth century, rulers derive their authority from God, not immediately, but through the medium of the people. The doctrine that they depend directly from God without the intervention of the collectivity was put forward by the sovereigns of centralized states (Henry IV, James I),

who wished above all to put an end to ecclesiastical interference
in political matters. It also owed its credit partly to the
tendency in Protestantism to make the king the head of the
national church in each State.[1] We must content ourselves
with this slight indication of the movement of ideas, for their
study does not directly concern this history.

§ 5—Religious Philosophies

449. Protestantism.—The weakening of the idea of an
ecclesiastical hierarchy, the Great Schism, the relaxation of
ecclesiastical morals, the exaggerated movements of mysticism, doubts concerning the value of the arguments put
forward to establish dogmas, and the discussions of Wyclif and
the Hussites all prepared the way for the Protestant Reformation. The latter is easy to grasp in its negative side : the
suppression of the ecclesiastical hierarchy, rites, and imposed
dogmas. Its positive side is more complicated : it advocated
a return to the primitive church ; just as humanism looked back
to antiquity, it inculcated a simple morality which in some cases
ended in puritanism ; and it brought the individual soul
directly face to face with God, and made the individual the
interpreter of belief.

The reformers joined with the humanists, though for different
reasons, in vehemently condemning the scholastic philosophy.
They considered it as the stronghold of the religion which they
wished to destroy. The theological controversies which they
aroused had an indirect influence on their philosophy, and the
latter took very varied forms (neo-Platonism, Stoicism, Aristotelianism, Pantheism). Each one made his own system of
doctrine, and naturally accommodated it to his own philosophy,
itself chosen just as freely.

450. The Reformers.—LUTHER (1483-1546) was not a philosopher. He forbade philosophy to meddle with theology,
and reproached scholasticism for having " sophisticated "
theology.[2] Justification by faith (*justitia Dei revelatur ex fide*)
is the master idea of his Christianity. Original sin corrupted

---

[1] Neville Figgis, *The Divine Right of Kings* ; and *From Gerson to Grotius*,
Cambridge, 1916, Ch. III-VI).
[2] On the relations between Luther and scholasticism, see Denifle, *Luther
und Lutherthum* in *d. ersten Entwickelung*, I, 2 (Mayence, 1904-1906).

man to the very depths of his being, only faith in the Gospel can restore him to justice and holiness. This redeeming faith, springing from individual inspiration, unites man to God, and leads him to felicity passively, without effort, and even without the concurrence of his works.

Nevertheless the dogmatic system of Luther implies a philosophy. The opposition between the flesh and the spirit leads to psychological dualism ; the passivity of man towards grace and absolute predestination lead to determinism.

ZWINGLI the Swiss reformer (1484-1531) agreed with Luther in regarding justification by subjective belief as the foundation of the new Christianity. He was a fervent humanist, and utilized neo-Platonism and Stoicism in establishing his doctrine. From them he derived the idea of the Divine immanence and the deification of man regenerated by the sovereign good. Seneca provided him with arguments in favour of the autonomy of the will, the absolute predestination of the good and the wicked, and moral determinism. The unity of divine revelation in the various religions, or universal Deism, was regarded by Zwingli as a natural conciliation between humanism and Protestantism.

MELANCHTHON (1497-1560) made use of Aristotle for the service of Protestant theology. He cultivated humanism in order to understand the philosophy of antiquity, and to build up on this basis an apologia for Christianity. His manuals on the dialectics, physics and ethics of Aristotle are remarkable for their order and their clarity, and won for him the title *præceptor Germaniæ*.

Melanchthon's peripateticism, which is comparatively pure in his dialectics, becomes tinctured with Platonism and Stoicism[1] when he deals with the theory of knowledge. Man possesses within himself a *lumen naturale* (against Luther),

---

[1] Dilthey, *Melanchthon und die erste Ausbildung des natürlichen Systems in Deutschland*, in *Arch. f. Gesch. Phil.* VI., p. 225. An Aristotelian in physics, Melanchthon ridiculed the discoveries of Copernicus. The pantheistic idea already advanced by Zwingli dominates the mystical anthropology of SEBASTIAN FRANCK (1499-1542, *Paradoxa, De arbore scientiæ boni et mali*) and above all the philosophy of JACOB BOEHME (1575-1624 ; *Aurora, Vierzig Fragen von der Seele, Mysterium magnum, Von der Gnadenwahl*). Boehme's originality consists in his metaphysical explanation of the simultaneous presence of good and evil. The opposition between these is a primordial and connatural fact in God, and hence necessary. The human soul is not a Divine creation (theism), but God Himself ; unique in all the representatives of humanity, it is the original state of God, the bottomless abyss, " containing heaven and hell in its immensity." (Deussen, *J. Böhme, über sein Leben und seine Philosophie*, Kiel, 1897 ; and Boutroux, in *Etudes d'histoire de philosophie*).

and innate principles teach us the great truths of the speculative and moral order (Stoicism, Cicero). The Greco-Roman philosophy, and especially peripateticism, has best deciphered the teachings of this *lumen naturale*. But it is still incomplete, inasmuch as original sin has darkened the intelligence of man. It belongs to faith and the Gospel to purify this source of knowledge and to restore to it its former brilliance. Thus faith completes reason (against Luther) ; Greek philosophy and Christianity teach the same truths in different degrees of clearness.

Melanchthon's *Ethicæ doctrinæ elementa* became the starting point for Protestant theories on natural and social right : the decalogue is the content of the *jus naturale*, and the State is of immediately divine origin and independent of the Church— a thesis which was vigorously combated by the Catholic publicists of Spain.

451. Deism.—The religious quarrels of the Reformation led to projects of conciliation between the various Churches. There was a stong conviction that all religions possess a common basis of essential truths concerning God, and that their content is to this extent identical.[1] Luther was hostile to this Deism, a kind of residue of the various Christian religions, but Zwingli and various sects in the Reformed Church favoured it. Moreover, Deism flattered the Renaissance spirit of independence, since it was simply naturalism applied to religion. Its followers wished to confine themselves to interrogating reason in order to discover religious notions. Deism had a great number of adherents, and its influence was felt in the moral, social and even the artistic life of the sixteenth century. In particular, it inspired the theories of the separation of Church and State, Indifference, and State toleration in religious matters.

Already at the court of Frederick II the identity of the great religions had been maintained (p. 107). ERASMUS propagated the thesis that the purified doctrine of Christ is identical with the religion of Plato, Cicero, and Seneca. GEMISTOS PLETHO, in the name of Platonism, REUCHLIN in the name of Judaism, and KONRAD MUDT (Mutianus Rufus) and the Erfurt humanists became the advocates of a primitive and integral Christianity identical with deism. In Holland, which had greatly suffered

---

[1] Dilthey, *Auffassung und Analyse des Menchen im* 15. *und* 16. *Jahrh.* (*Arch. f. Gesch. Philos.* 1894 and 1895) ; *Das natürliche System der Geisterwissenschaften im* 17 *Jahrh.* (*ibid.* 1895 and 1896).

from the religious wars, COORNHERT (born 1522) was one of the first to speak of religious peace and the reduction of opposed systems of dogma to common elements. This idea was widely supported. THOMAS MORE favoured it, HUGO GROTIUS stressed it, later on HERBERT OF CHERBURY developed it, and it became one of the favourite ideas of the philosophy of the seventeenth century.

CHAPTER III

Scholastic Philosophy

§ 1—*General Notions*

452. General characteristics.—(1) The dominant feature of Scholasticism in this period is the *prevalence of schools, parties, and routine*. The religious corporations accept the hegemony of one of their doctors. The universities flock to a standard, and it is not rare to find the choice of a philosopher determined by politics or intrigue. Officially the Faculties were restricted to nominalism or realism, or else the statutes gave the right to choose between the two *viæ*. Thus in 1452 a decree by the prince orientated the University of Heidelberg towards realism.[1] The University of Fribourg was nominalist at the time of its foundation (1456), but allowed realism after 1484.[2] The Faculty of Arts at Basle (1460) at first allowed the two methods, *paritas viarum*, but soon gave preference to nominalism.[3] The same is true of Ingolstadt (1472), where the administrative organization of the faculty was itself doubled[4]; the Duke endeavoured to restore unity in 1477. The choice between the *viæ* was left open at Tübingen (1477), where, however, the Scotist realists were more in favour. The same is true of Greifswald (1456). At Wittenberg, which received a University in 1502, the statutes of 1508 allowed the three scholastic methods, " vias scholasticorum doctorum absque differentia erigimus,"[5] those of the Thomists, Scotists, and Gregorians (nominalists). These latter were sometimes

---

[1] Ehrle, *op. cit.*, p. 177.
[2] P. 183.
[3] P. 185.
[4] P. 188.
[5] P. 231.

called Gabrielists, from Gabriel Biel, another disciple of Ockam.[1]

True, there always were from the fifteenth to the seventeenth centuries interpreters of Thomism, Scotism and Ockamism who displayed some originality, but it is easy to understand that these official classifications imposed wholesale were not favourable to individual work or reflection. The scholastic renaissance in Spain and Italy in the sixteenth century was a brilliant but ephemeral exception.

(ii) The *abuse of dialectical discussion* increased. The vital doctrines of scholasticism were neglected or else corrupted. In the seventeenth century manuals compared matter and form to lovers who courted, married, divorced, and contracted new unions. The merely verbal value of the theory of powers justified the sneers of Molière and his pleasantries on the dormitive power of opium. Similarly the misinterpretation of the " intentional species " was later on rightly criticized by Malebranche and Arnauld.

(iii) The scholastics defend themselves badly, or else not at all, against the philosophers of the Renaissance—and in such matters not to defend was to acknowledge defeat.

(*a*) Their attitude towards the humanists lacked foresight and vigour.

In the first place the scholastics were reproached for writing in a barbarous Latin, and making use of translations which were incorrect and devoid of elegance. If they had wished they could have profited by the just criticisms of the humanist philologists on this point, and their own philosophy would have benefited by it. On the ground of form, there was nothing to prevent an alliance with humanism. In point of fact there were a few interesting attempts in which the " Aristotelians " took the initiative, but they were the work of a minority, and did not succeed in changing the general mentality. At the end of the fifteenth century, two Parisian masters, James le Fèvre of Etaples (Jacobus Faber Stapulensis) and his disciple, Josse Clichthove of Nieuport (1472-1543), both ardent disciples of Aristotle as well as of letters, commenced a movement in this direction. They wanted to introduce a purer Latin into philosophy, substitute more elegant versions for those in circulation, and modify the Aristotelianism of scholasticism by Platonist elements. Clichthove edited the treatises of his

---

[1] " Indifferenter profiteatur via Thomæ, Scoti, Gregorii, p. 231.

master, Le Fèvre,[1] and only separated from him after 1520, when the former had become entangled in Lutheranism and was obliged to leave Paris. He himself retired to Chartres in 1526. The *introductiones* and *scholia* of Le Fèvre and Clichthove were adopted as manuals in many universities in France, Germany, and the northern Low Countries. At Paris they lead to a revival. But after Le Fèvre's expulsion and the departure of Clichthove, Parisian scholasticism returned to its former abuses. A reform in the Faculty of Arts at Vienna in 1492 is equally significant,[2] and again that introduced by royal decree of 1525 into the Faculty of Arts at Tübingen.[3] In both cases we recognize the beneficial influence of humanism.

But the humanists addressed a second reproach to scholastics, one which was more serious and not so deserved. Themselves fanatical servants of the cause of ancient letters, they accused scholastics of not philosophizing inasmuch as they did not know how to write. Whether from negligence or impotency, the scholastics did not protest against this accusation, which it would have been easy to rebut. They did not understand, or get others to understand, that the task of the philosopher begins where that of the philologist ends. It is not surprising that the humanist movement led to their confusion.

(b) The scholastics did in some respects accept the challenge of the Reformers, but the conflict was chiefly theological in character.

(c) As for the naturalist philosophies of Telesius, Pomponazzi and Giordano Bruno, these were not dealt with at all.

(iv) The scholastics kept themselves apart from the sciences, the revolutionary discoveries in which led to the ruin of the mediæval conceptions. Elaborated as they were outside scholasticism, these new doctrines were used against it.

Francis Bacon was fully aware that the Aristotelians did not concern themselves either with contemporary philosophy or with the progress of sciences. He reproached them for

---

[1] Clerval, *De Judoci Clichtovei neoportuensis doctoris theologi parisiensis et carnotensis canonici vita et operibus*, Paris, 1894. He wrote *Totius philosophiæ paraphrases, In terminorum cognitionem introductio*, and numerous commentaries on the works of Faber.

[2] Ehrle, *op. cit.*, p. 169.

[3] Pp. 197 *et seq.* It is a significant fact that the long list of scholastic authorities comprises representatives of all the groups, but excludes by name John of Mirecourt and John of Jandun ("non Monachum et Joannem de Gandavo"), i.e., the representatives of anti-scholastic tendencies.

this in exaggerated terms : " historiam vero et naturæ et temporis maxima ex parte ignorantes."[1]

453. Division.—The struggle between the Ockamist nominalists (§ 2) and the realists (§ 3), to adopt the terminology of the time, divided the Universities, and provides us with a first classification of the schools. The " realists," of course, were either Scotists or Thomists, and we can even include in this group adherents to the other philosophies of the thirteenth and fourteenth centuries. The chief event which dominated the sixteenth century was the revival of scholasticism in Spain and Italy. This was at once a restoration of the past and a doctrinal development (§ 4). The attitude of the scholastics of the seventeenth century towards Cartesianism and scientific discoveries forms the epilogue of a long and progressive decline (§ 5).

§ 2—Nominalism

454. Parisian Nominalism during the second half of the fifteenth century.—In 1446, the University of Paris had been placed under Parliament. The King, Louis XI, interfered in its philosophical orientation, and on the 1st March, 1474, endeavoured to suppress Nominalism by force. On the advice of his confessor (!), and instigated by the Realists, who seem to have been a minority in the Arts, but to have given the tone in the faculty of Theology, he forbade the teaching in any form of the philosophy of the *Nominales* or *Terministæ ;* he ordained that their works should be seized, and that the academic grades should be refused to anyone who would not swear to conform with his wishes. William of Ockam, John of Mirecourt, Gregory of Rimini, Buridan, Peter d'Ailly, Marsilius of Inghen, Adam Wodeham, John Dorp, Albert of Saxony, and their like (*suorumque similium*) were banned by name from the schools.[2] We can well understand that this made a great impression among the Terminists, who soon prepared to parry the blow. The collective work which they published in their defence in this same year 1474 is instructive in many ways. After establishing, in somewhat ordinary but at the same time piquant terms, the definition of *reales*

---

[1] Quoted by Brucker, *Historia critica philos.*, Vol. III, pp. 877-878.
[2] Ehrle, *op. cit.*, pp. 313 and 314.

and *nominales*,[1] they complain bitterly of the four persecutions to which the poor Nominalists have been subjected. The first was directed against William of Ockam, and although led by the Pope, John XXII, the University never dared to condemn philosophical nominalism.[2] The second, in Bohemia, was due to John Hus and Jerome of Prague, who obtained a decree expelling the Nominalists, which obliged them to transfer themselves to Leipzig. But the *doctissimi viri nominales*, Peter d'Ailly and John Gerson, reduced these two heretics to silence. The third persecution was connected with the predominance of Realists during the decades 1410-1430 and their *intransigéance*.[3] Lastly, the signatories of the protestation regard as a persecution the attitude of revenge which they ascribe to their adversaries in the matter of the Louvain master, Peter de Rivo : in his person Realism was condemned by the Faculty of Theology at Paris, and the Realists had never forgiven this.[4]

Moreover, the document concludes, the philosophy of the *Reales* is more dangerous than that of the *Nominales*, " ut patet in materia universalium, de æternitate propositionum et multitudine entium sine causa."[5] For one error met with in Nominalist doctrine there are four or five in Realism.[6]

The Nominalists won the day. Doubtless as a result of new influences, Louis XI changed his mind, and a decree of Parliament (1481) cancelled the royal edict. The books of the *nominales* were restored to circulation, and at the end of the fifteenth century Nominalism was in a flourishing condition at Paris. The numerous Nominalist works which issued from the Parisian presses are an evident proof of this. John Major took a leading part in this great publishing movement.

455. Nominalism in the other universities.—The end of the fifteenth century witnessed the entrance on the scene of the Spanish universities. Numerous students hastened from Spain and Portugal in order to study Parisian Nominalism and

---

[1] " Doctores nominales dicti sunt qui non multiplicant res principaliter signatas per terminos secundum multiplicationem terminorum. Reales autem, qui e contra res multiplicatas esse contendunt, secundum multiplicitatem terminorum etc." p. 322.

[2] " Dicta tamen universitas noluit eam condemnare, p. 323. Cf. also p. 177.

[3] Cf. p. 189. " Supervenerunt quidam Albertistæ qui, nullo resistente, doctrinam nominalium ejecerunt." (Ehrle, p. 325). The term *Albertiste* is here equivalent to Thomist.

[4] See later on.

[5] P. 326.

[6] *ibid.* The edict of Louis XI and the Nominalist document are published in full by Ehrle.

afterwards introduced it into their own countries at Salamanca, Alcala, and Coimbra. It was at Paris that Dominic Soto came into contact with Ockamism before entering the Dominican order. Of all the Spanish universities, Salamanca became the most famous, and a *catedra de nominales* was instituted there side by side with two others devoted to the exegesis of Scotus and St. Thomas. Gabriel Biel, Marsilius of Inghen, and still more Durandus were the standard authors. At the same time we must bear in mind that this Nominalist chair was a theological one, and that the sophistical logic so highly prized by the artists was not allowed.[1]

Nominalism similarly spread in the Italian universities, where it appealed to jurists and physicians as well as the artists. In 1494, Venice was a great Ockamist centre, and between 1494 and 1498 Bologna won the title *vera Nominalium academia in Italia.*[2]

As for the German universities, Nominalism maintained the reputation which it had enjoyed since their foundation. There was no place to which it did not penetrate.[3]

456. Principal nominalists.—The most prominent person in the group of Parisian Nominalists was the Scotch master, Johannes Major (1478-1540), regent of the College of Montaigu. He edited John Dorp's commentaries on Buridan, composed a *Propositum de infinito*,[4] various treatises on logic, and commented on the *Physics* and *Ethics* of Aristotle, and the *Sentences* of Peter Lombard. Among the numerous disciples to whom he imparted his zeal for Ockamist ideas were David Cranston of Glasgow ; the Spaniards, Antonius Coronel and Gaspar Lax ; and John Dullaert of Ghent (born about 1471-1513), the Aristotelian commentator of whom Vivès had such unpleasant recollections. It was Johannes Scotus Major whom Rabelais selected as the butt for his cheap ridicule of scholasticism.[5]

At Sienna, Olivieri, *doctor artium et medecinæ*, author of a *Tractatus rationalis scientiæ* (about 1491) ; his disciples, Alexander Sermoneta and Benedictus Victorius Faventinus ;

---

[1] Ehrle, *op. cit.*, p. 246, and *Die Salmantizenser Theologen, (Katholik*, LII, 500, and LIII, 503, 513).
[2] P. 247.
[3] P. 389-391.
[4] Duhem, *Léonard de Vinci*, II, 484.
[5] Not Duns Scotus as Plattard wrongly states in his work *L'ouvrage de Rabelais*, 1910, p. 6.

and the physicians Giacomo Ricci and Bernardinus Petri de Landuciis, adopted Nominalism. We must also mention the name of Cajetan de Thienis, and the Augustinian hermits, Paulus Nicolettus and Paulus Pergulensis (died 1451), all Venetian masters who, together with Petrus Mantuanus, were the most important representatives of Italian Nominalism. Marcus de Benevento, a Celestine monk, introduced Nominalism at Bologna about 1496, and in the same year edited the works of Ockam.

At Tübingen, Gabriel Biel (about 1425-1495), who is called the last of the scholastics, was a militant Ockamist. His chief work, *Epithoma pariter et collectorium circa IV Sent. libros*, or *Collectorium*, which is well known and has often been published, contains nothing original, but is justly regarded as a methodical and faithful exposition of Nominalism.

Henry Greve at Leipzig, Michael of Breslau at Cracow, John Altenstaig of Mindelheim, and Conrad of Buchen (died 1531), may be included in the long list of decadent Terminists which is being gradually extended by a scrupulous examination of documents.[1]

457. The end of Nominalism.—Nominalism collapsed before the combined assault of Humanism and the Reformation. Its defeat was a foregone conclusion. Its sophistical dialectic, paradoxes, and philosophical jargon collapsed before the ridicule directed against them, and as it was devoid of metaphysics, there was no doctrinal rampart behind which it could take refuge. It was otherwise with Thomism and Scotism, which, thanks to their metaphysical foundation, were not swept away, involved in the destruction.

458. Bibliography.—*Logica mag. P. Mantuani* (Venice, 1492). *Compendium* of P. Pergulensis (Venice, 1498). The last edition of the *Collectorium circa quatuor Sentent. libros* of Biel was in 1519 (Lyons). The treatise of Olivieri of Sienna was published in 1491. Editions of Johannes Major : *Quæstiones in veterem artem*, etc. (Paris, 1528), *Introductorium in Aristotelicam dialecticam* (ibid 1527), *In P. Hispani summulas commentaria* (Lyons, 1505, etc.), containing numerous dissertations on logic, *Commentary on the Sentences*,

---

[1] Prantl mentions other names : J. Wessl (died 1489) ; Antonius Silvester (died 1515) ; Stephanus de Monte, at Padua, in 1490 ; Judocus Isenacensis (died 1519) ; Bartholomæus Arnoldi (1532) ; etc. Completed by Ehrle, *op. cit.*

1519 and 1530.—V. Prantl, *op. cit.*, IV, pp. 194, 230 *et seq.*
On Biel, see article by C. Ruch, in *Dict. théol. cath.*, 1904,
Clerval, *op. cit.*, De Wulf, *Hist. Phil. en Belgique*, 1910, pp. 178
et seq. New matter in Ehrle, *op. cit.*

§ 3—*The Realist Schools*

459. Realism in the Universities.—Cologne and Louvain
remained faithful to the Thomist Realism they had followed
since their origin, and the history of these two sister universities is closely intertwined.

The Faculty of Arts at Cologne was devoted to Thomism,
and the movement of ideas consisted in controversies on shades
of meaning which are not very clear. We find the College of
the Mountain founded by Henry of Gorkum (1419) defending
Thomas Aquinas, while the Laurentian College sided with
Albert the Great, and opposed to the Thomists a *Schola
Albertistarum.* We shall later on point out some prominent
men in the two parties. Their disputes lasted till the sixteenth
century.

In its turn, the Faculty of Arts at Louvain endeavoured to
maintain in their entirety the statutes of 1427 forbidding the
teaching of Nominalism, and imposing an official list of Realist
interpreters of Aristotle, which included Averrhoes, Albert
the Great, Thomas Aquinas, and Giles of Rome. The University remained faithful to this spirit, not only during a celebrated
conflict which lasted for thirty years, but still in 1480, when it
threatened to suspend the masters who explained Aristotle
" ad intentionem Ockam et ejus sequacium."[1] From 1446 to
1476 there was an intestine quarrel at Louvain complicated by
intrigues, delations to the Roman Court, appeals to the Dukes
of Bourgogne, and consultations with the sister universities
of Paris and Cologne. The conflict began between a master of
arts, Peter de Rivo (born at Assche about 1420) and a theologian
Henry of Zoemeren or Someren, a professor from 1437 to 1472,
and concerned the truth of propositions relative to something
which may or may not happen, such as free acts. Aristotle,
and after him Peter de Rivo, said that such propositions could
be neither true nor false, for if they were true before the event,
the latter would be necessary and would lose its contingent

[1] Ehrle, *op. cit.*, p. 161.

character. The reason given contains a fallacy : we do not know, as a matter of fact, whether the event which is the subject of a future proposition will take place or not, but our ignorance does not prevent the proposition from being always either true or false. The question has theological applications, and it was these which aroused the theologians. If Peter de Rivo is right, prophecy has no truth, since it does not prevent the contingence of the event predicted, and God has no foreknowledge of future contingent events. Peter de Rivo defended his views in a *Quæstio Quodlibetaria* held in 1465. This discourse provoked a series of incidents which we need not relate here. Two parties were formed. Henry of Someren raised the cry of heresy (1470), but the University sided with his opponent, and as his own faculty of Theology was divided on the question, an appeal was made to the theologians of Cologne and Paris. The former decided for Peter de Rivo, and influenced the official opinion of the Faculty (Oct. 1470). Paris did not give any official opinion, although twenty-four theologians pronounced in favour of Peter de Rivo. The matter was taken to the Roman Court, it interested Cardinal Bessarion and François della Rovere (the future Sixtus IV), who both composed a *factum* on the subject. Henry of Someren was excluded from the University in November, 1470, but the affair ended in a retractation in due form (March, 1473) imposed on Peter de Rivo by the Roman Court.[1]

Peter de Rivo was a Realist, like his colleagues in the Arts, who had all sworn fidelity to Aristotle, and was regarded as such by the Parisian Nominalists,[2] but he had himself inherited the Nominalist turn of mind. His habit of opposing propositions which are true in Aristotelianism (*aristotelice veræ*) to those which are true by virtue of Divine foreknowledge (*veritate notitiæ divinæ*) betrays the secret complacency with which all Nominalists oppose reason and faith. The theologians of Louvain, Cologne and Paris who supported him displayed a similar sympathy for a philosophic attitude which they professed to combat.[3]

---

[1] On this affair see De Wulf, *Histoire de la Philosophie en Belgique*, pp. 155-158 ; Laminne, *La controverse sur les future contingents à l'Université de Louvain au XVe s.* (*Bull. Acad. Belg.* Classe Lettres, 1906), and Ehrle, *op. cit.*, pp. 126-135, who deals with new data. The history of this quarrel remains to be written, as the philosophical documents are as yet unpublished.
[2] Cf. above, p. 288.
[3] Ehrle, *op. cit.*, p. 136.

Together with Thomism, Scotism is described as a Realist philosophy in the university documents of the fifteenth and sixteenth centuries. In great university centres such as Padua, Pavia, Ferrara, Bologna, Vienna, Cracow, Cologne, Prague, and especially in Spain at Lerida, Valencia, Salamanca, Coimbra and Alcala, not to mention others, a special chair was instituted for the teaching of Scotism.

We have seen above that Scotist or Thomist Realism also developed in the German universities, especially in the faculties of theology, where the religious orders had representatives. Even in the Nominalist universities Realism was allowed.

460. The Thomist school.—HENRY OF GORKUM, educated at Paris (1418) and who ruled the College of the Montain at Cologne from 1419 to 1431 composed *Quæstiones in partes S. Thomæ*[1] in which he grouped various questions of the master, summarized his conclusions, and added to them personal commentaries. His disciple, GERARD TEUTEGEN OF HEEREN-BERG or De Monte (died 1480, Commentary on the *De ente et essentia*, author of an *Apologetica . . . qua ostensorem concordiæ inter S. Thomam et venerabilem Albertum magnum impugnat opprobriis, auctoritatibus et rationibus omissis*), LAMBERTUS DE MONTE (died 1499) and JOHN VERSOR were the Thomist leaders. The last mentioned wrote *Quæstiones super veterem artem ; Super omnes libros novæ logicæ*, and commentaries on the *De ente et essentia* and Petrus Hispanus. In the group of *Albertistæ* we find HEYMERIC DE CAMPO(died 1460), GERHARD HARDEWYK (died 1503, Commentaries on *Nova logica* and Petrus Hispanus), and ARNOLD OF LUYDE or of Tongres (died 1540, Commentaries on the *Organon* and Petrus Hispanus).

PETRUS NIGRI opposed the moderns in various German centres and drew up a *Clipeus Thomistarum* ; BARBUS PAULUS SONCINAS (died 1494) summarized Capreolus, commented on the *Isagoge* and the *Categories*, and composed *Quæstiones metaphysicales ;* JOHANNES A LAPIDE (died 1494) whom we meet with in turn at Paris, Basle and Tübingen, wrote commentaries on the *Organon*, treatises *De exponibilibus* and the *Sophistical Arguments ;* FRANCISCUS TÆGIUS wrote a commentary on St. Thomas's opusculum *De fallaciis* ; MICHAEL SAVARETIUS undertook the defence of Thomism against Scotism (*Quæst. de analogia contra scotistas ; Q. de universalibus;*

---

[1] Incunabulum undated, reprinted in 1473 at Eszlingen. Cf. Grabmann, *Hilfmittel*, etc., pp. 20-22.

at Fribourg in 1490 and at Rostock in 1520, Dominicans lectured on the magistral work of Thomas Aquinas.[1] Soon afterwards the *Summa* was imposed also at Louvain, Salamanca, and elsewhere.

Cajetan, Conrad Kollin and Peter Crockaert had introduced a new method, that of commenting on the *Summa*. Very soon the number of their imitators was legion. The works of the Dominican master received the same treatment previously given to the Sentences of the Lombard.[2] At the same time there appeared new abbreviations of the *Summa theologica* : CLEMENS DE TERRA SALSA wrote his *Conclusiones formales* (published at Cologne in 1486); in the sixteenth century JEROME DUNGERSHEIM OF OCHSENFURT (died 1540) also drew up the conclusions of the *Summa ;* the Italian Dominican SILVESTER PRIERIAS (died 1523), author of a *Summa Silvestrina*, various works against Luther, wrote a *Conflatus* or *Compendium operum S. Th. ex verbis ipsis doct. angelici concinnatum;* BERARD BONGEAN (died 1574) made a summary ; LUKE CARBONI (died 1597) wrote a *Compendium absolutissimum*, printed in 1587 and 1609; HUNNÆUS (died 1578) drew up *S. Thomæ totius summæ conclusiones;* the Dominican JOHN OF OCHOA (died after 1565), formulated *Primariæ conclusiones.* These works became a nuisance, for they were substituted for the original.[3]

463. The Scotist School.—Scotism remained the favourite doctrine of the Franciscans, who continued to combine the study of Duns Scotus with that of St. Bonaventure. Scotus also had followers outside the Franciscan order.

STEPHANUS BRULIFER explained St. Bonaventure at Mayence, and published *Reportata in IV 1. Sentent. S. Bonaventuræ.*[4]

---

[1] Ehrle, *op. cit.*, p. 208.

[2] Michelitsch, *Kommentatoren zur Summa Theologica des hl. Th.* (Thomisten Schriften, 2, Theolog. Reiche, Graz, 1924), mentions 218 commentators on the Prima Pars, 108 on the Prima Secundæ, 89 on the Secunda Secundæ, and 148 on the Tertia Pars. Commentaries abounded especially in the seventeenth century.

[3] In the seventeenth century the series of compendia of the works of St. Thomas was continued by the Jesuit Peter Alagona (died 1624), and the Dominican Dominicus Gravina (died 1543). Anthony Cloche (1628-1720) headed a revival of Thomism in the Dominican order. He published unfinished commentaries by Didaco Nuno Cabezudo (died 1614) on the Third Part of the *Summa theologica*, repeated the obligation to follow St. Thomas, and in the first years of the eighteenth century organized at Rome various institutions Thomist in character, founded through the liberality of Cardinal Casanate (1620-1700), and in particular a double chair of exegesis of St. Thomas.

[4] Basle edition, 1501.

LOUIS OF PRUSSIA, in his *Trilogium animæ*, was another admirer of the Seraphic Doctor.[1] Among the Scotists of this time we may mention PETER THOMAS (*Formalitates*), JOHANNES ANGLICUS (1483, commented on the *Quæst. de universalibus* of Scotus) ; ANTONIUS SIRECTUS (1484) and NICHOLAS TINCTOR, all thorough-going Formalists. The editor of the commentaries of the latter calls him " Scotisans subtilis plurimum." THOMAS BRICOT and GEORGE OF BRUSSELS, two men whose work was closely connected, approximated to the Terminist school. The same is true of JOHANNES FABER DE WERDEA (1500), and the secular PETRUS TARTARETUS (1494), the most remarkable Scotist of this time, author of commentaries on Aristotle, the Sentences, the *Quodlibeta* of Duns Scotus, and *Reportata* on the *Opus oxoniense.* The Aristotelian commentaries had a great vogue. A Scotist in metaphysics, the author derived his mechanical theories from the Nominalist school, and in particular from Albert of Saxony.[2] JOHANNES MAGISTRI (1432-1482), who wrote *Dicta introductoria in doctrinam doctoris subtilis* ; ANTONIUS TROMBETA (died 1518), who left a treatise *In Scoti formalitates, Quæstiones quodlibetales*, and an anti-Averrhoist work, *De animarum humanarum plurificatione ;* LYCHETUS OF BRESCIA (died 1520), a commentator on the *Opus oxoniense ;* MAURITIUS A PORTU (died 1513) ; JOHANNES DE COLONIA ; and a great number of other minor writers advocated a return to the purest principles of Scotism.

The seventeenth century witnessed a brilliant development of the Scotist school.[3]

[1] Minges, *Das Trilogium animæ des Ludwig von Preussen*, in *Franc. Stud.* 1914, pp. 291-311.

[2] Duhem, *D. de Soto et la scolast. parisienne*, B. Hisp. 1911, p. 160.

[3] So much so that Caramuel y Lobkowitz was able to write : " Scoti schola numerosior est aliis simul sumptis." (*Theol. fundam.*, II, disp. 10.) The soul of this movement was Wadding (born 1588), who in 1625 founded at Rome a celebrated Scotist college, and undertook in 1639 a complete edition of the works of Duns Scotus in twelve volumes, in which he utilized the works of Maurice du Port, Lychetus, and Cavellus. The Oxford Commentaries, printed since 1474, had been carefully edited by Hugh Cavell (Antwerp, 1620) ; Maurice du Port had printed in 1504 the treatises on logic ; other treatises existed separately. A general chapter held at Toledo in 1633 imposed the doctrines of Duns Scotus upon the Franciscan Order. Among the contemporaries and successors of Wadding, the best known were in Spain, Merinero (died 1663), professor of philosophy at Alcala, author of a complete and precise course of Scotist philosophy ; in Italy, Brancatus (1612-1693), of Lauria, who wrote eight volumes of commentaries on the two last books of the Sentences of Duns Scotus ; the Portuguese Macedo (1594-1681) who taught at Rome and Padua and left *Collationes doctrinæ S. Thomæ et Scoti cum differentiis inter utrumque*, etc. ; J. Poncius, a collaborator of Wadding, and author of a complete course of philosophy according to Scotus. In France, the principal defender of Scotism was Claude Frassen (1620-1711), a doctor of the

Clarissima singularisque totius philos. necnon metaph. Aristotelis expositio, or *Commentationes in Arist. secundum subtilissimi doct. Scoti sententiam* by Tartaretus appeared in several editions between 1494 and 1621 ; the *Dicta* of Johannes Magistri in 1490. *Quæst. quodlibetales* or *In Scoti formalit.* by Trombeta, Venice, 1493. Edition of Merinero, Madrid, 1663 ; of Brancatus, Rome, 1653-1662 ; of Macedo, 1671-1680, Mastrius, *Disputationes ad mentem Scoti in XII Arist. l. Metaph.* (Venice, 1708). The works of Frassen and of Hieronymus de Montefortino have recently been republished. Claudius Frassen, *Scotus Academicus seu universa doctoris subtilis theolog. dogmata*, 12 vols., Rome, 1903. Hieronymus de Montefortino, *J. D. Scoti etc. Summa theologica ex univ. operibus ejus concinnata, juxta ordinem et disposit. Summæ Angelici Doct. S. Thomæ A.*, 6 vols., Rome, 1900-1902. Prantl, *op. cit.*, IV, pp. 268 *et seq.* P. Dominic de Caylus, *Merveilleux épanouissement de l'école scotiste au XVIIe s.* (*Etudes francisc.* 1910 and 1911), valuable information. E. Longpré, *L'école franciscaine, histoire partiale, histoire vraie*, in *France francisc.*, 1923, p. 108 (deals with the Manual by Barbadette).

Burgus, *Henrici Gandav. doct. solemnis ord. Serv. Paradoxa theol. et philosophica* (Bologna, 1627); Gosius, *Summæ philos. ad mentem Henrici Gandav.* etc. (Rome, 1641), Sogia, *In I et II lib. Sent. mag. fr. Henrici Gandav. quæst. disput.* (Saceri, 1689-1697), and *opuscula theolog.* etc. ; Ventura, *Mag. fr. Henrici de Gand etc., philos. tripartita* (Bologna, 1701) ; Hieronymus Aymus, *Philosophia* etc. (Turin, 1667); E. Garcia, *Cursus* etc. (Rome, 1700); Jos. S. de Aguirre, *Anselmi Cantuar. theologia . . . illustrata* (Rome, 1679); *De virtutibus et vitiis in quibus accurate disputatur quicquid spectat ad philos. moralem ab Arist. traditam X lib. Ethic. ad Nicom.* (Rome, 1717).

§ 4—*Spanish Scholasticism.*

467. General notions.—The sixteenth century witnessed a brilliant restoration of scholastic theology and philosophy. The theological movement, which occupied the chief place, arose from a reaction against the Reformation ; it took shape in the deliberations of the Council of Trent (1563) and was based on the theological work of St. Thomas, whom Pius V in 1567 declared doctor of the Church. Theology was guided by the heresies in its choice of questions to be dwelt on and developed by preference.

The philosophical restoration, which developed parallel with the theological movement, was characterized in the first place by a return to the great systematizations of the thirteenth century and chiefly to Thomism. An inventory was drawn up of the great scholastic patrimony ; theories and arguments were collected and classified in order to subject them to a detailed criticism. On the other hand, the organic doctrines received a fresh interpretation, and new theories made their appearance. For these various reasons, Spanish scholasticism was an autonomous movement of ideas outside the frontiers of the Middle Ages, a neo-scholasticism inasmuch as it was an adaptation of old ideas to new times. Its representatives therefore must not be regarded as mere commentators, even if they themselves make this claim. Some of them were influenced by the new preoccupations of the Renaissance, but only in political and social matters. Lastly, the Spanish Scholastics restored to honour the pure and clear language, and sober and precise method of Thomism, and profited by the criticisms directed by the Humanists against their contemporaries and predecessors.

The philosophical restoration of the sixteenth century had its centre in Spain and Portugal, with ramifications in Italy. Its starting point was Salamanca, and still more Alcala, where Cardinal Ximenes founded a university in 1499 and gave a great impetus to philosophical studies. The university of Coimbra followed suit. Hence the designation, " Spanish scholasticism of the sixteenth century," used for the movement as a whole. In all these universities there were Thomist, Scotist, and Ockamist chairs. Many of the masters, before teaching in their own country, were trained in scholasticism at Paris, which attracted a goodly number of Spaniards and Portuguese. The first works produced were textual commentaries on the *Summa theologica*, which had replaced the Sentences of Peter Lombard ; and they were modelled on those of Cajetan and Silvester of Ferrara. But very soon a wider outlook was adopted, and the commentary gave place to independent expositions and systematic treatises which gave free scope to the individual treatment of the matter studied.

The Spanish restoration was centred in the Dominican and Jesuit orders.

468. Dominicans.—To FRANCIS OF VITTORIA (1480-1546) belongs the honour of having impressed upon the university of Salamanca, where he taught from 1526 to 1544, a new orientation towards Scholasticism. He had studied it at Paris, at the school of a man of some talent, Peter Crockaert of Brussels (p. 294). Francis of Vittoria desired not only to return to the doctrines of Thomism, but also to purify Scholasticism from its imperfect forms and give it a veneer of Humanism.[1] He edited the Commentaries of Peter Crockaert on the *Secunda Secundæ* of St. Thomas, and himself wrote various theological *opuscula*, besides commentaries on the *Summa theologica* and the Books of the Sentences.

Vittoria founded a school : Melchior Canus, Martin of Ledesma, and Andreas of Tudela were among his first disciples from 1527 and 1530. DOMINICUS DE SOTO (1494-1560) who taught with him at Salamanca from 1532, had perhaps known him at Paris, where he followed (about 1512) the lectures of the Nominalist Coronel (p. 289). He gives us valuable information on the scholastic systems in vogue, the *Nominales* and *Reales* (Thomists and Scotists).[2] He complains of the *barbaries sophismatum* which do so much harm to the *philosophia scolastica*,[3] but instead of repudiating the latter as did his compatriot Vivès, he advocated a vigorous return to the fundamental doctrines of the thirteenth century. Thomism was the basis of his philosophy. Nevertheless, he was to some extent influenced by Terminism especially in studying the dynamical problems which had attracted attention since Buridan and Albert of Saxony.[4] Besides numerous theological works, Dominicus de Soto wrote commentaries on the *Isagoge* of Porphyry, the *Physics* and *Dialectics* of Aristotle, the *De anima*, and parts of the *Summa theologica* of St. Thomas.

MELCHIOR CANUS (1509-1560), was first of all professor at Alcala and afterwards the successor of Vittoria at Salamanca (1546). He was the clearest writer of the group, and his

---

[1] He had sympathies for Erasmus, though he opposed him.   C. Getino, in *Ciencia Tomista*, Nov. 1910, p. 179.

[2] In particular he thinks it unnecessary to distinguish three schools, as Thomism differs little from Scotism : " Neque adeo existimo tres vias hic distinguere . . . cum inter S. Thomam et Scotum, parum admodum differat." (Comment. on *Physics*, Venice 1582, Vol. II, Præf.)

[3] See texts in Ehrle, *op. cit.*, no **473**, p. 636.

[4] Duhem, *Dominique de Soto*, etc., 1910, p. 284.

famous work *De locis theologicis,* contains a complete scheme
for the reform of theology and philosophy. To Bannez, who
reproached him for his elegance, he replied that the book
was directed against the heresies prevalent in the northern
countries, where its Humanist form would obtain its entry.[1]
Ehrle also mentions unpublished commentaries on the *Summa
theologica* of St. Thomas. BARTHOLOMEW CARRANZA, the
colleague and rival of Melchior Canus at Alcala, is principally
interesting for his theological works. Canus had as disciples
Bartholomew of Medina, Bannez, and the Augustinian Louis
de Leon (Ludivicus Legionensis).[2]

BARTHOLOMÆUS DE MEDINA (1527-1581), wrote a commentary on the *Summa theologica* which summed up the works
of his predecessors and became classical. His work, which
only dealt with the *Prima Secundæ* and the *Pars Tertia,*
was continued by his successor DOMINICUS BANNEZ (1528-1604)
who edited commentaries on the *Prima Pars* and the *Secunda
Secundæ,* thus making a complete commentary on the *Summa.*
Later on we find Italians ZANARDI (died 1642), and JEROME
MEDICES (died 1622, *Formalis explicatio S. Theol. S. Thomæ*),
the Portuguese ANTONIO DE SENA (died 1584, *In quæst. D.
Thomæ disputatas,* and works on the *Summa*), and JOHN OF
ST. THOMAS (1589-1644).[3] The last mentioned was a professor
at Alcala and Salamanca, and well known for his excellent
*Cursus philosophicus ad exactam veram et genuinam Aristotelis
et Doctoris angelici mentem,*[4] comprising logic, general and
special physics including psychology, still consulted with profit
by those who wish to study Thomism.

469. The Jesuits in Spain. Suarez.—The Jesuits established themselves in Spain about 1548, a few years after the
foundation of the Order. St. Ignatius, who had learned to
admire the teaching of St. Thomas at Paris (1533), chose him

---

[1] Ehrle, *op. cit.,* 1885, p. 99.

[2] We may also mention Vincent Varron (1550-1552), author of commentaries on the I. IIæ of the *Summa Theologica,* Diego de Chaves (de Clavibus)
who commented on the II. IIæ, and Dominicus de Cuevas, who assisted
Melchior Canus (1550-1552) just as Ambrose de Salazar and Juan de la Pena
assisted Bartholomew Carranza (1556-1560). Their works are mentioned
by Ehrle, *op. cit.,* pp. 105 *et seq.* The rivalry between the two professors led
to the formation of the Canist and Carranzist parties.

[3] Ehrle also mentions Pedro de Sotomayor, Mantius de Corpore Christi,
Petrus Fernandez, Juan Gallo, Juan Vincente, Dominicus de Guzman,
Alfonzo de Luna, Juan de Guervera, Pedro de Uzeda Guerrero, and Juan de
Medina. He points out that the study of the work of the disciples will throw
ight on that of the masters.

[4] Republished in Paris in 1883.

as the doctor of the Society. Following the precept of the founder, the General Congregation in 1593 imposed upon its members the duty of adopting Thomism in theological matters. It left them at liberty in questions of a purely philosophical character, but at the same time took precautions that they should not lightly depart from Thomism.

The Jesuits did not succeed in establishing themselves in the university of Salamanca, but they founded other centres of studies, such as the College of Coimbra, where PETRUS FONSECA (1548-1597), called the "Aristotle of Coimbra," was the first to occupy a chair. Under his direction there was produced and completed a great commentary on the philosophy of Aristotle known as the *Collegium Conimbricense*, or *cursus Conimbricensium*. This consists of an exegesis ideological rather than textual, divided into *quæstiones* clearly arranged and grouped together. At the same time it gives an excellent survey of the commentaries handed down by antiquity. SEBASTIAO DO COUTO (died 1639) worked on dialectics ; MANUEL DE GOES (1560-1593) dealt with the *De anima, Ethics*, and *Physics* ; MAGALLIANO the *De anima* ; FONSECA (died 1597) the *Metaphysics* and *Dialectics*. The *Tractatus de anima separata* by BALTHAZAR ALVARES is the last of the Coimbra commentaries.

Of all the Jesuit philosophers, the most famous was FRANCISCUS SUAREZ (*doctor eximius*), born at Grenada in 1548, died at Lisbon in 1617, after teaching in various universities, and chiefly at the Roman College (1580-1585), Alcala (1585-1593), Salamanca (1593-1597), and Coimbra (from 1597). His great philosophic work, *Disputationes metaphysicæ*, is one of the best arranged and most complete repertories of scholastic metaphysics. It is an original treatise on being, its categories, and causes, in which all who wish to make a close study of scholastic metaphysics will find a synoptic table of problems and solutions.

Suarez is also the most eclectic of the Spanish philosophers. His philosophy is an original interpretation of scholastic doctrines. In order to constitute it, he borrows a great deal of material from Thomism, but departs from it in important questions. Accordingly, he is not the " faithful commentator on the Angelic Doctor " which posterity was pleased to call him. To show this it suffices to enumerate some of the principal theses in his metaphysics and psychology. Contrary to St. Thomas, Suarez rejects the real distinction between essence and existence[1] ; and is consequently obliged to allow that existence can be composed of partial elements as essence is, and in particular that natural substances possess of themselves and without the determining act of the form, an existence of their own which God could conserve as such in a separated state. Suarez also departs from Thomism by this other thesis, that the constituent elements of each substance, and not prime matter, are the principles of its individuation. In psychology, we may confine ourselves to pointing out that under the influence of Nominalism, he allows to the intellect the power of obtaining a direct knowledge of the individual.[2]

As a publicist, Suarez occupies a distinguished place in the ranks of the Jesuits combating Protestantism on social grounds. He composed a treatise De legibus,[3] and in particular devoted his attention to the famous question, raised by the Protestants, as to the immediate origin of power. With Bellarmine he entered the arena to refute the theory of the " divine right of kings," in support of which James I of England had invoked theological considerations. To the Protestant conception that kings derive their power immediately from God, Suarez opposes the mediæval thesis of the initial sovereignty of the people : popular consent forms the original title of a prince's authority. In contrast with governmental omnipotence as set forth by Melanchthon, he recognizes in the people the right to depose rulers who are unworthy of the mandate conferred upon them.

---

[1] " Existentia enim substantiæ ita composita est, sicut essentia substantiæ et ideo sine ulla implicatione vel repugnantia, potest Deus sicut formam sine materia, ita et materiam sine forma conservare." (Disp. met. Disp. 15, sect. 9, n. 5. G. Saitta, La scolastica del secolo XVIe la politica dei Gesuiti Turin, 1911), is mistaken in thinking that this theory of Suarez destroys the notion of creation and leads to pantheism (pp. 135 and 136).

[2] The study of Suarez is really beyond the scope of this history, and accordingly we confine ourselves to this slight doctrinal treatment. Maréchal, Le point de depart de la metaphysique, I, p. 134, writes concerning his teaching : " Suarez, undoubtedly an eminent thinker, lived like his contemporaries in an atmosphere created by nominalism, and in spite of his definitely realist reaction in logic, he did not succeed in escaping completely in metaphysics from the secret poison which diminished—others would say it falsified—in advance the value of a meritorious effort. For Suarez, like Duns Scotus and Ockam, holds the thesis of the direct intellectual knowledge of the singular material thing, the individuation of sensible things independently of their matter, the real identity of essence and existence in creatures, the identity of matter and form considered in themselves, etc."

[3] D. de Soto, Molina, Lessius, and John de Lugo (died 1660), also wrote treatises de jure et justitia.

After Suarez, VALLIUS (died 1622), A. RUBIUS (died 1615), FR. ALPHONSUS (died 1649), P. DE MENDOZA (died 1651), and FR. GONZALEZ (died 1661) are personalities of secondary importance.

470. Jesuits in Italy.—The theological and philosophical movement of which the Jesuits were the promoters spread to the various universities which they founded outside Spain and Portugal.   In Germany, GREGORY OF VALENCE, author of a commentary on the SUMMA (1591) ; in Belgium BELLARMINE and LESSIUS championed the new tendencies.

But in Italy above all, important centres of studies were organized, the chief of which was the *Collegium romanum* founded by St. Ignatius.   Here taught JACOB LEDESMA (died 1575) and F. TOLETUS (from 1559-1569), the disciple of Dominic de Soto at Salamanca, author of excellent commentaries on Aristotle and of an *Enarratio in summam theol. S. Thomæ.* Here also we meet with GABRIEL VASQUEZ (died 1604), the rival of Suarez, and author of valuable *Disputationes metaphysicæ* and of a fine commentary on the *Summa theologica* of St. Thomas.

Under Vasquez and Suarez, from 1584 to 1588, studied COSMUS ALAMANNUS, who was born at Milan (1559) and afterwards taught there.   He published from 1618 to 1623 a *Summa philosophiæ* consisting of a didactic exposition of the philosophy of St. Thomas in which the author arranges the material in various sections (logic, physics, ethics, metaphysics) and carefully gathers together the texts of the master relating to each question.

PETER ARRUBAL, JOHN DE LUGO, ANTHONY PEREZ, NICHOLAS MARTINEZ, and SILVESTER MAURUS, all deserve special mention in the list of the professors at the Roman College in the seventeenth century.   MAURUS, born at Spoleto in 1619, began to teach in 1653, and continued to do so almost exclusively till his death in 1687.   In addition to several theological works, he wrote *Quæstionum philosophicarum lib. V*, and a paraphrase of the complete works of Aristotle.   We may say that these commentaries embody the thirteenth-century scholastic exegesis of Aristotle ; their concision and clearness make them models of their kind.[1]   Maurus based himself on the Greek text and the best Latin translations then extant.

---

[1] Preface to Vol. I in Ehrle's edition.

471. Other religious congregations.—The Franciscan order took an active part in the work of restoration (**463**). The Carmelites published the *Disputationes collegii Complutensis*, an encyclopædic commentary on Thomism.[1] The Cistercians (among them ANGELUS MANRIQUEZ, B. GOMEZ, P. DE OVIEDO), the Benedictines, Trinitarians, and others[2] followed the same philosophical traditions.

472. Conclusion.—The Spanish revival offers a pleasant contrast to the general poverty of scholasticism in the countries to which the movement did not extend. It led to an active current of thought which sufficed to show that the organic doctrines had not lost their vitality. Amid the general sterility, one branch blossomed forth and produced abundant fruit.

But this restoration remained local and ephemeral. It was unable to extend beyond Spain, Portugal and Italy. The divisions in the Central and Northern Europe resulting from the Reformation partly led to this check. Moreover, people were too much distracted by the varied tendencies of the time for Scholasticism to regain the ascendency. This would have necessitated Scholastics coming into closer contact with contemporary thought than was possible in Spain. What a pity the Spanish thinkers confined their researches to natural law ! They would have been a match for the anti-scholastics of their time. Their failure to adapt themselves to the new mental attitude arrested the influence of the Spanish movement.

473. Bibliography.—On the works of the Jesuits, see Sommervogel, *Biblioth. de la Compagnie de Jesus*, Vols. I-IX, (Brussels, 1898-1900). Editions of Vittoria at Pinciæ, 1561, Lyons, 1557, 1586, Salamanca, 1565 ; of Ledesma : Coimbra, 1555 ; of Dominic de Soto, Venice, 1572, 1582 ; of Melchior Canus, Salamanca, 1550-1558, numerous editions of the *De locis theologicis*, especially that of Serry in 1714, Getino, *El Maestro Fr. F. de Vitoria*, (Madrid, 1914) ; Duhem, *Dominique Soto et la scolastique parisien (Bulletin Hispanique*, 1910 and 1912), a study of the dynamical and mechanical theories of the master ; article on Melchior Canus by Mandonnet in *Dict. Theol. cath.* s.v. *Canus*, 1904.—Editions of Medina's

---

[1] The Carmelite Philippus a S. Trinitate (died 1671) is considered to be an excellent interpreter of St. Thomas.
[2] Manuel da Natividade, of the Order of Our Lady of Ransom, wrote a *Philosophia sec. mentem angelici præceptoris* which has not been published. See Ferreira, *op. cit.*, p. 313.

Louvain, Van Gutschoven (1615-1665), Philippi (about 1660-1665), and above all Arnold Geulincx (1624-1669) defended the new ideas against Froidmont and Plempius (died 1671). Geulincx of Antwerp, an original thinker who taught Occasionalism in psychology before Malebranche, and a theory of resignation in ethics,[1] was very sarcastic at the expense of the Aristotelians. His opening discourse at the " Saturnalia " in 1652, and his address at Leyden in 1662 consisted of a merciless satire on their physics and metaphysics, sayings and axioms, language and didactic methods.

The official censure on Cartesianism in the Southern provinces (1662) did not impede its development. It was equally prominent in the two universities of the Northern provinces, Leyden and Utrecht, and its progress here was even more rapid. At Utrecht the Cartesians Reneri and Anthony Æmilius, opposed the Aristotelians De Maets, Voetius and Senguerdius. At Leyden, where Geulincx took up his abode when sent away from Louvain, Cartesianism easily won the day.

From the campaign waged by Geulincx and others against Scholasticism, and information contained in the Aristotelian manuals of the seventeenth and eighteenth centuries, we may draw several conclusions. Geulincx's parody, like every caricature, sinned by excess, but was not beside the mark. Important scholastic ideas were disfigured by the Aristotelians of the decadent period, notably the theory of matter and form, and that of the faculties. Dialectics occupied an exaggerated place in teaching, and towards the end of the seventeenth century, students, with the full knowledge of their professors, filled their notebooks with pictures intended to " illustrate the text." [2] All these are faults which are imputable to the Aristotelians, and not to Aristotelianism. Geulincx's criticisms apply to individuals and not to the great doctrines of mediæval scholasticism. The *parerga* or " useless ornaments " of which he complained were the products of the decadent period. In order to explain the theory of demonstration or of individua-

---

[1] See De Wulf, *Historie de la Philosophie en Belgique* : pp. 221 *et seq.*

[2] Dialectics was represented as a corpulent matron ; genera and species, substance and accident, the figures and modes of the syllogism, etc. all had their symbols, and it is scarcely necessary to add that the doctrines themselves were disfigured and not explained by these schemes and designs. We have reconstituted the complete series of these pictures, which booksellers sold in sets like picture postcards, and of which the students made full use. On this curious subject see De Wulf, *Histoire de la Philosophie en Belgique*, pp. 207 *et seq.*

tion, it was not necessary to refer to facts in the life of the Saviour, or to speak of Alexander's horse, as was done then. The use of phraseology of which the sense was not understood, the citation of strings of texts the meaning or source of which was unknown, and the habit of giving lengthy introductions, were dialectical methods having nothing in common with those practised by Aristotle and the great Scholastics.

Again, the philosophical doctrines ridiculed by Geulincx, do not correspond to the psychological and metaphysical ideas of the thirteenth century. Matter and form are not at all like married couples, their union does not resemble a wedding, and powers and faculties are not solemn futilities. In the same way, genera and species cannot be represented by emblems, and the *pons asinorum* or the theory of the figures of the syllogism do not possess the tremendous importance ascribed to them. The discussion between the Cartesians and the Aristotelians of the seventeenth century did not affect the fundamental doctrines of mediæval Scholasticism.

The same is true of the controversies between scientists and Aristotelians. Of slight importance in themselves, the events connected with them have derived their significance from the circumstances in which they took place.

475. Scientific discoveries and their relations with scholastic philosophy.—The great discoveries of Copernicus, Galileo, Kepler, Newton, Torricelli, and Lavoisier revolutionized physical and mechanical astronomy, physics, chemistry, and biology, while Descartes, Newton and Leibniz reconstructed mathematics on new foundations. This involved the condemnation of the greater part of the theories of celestial and terrestrial physics which the Middle Ages had incorporated into its conception of the universe. For the geocentric system Copernicus substituted the heliocentric system. The telescope discovered stars freely moving through space, and thus destroyed the theory of the solid heavens. The elliptical movements of the planets exploded the old notion of the perfection of circular motion. Observation showed the falsity of the current ideas concerning the nature of the heavenly bodies : in various constellations Galileo discovered new stars ; in 1611 he discovered sunspots by means of the telescope, and from their displacement on the sun's disc inferred the rotation of the sun itself ; then he discovered the phases of Venus, thus providing an experimental confirmation for the predictions

Aristotelians thought that it was impossible to do anything to an age-long tree, and that to despoil it of a dried-up branch would be to deprive it of its life.

Scholasticism was vanquished for want of men, not for want of ideas.

478. Bibliography.—Monchamp, *Histoire du cartésianisme en Belgique* (Brussels, 1886), and *Galilée et la Belgique, Essai historique sur les vicissitudes du systeme du Copernic en Belgique* (Brussels, 1892) ; Féret, *L'aristotélisme et le cartésianisme dans l'Université de Paris au XVIIe s.* (*Annales de Philos. chrét.* April, 1903) ; Picavet, *Galilée, destructeur de la scolastique et fondateur de la philosophie scientifique,* in *Conférences de Société d'études ital.* (Guenard, 1895, pp. 116-130), a misleading title. De Wulf, *Hist. de la philos. en Belgique,* pp. 235 *et seq., Introduction to Scholastic Philosophy,* § 19. Proost, *L'enseignement philosophique des bénédictins de Saint-Vaast à Douai à la fin du XVIIIe s.* (*Revue bénédictine,* Jan., 1900) ; Maritain, *De quelques conditions de la Renaissance thomiste* (*Ann. Institut philos.,* Louvain, 1920, pp. 573-604).

CONCLUSION

The twelfth and thirteenth centuries marked both the height of mediæval civilization and the golden age of that philosophy which was its most characteristic product. The preceding period prepared at length for this triumphal hour, and collected together the various materials from Greek sources. The new peoples who, under the guidance of Christianity, derived from them new ideas, displayed the fresh and vigorous qualities of young races, which were the germ of the modern nations. Everything was at once Greek, Christian, neo-Latin, and Germanic in the great syntheses abounding in the thirteenth century. Running through the philosophies of a Bonaventure, a St. Thomas, or a Duns Scotus, we find a doctrinal patrimony common to all, a series of ideas which gives them a family likeness, but which each stamps with its own imprint. The finite and the infinite, act and potency, matter and form, essence and existence, individuality and individuation, efficiency and finality, sensation and thought, the spiritual soul and material body, constitute a framework in which the Scholastics constructed their thought.

The fourteenth century continued to feed on these strong doctrines of the mind, but little by little, for many and various reasons, they lost their savour. Their objectivity was called in question by Ockamism, and straightway their value descended several degrees. The order of essences, the fixity of which the thirteenth century doctors founded on the very essence of God, gradually became a matter of symbols, constructed by the human mind, and only valid for it. True, the Thomists and Scotists defended against this Nominalism the metaphysic which was the great creation of the thirteenth century. But they were a minority, and could not withstand the Nominalist current, nor even keep themselves wholly free from its influence.

BRISTOL : BURLEIGH LTD., AT THE BURLEIGH PRESS